~

WILLIAM HENRY JACKSON'S

"THE PIONEER PHOTOGRAPHER"

~

THE UPPER TWIN LAKE, COLORADO. JULY 26, 1873.
Copy of modern print from wet plate negative.

William Henry Jackson's

"THE PIONEER PHOTOGRAPHER"

~

Compiled, edited, and annotated by

BOB BLAIR

With original text from the 1929 edition

by William Henry Jackson in collaboration with

HOWARD R. DRIGGS

~

Foreword by Lee Whittlesey

MUSEUM OF NEW MEXICO PRESS ~ SANTA FE

Project editor: Mary Wachs
Manuscript editor: Dawn Hall
Design and production: Deborah Flynn Post
Composition: Set in Stempel Garamond
Manufactured in: Singapore
10 9 8 7 6 5 4 3 2 1

Museum of New Mexico Press
Post Office Box 2087
Santa Fe, New Mexico 87504

Front cover illustration: *The Anna,*
ca. 1920–1930 (color plate 11). Back cover
illustration: *Expedition of 1870,* ca 1920–1930
(color plate 8). Photographs by William
Henry Jackson, from *William Henry
Jackson's "The Pioneer Photographer."*

Library of Congress Cataloging-in-Publication Data

Jackson, William Henry, 1843–1942.
  [Pioneer photographer]
  William Henry Jackson's "The pioneer photographer" / compiled,
annotated, and edited by Bob Blair ; with original text from the 1929
edition by William H. Jackson in collaboration with Howard R. Driggs ;
foreword by Lee Whittlesey.
     p. cm.
  Originally published: Yonkers-on-Hudson, N.Y. : World Book Co., 1929.
Includes additional sketches, photos, and paintings by Jackson and
commentary.
  Includes bibliographical references and index.
  ISBN 0-89013-435-9 (clothbound : alk. paper) -- ISBN 0-89013-436-7
(paperbound : alk. paper)
  1. West (U.S.)—Description and travel. 2. West (U.S.)—Pictorial
works. 3. Jackson, William Henry, 1843–1942—Travel—West (U.S.) 4.
Geological and Geographical Survey of the Territories (U.S.) 5.
Frontier and pioneer life—West (U.S.) 6. Photography—West
(U.S.)—History—19th century. 7. Photography—West
(U.S.)—History—20th century. 8. Jackson, William Henry, 1843–1942. 9.
Photographers—United States—Biography. I. Blair, Bob. II. Driggs,
Howard R. (Howard Roscoe), 1873–1963. III. Title.
  F594.J165 2005
  917.8'0022'2--dc22

                                   2004016823

Contents

Foreword

It is a pleasure to write this foreword to Bob Blair's new edition of William Henry Jackson's classic book *The Pioneer Photographer*. First published in 1929, the book has long been considered one of the most important statements from Jackson himself about his now-iconic photography of the American West. It, along with his *Time Exposure* (1940) and his personal diaries, have been utilized by generations of historians as they look at Jackson, photographer for the Hayden surveys 1870–79 and now known as one of the most important landscape photographers of the American West. His photos received credit as the earliest photographic record of the Yellowstone National Park, and they played a large role in the establishing of Yellowstone as the world's first national park.

Unfortunately, as historian Marlene Merrill has noted in her book *Yellowstone and the Great West*, some of *The Pioneer Photographer* is a "misremembered recollection." Both it and Jackson's *Time Exposure*, as well as some of Dr. F. V. Hayden's works, says Merrill, "omit important facts" and "contain errors and misleading claims concerning the survey's discoveries and accomplishments" (1999, xv). This is not surprising, as Jackson waited more than fifty years to write the book, and he wrote *Time Exposure* even later. That gave him adequate time to forget things and to mix up his memories of 1871 with 1872. His biographer Peter B. Hales called these two books "significant fictions" (1988, 302n2). And it is unfortunate that late in Jackson's life, according to Dr. Merrill, he and his son Clarence destroyed a great deal of his personal materials, perhaps even including his 1871 diary that he claimed not to have kept (1999, xvi; Hales, 6).

Thus, it is nice to finally have a corrected edition of *The Pioneer Photographer*. According to Peter Hales, it is "the more trustworthy" of Jackson's two books, "because of its earlier date" and because it came from materials Jackson put together for it around 1920 (Hales, 1988, 302n2). Hales has called *Time Exposure* "a strange amalgam of fact, romance, anecdote, shaded truth, and sheer fiction" (294). *Pioneer*

WILLIAM HENRY JACKSON. Circa 1929. Type of print unknown.

This photograph depicts Mr. Jackson near the time *The Pioneer Photographer* was first published. The signature comes from a signed copy of his second autobiography, *Time Exposure* (Jackson [1940] 1994). Courtesy National Park Service/Grand Teton National Park.

Photographer was and is a better book. It was used in the 1930s, along with Jackson himself as speaker and living pioneer, to "bring a heritage consciousness to Western residents" (Hales, 288). So, too, were Jackson's drawings and paintings used, and some of them are reproduced in this new version.

Personally I remember using Jackson's wonderful statement in one of my own books about his hearing of Yellowstone on the Oregon Trail. "In 1866, when I was traveling over the Oregon Trail," Jackson recalled, "old frontiersman told me of the great lake, the waterfalls, and the geysers not far away to the north and I remember that at the time I had a longing to go there." As a budding historian, I read this Jackson comment thirty years ago, and it started me on the personal quest of attempting to find other references to the Yellowstone country that might have been told to Oregon Trail travelers besides Jackson. But alas, years of searching have not turned them up. One would think that the many fur trapper guides who conducted the thousands of travelers on the famous trail would have mentioned Yellowstone to some of those people, but if it happened those travelers apparently did not write about it in any of thousands of known diaries.

Certainly William Henry Jackson lived for so long (1843-1942) that he came to know that he was a celebrity. Later he experienced sadness over the loss of control of his own history and even of his own persona, so bound up with the Hayden surveys, the Oregon Trail, and the West in general had he become in the public mind. By 1940, he was in danger of "disappearing into his own image." A "caretaker of western myths," Peter Hales has written, "he was becoming lost in their latest incarnation" (294). Thus has it become difficult to separate Jackson the man from Jackson the myth. But even long after his death he continues through his pictures as a powerful spokesman for the importance of landscape to American culture. He generated myths beginning in the 1860s but he also transformed myths and tended myths throughout his important life.

Join us now in reading Jackson's own thoughts during episodes of his truly remarkable time.

Lee H. Whittlesey
Park Historian, National Park Service
Yellowstone National Park, Wyoming

Editor's Preface

During the summer of 1977 while I was employed as an interpretive river guide in Grand Teton National Park, I became familiar with William Henry Jackson while researching park history. One evening I returned home to find my wife reading a copy of *The Pioneer Photographer,* which she had purchased earlier in the day. Over the years I read Jackson's story several times. I began to pay attention to his photographs. I started to explore the exact locations where he had created images. While on a hike in the Grand Tetons to locate one of Jackson's "high places," it struck me that others deserved to see and hear this wonderful story. The efforts to see this dream become reality followed.

This adventure was lived by Jackson—it is his perception of events. The story covers his childhood and the years he spent as the official photographer for the Unites States Geological Survey of the Territories under Dr. Ferdinand V. Hayden. The free-hand artwork spans almost ninety years of creative endeavor. It is notable for its vivid imagery and its historical content. Jackson thought of himself as an artist who happened to become famous as a photographer. He began and ended his life pursuing a passion for sketching and painting. Nonetheless, he is remembered for his photographic "views," which are viewed to this day. As time passes the sketches, paintings, and photographs become more valued as a window into nineteenth-century western America.

A prolific writer, the man was absolutely convinced of his inability to write well. In 1940 Jackson published his second "autobiography," *Time Exposure* (Jackson 1994). A ghostwriter, Carl Brown, wrote the text. "And here is where I am having the most brain-racking job I ever tackled in checking over the first draft of the manuscript. You can imagine how hard it is to keep within bounds the ideas and fancies of a writer who has no background of experience or knowledge of his subject. About all I can do in the present is to cross my fingers and hope for the best" (Jackson,

February 11, 1925). They collaborated well; the book is currently in print after sixty years.

No man is without fault, William Henry Jackson included. Over his long and productive life span, some of his stories were embellished or altered. Records, catalogues, and writings were transcribed inaccurately. Documents were misplaced and lost. More accurate scientific information has been gathered since the era of the Great Surveys of the American West. Fortunately, *The Pioneer Photographer* is thought to be a relatively accurate description of this early part of Jackson's distinguished career, even though it was written half a century after its occurrence.

When acquiring an image made by another photographer, an acceptable practice in the early days of photography was to claim it as one's own without crediting the creator. There are photographs in this book for which Jackson is commonly given credit that were taken by others. Jackson's assistants undoubtedly took some images. In 1877 the United States Geological Survey of the Territories published *Miscellaneous Publications No. 9; Descriptive Catalogue of Photographs of North American Indians* (Jackson [1875] 1978). Yes, he compiled the photographs and organized the manuscript, but other photographers created the majority of the images. They are not credited for their work. With the passing of time it has become a daunting task to give proper recognition to the original photographers.

After his work with the Survey, Jackson continued to pursue an active career in photography, first in Denver (1879–97) and later as a vital part of the Detroit Photographic Company until its bankruptcy (1897–1924). In Detroit he supervised production after discontinuing his work as a professional photographer in 1903. Upon retirement he spent endless hours researching the early westward expansion of the United States, sketching and painting his impressions. His photographs were often the basis for these paintings. He became a leading authority on the history of the Oregon Trail. His paintbrush remained active into his ninety-ninth year. He was buried in Arlington Cemetery on April 30, 1942.

In republishing *The Pioneer Photographer* an effort has been made to synthesize all of the artist's creative accomplishments. The format of the first edition of *The Pioneer Photographer* has been altered, although the entire autobiography remains in this current edition. Most of the additions made in this printing are the work of Bob

Blair. Jackson's additions and corrections to the published text have been silently added to the text. They come from his personal copy of the book, residing at the Harold B. Lee Library, Brigham Young University. Unless otherwise noted all quotes come from a variety of his original writings. They are included as image captions, sidebar text, and endnotes. Some caption text is as it appeared in the first edition in Jackson's voice. Added editorial notes within the original main text are encased in brackets. Any errors in this publication lie with me as editor/compiler and with the original authors, who are no longer here to share this responsibility. The desire is to give the reader an appreciation and understanding of the events detailed in this incredible narrative as experienced by the author—William Henry Jackson.

This republication is a product of the efforts of many individuals and the resources of many institutions. In particular I would like to thank the following individuals: Ann James, U.S. Department of the Interior Museum; Diana Wiggam, park ranger, Rocky Mountain National Park; Dan Davis and Leslie Shores, photo archivists, American Heritage Center; Thomas H. Harrell, historian; Wayne Johnson, historian; Dean Knudsen, historian, Scotts Bluff National Monument; Joe McGregor, senior photographic librarian, U.S. Geological Survey; Marlene Merrill, historian; Monica Miller, office supervisor, Harold Warp Pioneer Village Foundation; Richard Niemeyer, technical assistant; Eric Paddock, historian, Colorado Historical Society; John Irwin, senior librarian, The Denver Public Library; John Richardson, historian; Richard Rudisill, curator of photographic history, Museum of New Mexico; Andrew Smith, Andrew Smith Gallery, Santa Fe, New Mexico; Don Snoddy, curator, Union Pacific Museum, Omaha; Bill Swift, chief of interpretation and Christine Jacobs Landrum, museum curator, Grand Teton National Park; Hallam Webber, historian; Tom Wells, Special Collections and Manuscripts, H. B. Lee Library, Brigham Young University; Joseph Struble, assistant archivist, George Eastman House; and Lee Whittlesey, historian, Yellowstone National Park. Finally, Sally Blair deserves special thanks for providing the spark that created this project, and for the technical assistance and emotional support she provided.

—Bob Blair

ALONG THE UNION PACIFIC. Circa 1920–1930. Hand-tinted colorized glass lantern-slide.

The photographer and his working outfit along the line of the Union Pacific Railroad in 1869. The developing box, chemicals, various pieces of photographic equipment, and camp tools are visible in the foreground. The tent was used for both workroom and living quarters. Courtesy National Park Service/Scotts Bluff National Monument.

Introduction

More than half a century has passed since Howard Driggs wrote the following introduction in the first edition of *The Pioneer Photographer*. The ideas, feelings, and images he created remain relevant today.

"The marvelous process of taking pictures has become so common that with most people it has ceased to be a marvel. Even kindergarten children today can manipulate a kodak, and practically every home possesses its album of snapshots by members of the family. Newspapers, magazines, and books are filled with photogravures; entertainment and instruction are being given daily to millions by means of moving pictures. . . .

"Pioneer photographers who have lived through the whole intriguing story of the days of tin types to television [were] not readily found [at the time this story was written]. Happily, one of them, well up in his eighties but with his photographic memory keen and clear, . . . [told] us about the beginnings of this art that has come to play so vital a part in our everyday lives. Nor, did he have to rely on his memory for the story; for with rare insight, by means of copious notes, sketches, and photographs made on the spot through all the earlier days, he has preserved with fidelity a most satisfactory cross section of the whole record of pioneer photography.

"This volume presents some of that record, not as a matter-of-fact treatise but as a gripping story of adventure and achievement. It tells the life of a real American boy born in a picturesque part of New York of parents with a bent for things artistic. It tells of this boy's early apprenticeship in pioneer photography; of his serving his country as a volunteer from the Green Mountain State during the Civil War; and then of his adventures as an itinerant photographer on his way out into the wilds of the West. It relates the story of his playing the roles of bullwhacker and vaquero, until he returns to frontier Omaha to take up his chosen life work, that of landscape photography.

~

"Before the present era of facile photography . . . it was quite different in actual practice, and there are not many who know, or fully realize, how onerous were the conditions imposed on the old-time photographer. . . . The 'wet plate process' was, briefly, making on the spot the sensitive plate for each exposure. This required a portable 'dark room' (box or tent) to work in, and nearly all the appliances ordinarily used by the sedentary photographer in his 'gallery'—all of which had to be condensed into our very limited carrying capacity. . . . [A typical] outfitting was for three series of negatives, 11 × 14, 5 × 8 and stereoscopic. The glass alone —some 400 pieces, was no inconsiderable item, with collodions, silver nitrates, iron sulphates and a score or two of other chemicals and articles, made up in bulk what they lacked in weight" (Jackson 1926, 11–12).

~

THE PIONEER PHOTOGRAPHER. Circa 1940.
Oil painting.

This black-and-white oil painting done by William
Henry Jackson was used as the embossed cover of the
first edition of *The Pioneer Photographer.* Courtesy
Brigham Young University.

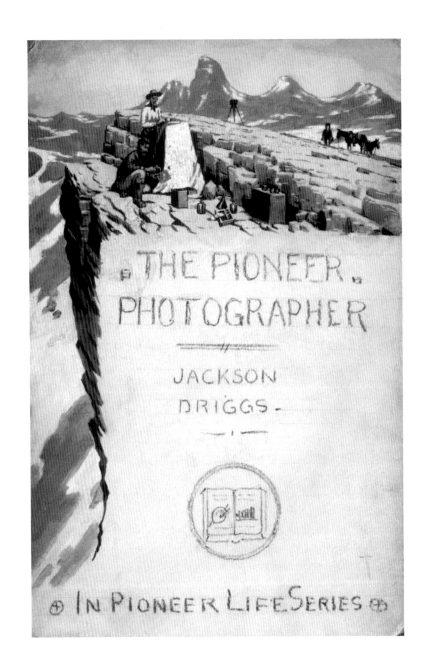

"It was just after he had been making a picture record of the building of the Union Pacific Railroad that he came in touch with Dr. Hayden, then head of the United States Geological Survey. This meeting resulted in the performing of a signal service for our country and the world at large. Photography was brought into the work of revealing the wonders of the newly opened West. The region of the Rockies became the scene of action for our pioneer photographer.

"In those stirring days of the eighteen seventies, the Indians were not yet quite tamed. Nature still held sway over the western mountains and valleys and plains. To be one of the very first men to carry a camera into this little known realm was a rare adventure. To be able to bring out, at the cost of difficult and dangerous work, the photographs that were to give the world something of a thrill, was a privilege. It was through his work that we obtained our first photographs of the Yellowstone Wonderland, the Grand Teton, the Mountain of the Holy Cross, and the land of the Cliff Dwellers.

"The book of story and picture we are presenting . . . is composite in nature. Those who like adventure will find in it adventures of a stirring kind. Those who enjoy history may get from it some humanistic pictures of our country in its making. For those interested in geography, it will bring vivid descriptions of our land from East to West; while those who like to take photographs will find a charm in the major message of the volume, which is to tell the story of the photographer of the early days.

"Back of it all is the man who lived the story. . . . To read of his trips into the craggy canyons, his climbs up to the snow capped peaks, his bivouacking in storm and shine with faithful companions out in the open plains and high hills, is to understand in part how he managed to maintain his springy step and keen mind all these years. It is truly a pleasure to be able to introduce . . . William H. Jackson."

—Howard R. Driggs (Jackson 1929b, v–viii)

WILLIAM HENRY JACKSON. July 1872.
Type of print unknown.

In his second autobiography the following notation appears: "In 1872, while a member of the U.S. Geological Survey exploring the Teton country, I set up my camera, then stepped into this picture as an assistant uncapped the lens" (Jackson [1940] 1994, 208). Courtesy National Park Service/Rocky Mountain National Park.

THE LITTLE WEATHER-BEATEN SCHOOLHOUSE. n.d.
Pencil drawing.

It is seen at the crossroads at Peru, New York, where I
first tackled the three R's (about 1850). Jackson claims it
was "a little one-room schoolhouse half a mile from
home. There were no more than a dozen or fifteen
pupils, and the teacher was a girl of perhaps nineteen—
who seemed very old indeed to us children" (Jackson
[1940] 1994, 10). Courtesy National Park Service/Scotts
Bluff National Monument.

Chapter One

Early Experiences

April 1843–April 1866

IT seems rather the natural thing that I should have become a maker of pictures.
My birthplace, the village of Keeseville, New York,[1] was set between the picturesque Ausable Chasm and the wooded Adirondacks. My mother had graduated
from the school that is now named the Emma Willard School for Girls in Troy, as
an accomplished painter in water colors; and my father, about the time I came into the
world in 1843, was experimenting with the newly discovered process of making
daguerreotypes, the forerunner of photography. I remember, as a small child, having had parts of a camera as playthings. Picture making was therefore a kind of inher-
itance; but never, even in my wildest boyhood imagination, did I dream that the
desire to sketch and to paint pictures would carry me finally into every part of our
country and over most of the world.

My feet were set in the ways of travel earlier than I can recall, for about the
time I was one year old my parents moved to Columbus, Georgia. Our stay in the
sunny Southland was so brief that I have only one vivid impression of it—that of
being carried to the deck of a river steamboat, where under a bright full moon I
gazed out over dark waters, palmettos, and moss-draped trees. This was probably
a scene on the Chattahoochee, down which we sailed when we were returning to our
home in northern New York. The balmy beginning of that return trip was quite in
contrast with its end, when, as mother used to tell us, we made the last stage of the
journey from Whitehall to Plattsburg by sleigh over the smooth, glassy ice of Lake
Champlain.

The years that followed at Plattsburg and at the old farm in Peru Township,
about twelve miles south of Plattsburg, were such as make for sturdy health and for
a love of the great outdoors that has never left me. I had all the experiences of

Whittier's barefoot boy around the historic homestead with its Revolutionary memories. The house was set back about three hundred yards from the roadway and was approached through a lane with ancient poplars. These trees remain a vivid picture with me, for one of my biggest chores came when they were cut down and I had to stack up the firewood made from them in orderly piles. For that rather hard task I was given as a special reward a silver three-cent piece.

My early school days were spent in a little weather-beaten schoolhouse at the crossroads some distance away. Of these days I remember little; but I do recall distinctly my later school days in the old Fourth Ward School in Troy. It was not studying books, however, which interested me most. I much preferred to draw pictures for the amusement of my classmates. I did not remain in school beyond the eighth grade. An urge to get out and put to practical use my talent for making pictures, coupled with the fact that I was the eldest of an increasing family, was the thing that decided the question. From the age of fifteen I took my training in the school of experience.

Various kinds of picture making occupied my time for a while. I made family portraits; I painted landscapes on window screens, a fashion in those early days; and I painted a row of big jars as part of the stage scenery for "The Forty Thieves" of the old Arabian Nights. The chief scenic artist for the local theater gave me an approving slap on the back for my good drawing in this first attempt at scene painting.

None of these beginnings brought in much money, but they were good practice. To this hit-or-miss art training was added a few months' work in the studio of a portrait painter, which improved my technique somewhat. My ambition was to study art for the sake of art, but I was soon forced to turn to the humbler work of coloring photographs for a more dependable income. At length I found steady work with a photographer named Mowry in Rutland, Vermont.[2] My pay was six dollars a week, but as board was only three dollars and a half a week, I felt that I was doing very well.

Mowry had recently advanced from making daguerreotypes to making tintypes and the popular *cartes de visite,* which were portrait photographs somewhat larger than a visiting card. Now, with my assistance, he undertook the making of oil-painted enlargements; and I also helped in the regular work of the gallery. Incidentally, I was making friends among the young folk of the town, and many delightful times

RUTLAND CRONIES. 1865. Albumin carte de visite.

The author [is] seated at the right. Verso information on the photograph, written by Jackson, dates it as 1864. Courtesy Brigham Young University.

~

Will Jackson's Civil War diary points out the daily drudgery and uncomfortable living conditions brought on by war. Many of the entries speak of dealing with the natural elements — marching in the mud or dust, sleeping in wet tents, enduring the snow and cold of winter or the heat of the dry camps in summer. He writes about preparing for inspections, participating in drills, and moving camp. He discusses stealing food to supplement the sparse military rations. Occasional close calls broke the monotony:

"Sunday . . . received orders . . . to be in readiness to march at a moments notice. Cartridge boxes were inspected and filled to the full 40 rounds. About 6 PM were marched out by the flank through the village on the road to Washington. About half a mile beyond were filed off to the right in a field and occupied a line of breastworks facing Washington. . . . Remained standing on the line until about nine o'clock when the Gen. ordered guns loaded & for our two exposed companies to lie flat on the ground. The general gave particular instructions how to fire to repel cavalry. Soon after, while watching the road we heard a hurrah! Two or three shots & then a volley — silence following. This occurred some two or three hundred yards ahead of our line and the flash of the guns of the skirmishers could be plainly seen. We lay in breathless silence expecting at any moment to see the enemy come dashing over the hill. We were ready for them, our guns pointed to the spot where they were expected to appear. The moments passed away however and nothing more was heard of them. The General rode up there & said our advance skirmishers had repelled the charge of two companies & had used them up badly. After that — although we expected them to appear at any time — nothing more was seen of them" (Jackson [1862–1863] 1915, December 28, 1862).

~

we had during those days I spent in Vermont. Our little social club made frequent excursions into the Green Mountains to picnic, to fish, and to climb the pine-clad hills to their rocky summits. Best of all were the buggy rides with a sweetheart along the beautiful mountain roads.

These pleasures of youth were broken into all too soon. The tragic days of the early sixties had come, and young men were needed. I continued to sketch and to paint during my spare time, but with the other boys I watched anxiously the darkening war cloud. Then came "Father Abraham's" call for "300,000 more," and I joined the Rutland Light Guard. A little later my brother Ed from Troy joined me and together we entered Company K, Twelfth Vermont Infantry, which with other regiments formed the Second Vermont Brigade.[3] We were soon on our way to Washington.

My soldier days were not particularly exciting. We never got into the thickest of the fray. At Fairfax Court House Mosby, the daring Confederate leader, raiding at midnight, carried off our brigade commander from right under our noses,[4] and we had some skirmishes with raiders along the railroad, but that's all. I had time enough between these activities to indulge in my favorite occupation of making sketches. When our colonel took note of my talents, he detailed me to his headquarters for a while to continue this kind of work.

I was sent one day to make a sketch map of the picket lines we were then holding along the Bull Run.[5] This was a rather difficult and dangerous undertaking for a boy of nineteen. Following instructions, I made my way laboriously through thickets and woods from post to post until I found a raft concealed under overhanging bushes. Appropriating this raft, I paddled quietly down the sluggish stream and managed to escape the attention of enemy scouts. I was getting along with my work when suddenly I was halted by the clicking of guns and commands of our own pickets, who perhaps mistook me for a spy. Taking me ashore, they questioned me sharply until they learned what my particular duty was, then turned me loose, with a sober warning to keep away from the river, or some enemy might get me.

Our first real contact with the war came when our brigade, now commanded by General Stannard, marched north to help head off General Lee.[6] The Confederate leader, bent on carrying the conflict to Northern soil, had swept across Maryland into

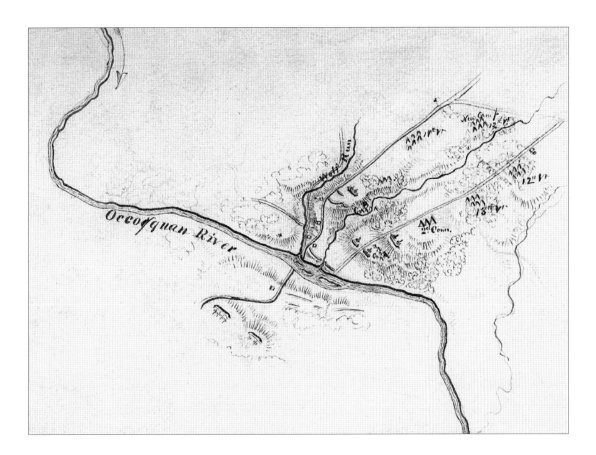

CIVIL WAR MAP WORK. 1863. Pencil drawing.

"Several of the officers had already shown an interest in my [art] work, and there had been rumors that I might get a chance to do some military drawings. . . . The chance came on February 20 [1863], in the form of a summons from Colonel [then Captain Charles Edward Blunt, of New Hampshire]. When I reported to him, I was ordered simply 'to sketch or draw.' The assignment gave me almost *carte blanche*. The Colonel wanted, as much as anything a record of camp life; consequently, I was free to draw anything I pleased, as I pleased. It is hardly necessary to add that I applied myself diligently. But I did more than make pictures of the surrounding camp and its occupants. I mapped the surrounding countryside, and the finished work was of substantial aid to the commanding officers in planning breastworks and trenches" (Jackson [1940] 1994, 58–59). This map shows Jackson's rendering of Wolf Run. It survives as an example of the topographic work that he produced. Courtesy National Park Service/Scotts Bluff National Monument.

Pennsylvania. Achieving a victory there, he might sweep back upon the capital, and the Southern Cause might emerge triumphant. The Union forces were bent towards defeating the Southern army in this purpose. Our Green Mountain boys, with the other troops, were hurried back across the Potomac.

A few days later, on July 1, 1863, we arrived on the outskirts of Gettysburg. Here our brigade was divided, three of the regiments going forward to take a position on Cemetery Ridge, another being assigned to picket duty, while ours was detailed to guard the baggage trains. The air was full of battle rumors; according to

~

"On July 7 [1863] the regiment started north. Our enlistment time was up, and we were being returned to Brattleboro, where we mustered in. We rode from Baltimore to the Jersey shore on box cars …they were so crowded that some of us had to ride on top—but it was a pleasure to be outside. All of us had a gay time along the way. The good news of Gettysburg, along with Grant's capture of Vicksburg, brought enthusiastic crowds to the stations to look at part of the army that had at last won a real victory. I considered with some amusement the fact that many of us had spent the best part of a year at the front without once firing our guns at the enemy" (Jackson [1940] 1994, 68).

~

Double exposure. 1865–66. Carte de visite.

William Henry Jackson is pictured (seated and standing) in the Frank Mowry photographic studios where he was employed as a photographic assistant. Courtesy National Park Service/Scotts Bluff National Monument.

one of them, Stuart, the dashing Confederate cavalry leader, was raiding the vicinity and was likely to pounce upon the supply trains we were protecting.[7] To prevent this, we spent nearly all night "double-quicking" with the wagons to the rear, but the anticipated attack did not come. The next duty assigned us was to pick up twenty-five hundred prisoners and escort them to Fort McHenry at Baltimore.[8] These moves took us completely out of the battle then raging around Gettysburg.

The other regiments were in the thickest of the fight, however, and the boys of the "paper-collar brigade," as Stannard's command had been dubbed, gave a good account of themselves. In a flank movement by two of the three regiments on the front of the firing line did signal service in meeting General Pickett's charge and helped in bringing about the repulse of that courageous commander and his brave men in gray.[9] Our boys captured hundreds of prisoners and many battle flags. They won rare praise from General Doubleday for their work on the crucial day that brought disaster to the high hopes of the Confederate army.

When the terms of enlistment had expired, we received our honorable discharge from military service and returned to the Green Mountain land. It was a time of happy reunions and sad ones, for some of our boys did not return. There was naturally a demand for pictures of these loved ones and of the popular military heroes of the day; so I found ample work in photography and portraiture to keep me busy.

A position was soon offered me by Styles, who had a gallery in Burlington.[10] Styles supplemented his good town business by taking his horse and buggy and canvassing the country around for pictures to enlarge and color. He generally came back with enough old daguerreotypes, tintypes, and other antiquated pictures to keep me constantly employed.[11] I was now paid twenty-five dollars a week, a royal sum for those days, and I was contented enough.

The rosy happiness and the promise of prosperity for me, however, were suddenly dispelled. In the spring of 1866 a new turn in my love affair through the breaking of my engagement to this young lady I was soon to marry caused me to pull up stakes and drift away from Vermont for a long, long while. It just seemed that I had to get away from those memory-filled scenes; but I had no idea that this misfortune was to send me to such far-away paths of adventure.

"Suddenly, my snug little structure crashed at my feet. On the second Sunday in April, I had, as usual, gone to Rutland to spend the day with Miss [Caroline 'Caddie'] Eastman and her family. Some time during the afternoon we had a difference, a difference so slight that I haven't the remotest idea now of its origin. She had spirit, I was bull-headed, and the quarrel grew. When I started for the depot after supper Miss Caddie said coldly, 'Good night Mr. Jackson.' With equal formality I responded, 'Good night, Miss Eastman,' and bowed at the hips. All the next week I was upset. I arranged to take Saturday off, and late Friday afternoon I went to Rutland, hoping that I could mend the breach. If I had possessed the whit of a squirrel I would have acknowledged my fault —whatever it was —and been forgiven. But at twenty-three I knew hardly more about the feminine mind than I do today, and I failed miserably. I was, so to speak, discharged. And since I found it impossible in my shame to face the world, I renounced it" (Jackson [1940] 1994, 81–82).

DAY DREAMS. 1866. Pencil drawing.

Will Jackson could not let go of his relationship with Caddie Eastman. It haunted and drove him for years to come. The dreams they shared of settling into family life were suddenly shattered. Life no longer felt in control. Courtesy National Park Service/Scotts Bluff National Monument.

Chapter Two

A Plunge into Unknown Fields

April 1866–June 1866

The sudden ending of my romance proved to be the opening of a new world to me. Youth-like, I took it all so seriously that nothing else for the time mattered. Only one thing was clear; I must get away from old scenes and old friends and seek forgetfulness elsewhere. Acting on this impulse, I took the first train leaving Burlington, caring little where it went, and the next day I found myself in New York City. With the same purposeless mind I left the train and wandered down from the station to City Hall Park, where I put up at Lovejoy's on Park Row.

The day after my arrival I chanced to meet a former comrade of my old Company K, a fellow we called Rock for short.[1] We had not been together long before he asked me why I was loafing around New York. I told him frankly about the reason I had cut loose from Vermont and the uncertainty of my next move. He became confidential also, saying he had been out of work for a long time and was thinking of striking out for the gold-mining camps of Montana. "What do you say to going there?" he asked.

The proposition seemed to offer just the thing for me. Rock added to the attractiveness of the plan by saying that he had inside information concerning some companies, with headquarters in the city, which were sending men out to their mines, with all expenses of the long trip paid. I needed no further urging and together we investigated this opportunity for free travel.[2] The result, as might have been expected, was failure. None of the several companies we interviewed had any such employment to offer. Our efforts, however, served to whet our desire to go west, and we picked up a good deal of information as to how we might, "by hook or by crook," work our way to that goal of our ambitions.

About the time we had fully made up our minds to go west, Rock introduced me to a chum of his, whom he called Billy. Billy was then a clerk with a prominent New York firm, but because he led a rather wild life, was losing the confidence of his employers. He wanted to get away from it all into a clearer atmosphere, and we gladly took him into our party.[3]

The three of us were now in frequent conference as to how we were to get to the Rockies. The problem was simply one of money, and none of us had enough of that necessity to see us very far on the long trail. I left Vermont with about thirty dollars, but just at this time I lost nearly all that remained—probably the work of a pickpocket. Rock was dead broke; and Billy, living from hand to mouth, delayed our departure a day or so to get his week's wages. In this emergency I sold my watch, which with Billy's contribution would have taken us to Chicago on second-class fares. But we bought tickets as far as Detroit only, for Billy assured us that when we got there he could get a hundred and fifty dollars from his prosperous sister there, just by asking for it.

Relying on this promise, we left New York in high spirits; but our hopes were not to be realized, for on arriving at Detroit we soon learned that Billy's expectations were a sorry delusion. His sister would lend him no money. She was strongly opposed, indeed, to his going west at all.

Then followed a period of hopes and disappointments. We shifted from one cheap hotel to another as our funds became exhausted, and even resorted to the pawning of portions of our clothing to pay for occasional meals. On a snowy night we walked the streets for some time without a penny to pay for lodgings, until finally we interviewed a policeman. He advised us to go to the police station, where the men not only provided cots for the night, but also contributed a little money for our supper.

This proved to be the culmination of our troubles in Detroit. The next morning Billy, who had been living with his relatives, came to us with the joyful word that his brother-in-law had given him twenty dollars and a pass to Chicago, but wanted nothing more to do with him. Elated over this little lift, we had a good meal, then redeemed our pawned clothing, and sat down to plan for the journey ahead of us.

~

An article titled "Strapped" appeared in the *Detroit Daily Tribune*. Jackson was impressed enough by the event to paste the clipping in his diary. It read: "Yesterday two young men from New York, named Ruel Rounds and Wm. Jackson, called at the police station and told a story of want, curious in parties of their appearance, yet apparently truthful. They were 'strapped' and a long way from home. They stated that in company with W. H. Crow [Crowl], who resided in this city, they started from New York to go to Montana Territory. They paid Crow's fare to this city upon the strength of representations that he had friends here who would supply them with the 'needful,' so that they could reach their destination. Crow and the New Yorkers were thus left destitute, they originally having only funds enough to bring them to Detroit" (Jackson 1866–1867, May 12, 1866).

~

IMMIGRANTS ON THE C&RI. RR. May 1866.
Pencil drawing.

Drifting westward, Jackson and his companions spent
most of their time scraping together enough money to
continue chasing their Montana dreams. Jackson spent
three weeks traveling with a wealthy thirty-year-old art
and photography student, Mr. St. Clair. He makes his
feelings toward the man very plain: "There has been so
much fussing around. . . . He is a perfect old Granny"
(Jackson 1866–1867, May 26, 1866). "St. C. and I bitch
badly. I have a very strong antipathy to the man and can
not rid myself of it. He has such a grim awkward
hesitating manner that I get out of all patience entirely"
(Ibid., May 29, 1866). They were riding on the Chicago
and Rock Island Railroad when this sketch was created.
Courtesy National Park Service/Scotts Bluff National
Monument.

On taking stock, we found that there was not enough left to take all of us to
Chicago, where we expected to get work. It was decided, therefore, that since I had
provided most of the funds for the trip thus far, I should take the pass and a few dollars and proceed at once to Chicago. Billy and Rock, after waiting a few days for some
money Rock expected, would follow me.

Arriving in Chicago, I soon found a job of sign painting.[4] A week passed, but
no word came from the boys in Detroit. I was getting a bit concerned as to what had
happened to them when one morning a pair of fagged and sorry-looking individuals came dragging up to the Sherman House, which we had named as a rendezvous.
They had been a week on the road, taking the "hobo" way to Chicago. Rock's expected remittance had not come; and a news item that appeared in a Detroit paper telling
of our police station experience and dilemma had hastened their departure. Following the railroad, they had boarded every train, freight or passenger, they could get on,
and had been just as regularly put off by the train crews, once at midnight in a drenching rain. But by getting some short rides and taking long walks and by subsisting on
occasional meals and "handouts" from farmers along the way, they had managed to
reach Chicago with their "plug hats" and clothes sadly in need of repairs and a good
cleaning.Fortunately I was now in a position to supply the boys with means to fill
their empty stomachs and get them comfortable lodgings. I continued another week
at sign painting, while Rock got work just outside of Chicago, at his former trade of
marble cutting. He took Billy with him. Our agreement was to keep in touch with
one another and to strike out again as soon as we had earned enough to pay our way
to the end of the railroad at St. Joseph, Missouri.

A day or so after we separated I chanced to meet a young man who wanted to
go into the colored photograph business. Learning of my experience, he asked me
to give him a course of instruction and then go out into the country to assist him in
working up the orders he would get by canvassing. This promised a way of getting
more money and also of moving on towards the West. After about three weeks of this
fieldwork, I parted from my pupil at Davenport, Iowa, on the banks of the Mississippi, with enough cash in hand to buy a through ticket to St. Joseph.

Rock and Billy, meanwhile, had written that they had their tickets to St. Joe and
suggested that we meet at Quincy, Illinois. Boarding one of the river packets, I went

down "the Father of Waters" and arrived at Quincy late the next evening to find the boys waiting for me. There was an immediate conference as to the state of our finances, which disclosed $3.50 as the total of our combined wealth. The train westward did not leave till morning; but since we were again about down to bedrock, we decided to save expenses by sleeping, as best we could, on the hard benches and trucks about the station.

The next morning we were off on a train pulled by one of the little wood-burning engines of those earlier days. The tracks were not the smooth ones of today, but we were glad enough to find ourselves bumping along over them. Our ride across the rolling prairies of Missouri was enlivened by several spectacular thunderstorms. A particularly impressive one came just before dawn as we were approaching St. Joe. The booming, rumbling thunder seemed to shake the very earth, while the almost incessant flashes of lightning gave us snapshot impressions of the far-away prairie in distinct and vivid contrasts of light and shade.

At daybreak our train reached its western terminus on "the Great Muddy"— then the farthest point west the railroad ran. We got up stiffly out of the uncomfortable seats on which we had dozed through the night—there were no sleeping cars on that line—and made our way along the unpaved, muddy streets from the station down to the business center near the river. After some reconnoitering while the town was waking up, we picked out the City Hotel as one that came within our limited means. Here we washed up and had breakfast. This gave us a little more courage to face the next problem of finding in this frontier town some way of getting on into the wilds of the farther West.

An advertisement in the Morning Herald—WANTED: TEAMSTERS FOR THE PLAINS—caught our attention.[5] Following up this lead, we learned that it was for bullwhackers—that is, ox-teamsters—to drive from Nebraska City to Montana at twenty dollars a month. This was what we were looking for, but decided to prospect further before making applications. Billy had a letter of introduction to a St. Joe firm that held possibilities for something better than bullwhacking. Nothing came of that, however, except the loss of half a day while we waited vainly for the man who, according to information, was about to take a mule train through to Montana.

ED OWENS, WAGON BOSS. Circa 1866. Pencil drawing.

Jackson describes the man in charge of the wagon train. The "boss . . . was the wagonmaster. Ours turned out to be a handsome gentleman named Ed Owens, with wavy, shoulder-length hair. But Owens, for all his tumbling hair and the leather leggings he rode in, was not only sound but one of the most patient men I have ever known. In a vocation resounding with profanity and explosions of bad temper he almost never raised his voice in anger; nor did I ever hear him berate even his slowest teamsters" (Jackson [1940] 1994, 109). Courtesy National Park Service/Scotts Bluff National Monument.

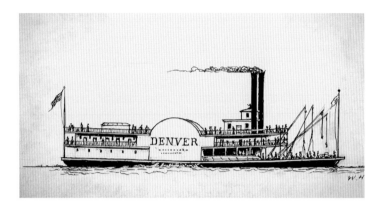

RIVER BOAT. n.d. Ink sketch.

On June 23 . . . the three drifters . . . head[ed] toward
Nebraska City to be initiated into bullwhacking. "When we
boarded the steamboat *Denver* Saturday night we found it
loaded to the guards with Mormons on their way to Salt Lake
City. We teamsters were herded together upon the hurricane
deck, with strict orders not to go below. That was very
pleasant during the night and in the cool hours after dawn.
But the climate in the Missouri Valley is not really agreeable in
late June. By noon we were soaked with sweat and beginning
to be sunburned. The boys started to slip below for ice water.
Soon all of us were circulating about the main deck—and by
no means confining our attentions to the water cooler. . . . The
Mormons at that time were a sect in whose religion and
economy a surplus of women had become an extremely
important factor. Even on the good ship *Denver* they had
their customary surplus. And soon most of the boys in our
party were trying for the attention of the extra ladies
accomplishing their purpose with no objection at all—except
from certain male members of the group who seemed to be
running the party" (Jackson [1940] 1994, 106–7). Courtesy
National Park Service/Scotts Bluff National Monument.

We made the rounds of the corrals and other places seeking chances to get in with
a horse or mule outfit, but no such job came our way. It was little wonder, for our
"plug hats," "paper collars," and untanned skins were not likely to impress the beard-
ed, roughly clad wagon bosses who had the job of picking their teamsters. Somewhat discouraged, we finally turned back to the first job and put down our names
as bullwhackers. Here we were met with a demand for a fee of a dollar and a half each.
This baffled us for the time being, for, after paying for our breakfast, we did not have
the price among us of even one fee.

We decided to save what little we had left by spending a supperless night in the
railroad station and to prospect in the morning for more funds. The next day we tried
out plan after plan in search of the few sorely needed dollars until Billy and I gave it
up as a hopeless task. We had returned from our fruitless quest and were idling at a
street corner, tired and hungry, when suddenly Rock appeared waving a five-dollar
bill before our astonished faces.

Where did he get it? A man by the name of Smith, with whom we had hob-
nobbed a little during the day, and who at first professed himself to be dead broke like
ourselves, had finally yielded to his sympathies and shared with us some of the little
money he had kept hidden away, almost from himself, for emergencies. He produced
the money *sub rosa,* as it were, to pay the fees for our jobs; then out of generosity
lent us another five dollars to help us get a few supplies for our journey up the Missouri to Nebraska City.

Overjoyed at this kindness, we soon joined the group of teamsters who were
now starting for the Far West. After a good square meal, we laid in a supply of provisions for the boat trip—crackers and cheese entirely. On the boat meals were served
to cabin passengers only. At ten o'clock we went on board—about twelve of us all
together. Ordinarily, as second-class passengers we would have stayed on the lower
deck, but this happened to be fully occupied by two or three hundred Mormon
immigrants, who were on their way to Salt Lake City. So we were assigned to the
upper deck with strict injunctions not to intrude on the cabin section below. We were
more interested, however, in our Mormon fellow passengers than in anything else.
They were from several north European countries but mostly of English stock, and
some were of refined and well-bred appearance.

WE INTERVIEW THE [WAGON] *BOSS.* n.d.
Ink wash and graphite sketch.

The three drifters are seen interviewing Ed Owens at St. Joe [Missouri] in hope of getting a job at bullwhacking. They talked to the teamsters who were around the corrals. "Got pretty well discouraged and the boys about there didn't give us much encouragement. Our tall hats & paper collars went against us very much I know. Our appearance for teamsters was not very favorable. Decided at last to stick to the first application & see what we could make there [the next day]" (Jackson 1866–1867, June 22, 1866). They finally took jobs as bullwhackers, the lowest of available jobs. Courtesy Brigham Young University.

MAP SHOWING THE LOCATION OF THE PIONEER PHOTOGRAPHER'S ACTIVITIES IN THE ROCKY MOUNTAIN REGION.

This map appeared in the first edition of *The Pioneer Photographer.*

ROUTES FOLLOWED BY THE AUTHOR ACROSS THE WESTERN PLAINS AND MOUNTAINS.

The scene of the author's experiences in 1866–67. This image was reproduced from the first edition of *The Pioneer Photographer.*

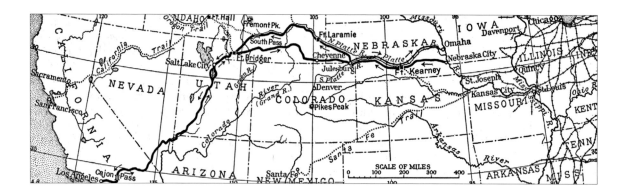

"Matt Ryan's train carrying groceries, sugar, oil, whisky, and sundries was as trim an outfit as ever crossed the plains. In line with accepted practice, it consisted of exactly twenty-five wagons—but not the traditional prairie schooners, those immense, unwieldy conveyances, which still typify the covered-wagon days to most people. Instead we used Studebakers, Brains-Murphys, and Schutler's along with the latest Jackson 'back-action' wagons (made in Jackson, Michigan)—two light, strong sections designed to be hooked together as a rolling unit. Such a wagon as the Jackson was far easier to control on grades and curves, and it had the additional advantage of packing a bigger pay load without increasing the gross burden of its 12-bull-power motor" (Jackson [1940] 1994, 114).

After chugging up the twisting Missouri for two long scorching days, we arrived at our destination, Nebraska City. It was after midnight when the old packet reached the landing. We piled off and marched up the street into the quiet place—not a light or a sign of life anywhere. Distributing ourselves over sidewalks, porches, and doorways, we slept—or tried to—until daybreak when an agent came and took us to the Cincinnati House for breakfast.

No time was lost in making ready for the journey. We were first taken to an outfitting house to get our personal equipment. I got a pair of blankets, raincoat, shoes, a Colt's revolver, cartridges, and some other things, amounting in all to about forty dollars, which was charged against my wage account.

The outfit hiring us was said to belong to Matt Ryan of Nebraska City. It consisted of twenty-five Jackson wagons with trailers, making twenty-five teams of six yoke—that is, twelve oxen to each wagon. Staple groceries and liquors made up the greater part of the three to four thousand pounds of freight in each wagon. The destination was Virginia City, Montana, and there were intimations that we might go by way of Salt Lake City, in case the Powder River cut-off to the Montana country proved too difficult on account of Indian troubles.[6]

Chapter Three

Bullwhacking across the Plains

June 1866–December 1866

The following letter, preserved for more than three-score years, brings back with vividness my experiences as a youthful bullwhacker on that thousand-mile journey from the Missouri River to the valley of the Great Salt Lake.

GREAT SALT LAKE CITY,
October 30, 1866

DEAR FATHER AND MOTHER:

In my letter of the 24th I said nothing of my journey across the plains to Salt Lake, but promised to do so in another letter. I intended writing again at once, but I had used up all my paper and was not able to get more until today.

As in my first letter, I keep my diary before me and will tell my story, as well as I can, directly from it. I am not sending any of my sketches, as most of them are too large to send with this letter. Before I leave, however, I will send all of them to you. If I attempt to carry them about with me much longer I may lose them; I have lost too many already.

We arrived at Nebraska City Tuesday morning, June 26, a little after midnight, and when the stores opened up were outfitted with blankets, additional clothing, firearms, etc., and were then marched out on the plains some three or four miles where the wagons were all loaded ready to start out. Prepared our own dinner at once. Baked bread in Dutch ovens, fried bacon, and made coffee. Ravenous appetites from the long walk made it seem the best meal I had ever eaten. Afterwards we were assigned our yokes, chains, and other things required for driving, and at night made our beds in the wagons on top of the loaded freight.

YOKING A WILD BULL. November 26–December 9, 1866. Pencil and ink sketch.

While the memories were still vivid, Jackson was documenting his recent employment as a bullwhacker. Living with the Birch family near Salt Lake City and doing odd farm chores gave the young artist time to document his experiences. Long hard days with the wagon train had left little time for doing artwork in the field. Courtesy National Park Service/Scotts Bluff National Monument.

⌣

As a novice it took Will Jackson nearly eight hours to complete the task of yoking and hitching his bulls. "The morning after our arrival at the camp we were routed out of our wagons by stentorian commands to 'Roll out! Roll out! The bulls are coming.' Our first sight of the cattle as they came crowding into the corral in the dim, dusky light preceding dawn—bellowing, ramming around and prodding each other with their horns in vicious unruliness—was not an assuring one.

"... each team was made up of six yoke ... The Leaders were the brains of the team ... The Swing contained all the unbroken riff-raff, controlled to some extent by the Pointers, while the Wheelers were the main reliance in emergencies.

"The regular procedure was, first, to get the Wheelers yoked up and hitched to the wagon wheels. Then, beginning with the leaders and attaching them to the wagon in the same way, the other four yoke were added successively, connecting each pair with heavy chains running from yoke to yoke. The wagons being parked with the tongues pointing outside the corral, the Wheelers were first taken out and put in place, and then the long string of the five yoke had to be maneuvered out of the crowded corral and around to their place in line so precisely that the driver could hook the Pointer's chain on to the end of the tongue while this movement was under way—not an easy trick. . . .

"It was with a sinking heart and with the courage sustained by grim determination that I shouldered a yoke and ventured out into the turbulent mass of bovines for the off-wheeler that was pointed out to me as the first of my team" (Jackson 1923, 5).

⌣

The following morning, when it was barely daylight, we were routed out of our wagons as the bulls (all oxen are called bulls out here) were driven in, and the operation of yoking up began at once. There was no time for breakfast. Among the cattle were many longhorns that had never been yoked, and all of them had been running the range all winter. You can possibly imagine the kind of time we tenderfeet had who had never so much as seen an ox yoked.

The wagons were parked in a circle, with openings on opposite sides, forming an enclosure called a corral, which was just about large enough to hold the 325 head that comprised our outfit. It was no light undertaking for a greenhorn at the business to go out into this corral, crowded with restless and excited bulls, and with a heavy yoke over my shoulder pick out and yoke up, first the wheelers, then the leaders, swing, and pointers that comprise the six yoke of my completed team, and make no mistake as to the right ones.

Sometimes it happens that, after a long chase through the milling herd for a particular steer that has been pointed out by the wagon boss as part of my team, I have him cornered between some wagons and finally, by careful maneuvering, succeed in getting the bow and yoke fastened together around his neck. Just then some wild bull gives a vicious dig into the ribs of the one I am gently urging up to my wagon, and sends him kiting off into the thickest of the herd. I hang on to the yoke as well as I can for a while, and am dragged and bumped about until I can stand it no longer, and then leave my ox to his own devious ways. Sometimes momentary safety from being trampled underfoot is had by jumping on the back of the nearest steer. Many of the bulls are so unmanageable that they have to be lariated and pulled up to a wagon wheel to be yoked.

There was some queer driving our first day out on the road. What with contrary and unbroken steers, who gee when they should haw, and disregard entirely the whoa, jamming right ahead and getting mixed up with other teams to the exasperation of other drivers, one begins to think he is earning more than twenty dollars a month and his grub. There were no smash-ups, however, except a few broken tongues on the wagons.

At first we made but one drive a day, green drivers and unbroken steers all making for a late start in the morning. Later, when we were more accustomed to the work, two drives a day was the rule, fifteen miles being a fair average for the day. The roads in eastern Nebraska were excellent; I never saw finer ones, broad, level, and smooth, and yet entirely unimproved. At first we traveled over a rolling prairie until we reached the valley of the Platte River, about forty miles below Fort Kearny.[1] Along the Platte it was nearly a dead level with only an occasional arroyo to cross. Our greatest trouble and annoyance was the dust, rising so thick at times, when there was no wind, that we could not see the length of our teams ahead. At the end of the day's drive we were coated with it to a uniform grayness, more like clay images than human beings.

From about this time, after passing Fort Kearny, I began to think myself a full-fledged bullwhacker. Great times I had with those twelve bulls of mine; but before long I had them so well broken that they gave comparatively little trouble. The hardest work at first was to keep up with the teams ahead. Much urging was required to do this, particularly in crossing sloughs or climbing hills, and I was a long time learning to use my whip effectively. The bull whips in use on the plains are enormous, intended apparently to reach out nearly the whole length of a team. They are of plaited rawhide, about twenty feet long, with a strip of buckskin as a popper at the end of the lash, and with a stock, or handle, some twenty-five or thirty inches in length. The professional bullwhacker takes pride in the expert use of this whip, and can make that strip of buckskin pop like the report of a pistol; and when directed against an ox that is not pulling as he should, it will make him hump up and almost go through his yoke.

The first two or three weeks were the hardest. A green team (with a greener driver) requires constant attention, and for my part, I had to be at them constantly, with whip and voice, frequently jumping over the tongue to the off side—herding them along, as they called it. For a while many of us were so hoarse from the constant repetition of whoa-haws and objurgations that we could hardly speak at all after getting into camp at night.

The program of a day's work will give you some idea of the kind of life we have been leading. In the morning, just as day is breaking and when sleep lies heaviest upon us, the night watch makes the rounds, pounding on the wagons and shouting, "Roll out! Roll out! The bulls are coming." As the turbulent herd crowds into the corral,

～

"Just a day or two before reaching the fort [Kearny], Billy [Crowl], had the honor of engaging in a personal 'encounter' with an Otoe brave. As we were halting for the midday rest, half a dozen redskins galloped up and began their usual begging for 'tobac.' Billy accommodated one of the half naked gentlemen by tossing him his chewing plug — whereupon the ingrate wheeled his horse and would have gone off with the entire pound had not Billy caught the bridle. Whipping out his colt, Billy called the Otoe every name he had learned from the professional bull whackers, plus several more he had brought from New York. He got back his property.

"At this time we were all so engrossed in the humor of the situation that we failed to observe a much more significant item of behavior. While Billy and his tobacco devotee were putting on their act another Otoe was circling the camp. After all of them had gone away the boss called us together. Owens looked at us for a long moment before he spoke.

"'Indians don't drop by in this country for a cup of tea, gentlemen,' he drawled. 'Nor just for tobacco, Mister Crowl. But they sometimes do count up the men in a wagon train. That's one reason why you carry Colts. That's one reason why we've got a stand of carbines with us. Never forget it, never forget it!'" (Jackson [1940] 1994, 117).

～

⌒

Jackson's second thoughts plagued him as he struggled west with the wagon train. "Well, here I am some fifty miles out in the plains bound for Salt Lake City & Montana. Little did I think I should ever come to this. I am now a veritable 'Bull Whacker' & heartily sick of the job in the bargain. Good enough for me. I tell myself I had no business to go. . . . It can't be helped now however. I am in it for a vengeance" (Jackson [1866–1867a] n.d., July 2, 1866).

⌒

I mentally, and sometimes quite audibly, "damn the bulls." But there they are and I must get up. Sometimes there is a desperate resolution to turn over and go to sleep again, let the consequences be what they may; but with another "Roll out! Roll out!" I conclude that I had better turn out with the others. So I stretch and yawn while feeling around for my old hat; then pulling well-worn shoes on still-aching feet, I back out of my wagon only half awake.

Shouldering one of the heavy yokes, I begin looking for my old off-wheeler. It is hardly light enough yet to distinguish objects clearly and I have some difficulty at first in telling one ox from another. But I finally get my last pointer yoked; and having previously put the wheelers on to the tongue, I drive around the other five yoke, connected with chains, and hitch them on ahead. I am ready to pull out, usually just as the sun is appearing above the horizon. When I am ready before those ahead of me have pulled out, I slip around to the mess wagon for a bit of cold bread and bacon, if any is left over. Sometimes I lay it by the night before, for I am always as hungry as a wolf before we stop for a midday meal.

About ten o'clock the train is corralled, unyoking quickly done, and the cattle turned out to graze in charge of herders, and we proceed at once to get breakfast. The train is divided into four messes, the men taking turns at the various duties. This is frequently accompanied by a good deal of contentious wrangling because there are always shirkers that fail to do their proper share of the work. The details bring the wood and water. The cooks for the time being bake bread in the big Dutch oven, make two or three gallons of coffee, slice up half a side of bacon, and with this and that done, find it hardly necessary to shout "Grub pile!" for the whole mess is right there, impatiently waiting. Each one helps himself with tin cup and plate, and retiring to the shady side of a wagon experiences for a brief half hour complete satisfaction.

The afternoon drive sometimes brings us into camp so late that it is quite dark by the time we get supper. One of the greatest difficulties in cooking is the matter of providing fuel. Wood is scarce, and along most of our route, entirely lacking. The only substitute available is buffalo chips, the hard dry manure of buffalo or cattle that is found scattered all over the plains. It makes an excellent fire for cooking purposes when entirely dry, but when damp or wet is the meanest stuff imaginable to get along with, trying the patience of the cook to the utmost. When chips are the only recourse,

those drivers who have detailed to provide fuel for the cook, hang a gunny sack on
their wagon and during the day's drive usually pick up enough along the road to fill
the bag by the time camp is made.

My heavy suppers with the great quantity of strong coffee I drink just before
going to bed frequently result in dreams that verge on nightmares. At first, when the
novelty of my adventure with its attendant work and worry was uppermost in my
mind, I had lurid dreams almost every night, and invariably they related to my team
of bulls. Sometimes I imagined them out of control and about to plunge over a great
precipice. Wild with terror, I tumble out of my wagon in a desperate attempt to head
them off from destruction, only to be yanked back by my bedfellow or brought to
my senses by the night watchman. Billy and I slept on a buffalo robe with long shaggy hair. On one occasion I began tugging at this robe so violently that I nearly threw
Billy out of the wagon. Of course he was in a high dudgeon and wanted to know
what I thought I was doing; dreaming still, I replied, "I can't get my confounded
leaders' heads around."

LIGHTNING STORM. November 26-December 9 1866.
Ink wash drawing.

Jackson's own vivid description attests to the fury of this
storm two days prior to reaching Chimney Rock,
Nebraska. "The lightning was almost incessant & when
that flashed our fire looked pale and silky. Sharp,
deafening thunder followed close upon it & from that I
knew it was unpleasantly close upon us.... In the center
of our corral was a telegraph pole, the wagons being
formed around it. While a group of us were standing
close to the fire, a blinding flash & a deafening roar
seemed to break the night over our very heads. [Billy]
Crowl jumped so that he knocked me over. I excused
his nervousness somewhat when we saw that the
telegraph pole in our midst had been shattered. . . ."
(Jackson [1866-67a], n.d. July 30, 1866). Courtesy
National *Park Service*/Scotts Bluff National Monument.

Nothing of particular interest occurred while on our way along the Platte Valley until we reached the crossing of the South Fork near Julesburg.[2] Our camps were
usually near the river with frequent opportunities for bathing. The water was very
muddy, flowing in strong currents, spreading out sometimes to two or three miles
in width and so shallow that it could be forded at almost any place.

With the exception of a few plains Indians, Otoes or Pawnees, that we met a few
days out from Nebraska City, we saw none of the hostile redskins we had heard so
much about. Many rumors were floating about of their intention to clean up the whole
valley, and some confirmed reports of actual depredations. At Fort Kearny the military command enforced a regulation that not less than thirty wagons would be permitted to pass on up the valley and every man must be well armed. I had a Colt's
revolver and also a Spencer carbine and was therefore "well heeled." A waiting train
of ten wagons made the necessary reinforcement to our numbers.

We arrived at the crossing of the South Platte, some three miles above Julesburg,
on July 24th. The river at this place is more than half a mile wide and not more than
four feet deep where the current runs the deepest and strongest. There were a number of other trains gathered there, engaged in crossing or preparing to cross. The river
was filled from bank to bank with teams, a dozen drivers to each, wearing but a single garment. The scene was an exciting and intensely interesting one, and it will be
almost impossible for me to give you an adequate idea of it by words alone. I have a
sketch, which I will send you, that will perhaps give you a better idea of what was done
than my descriptions, but still conveys little of the real life and action of the scene.

For our own preparations, the trailer wagons were uncoupled and to each single wagon the teams were doubled; sometimes even eighteen yoke were used. The
first plunge into the river was into the deepest part. The cattle were excited and reluc-
tant to enter the water; and when we got them in, it was difficult to make them string
out and pull, as they should.

The river bottom is a shifty quicksand, and if the wagon is allowed to halt too
long, it will sink into the sand so as to be almost immovable. When this is about to
happen, there follows a perfect pandemonium of shouting and yelling, with crack-
ing of whips and thumping with sticks, as the drivers, up and down the line on both
sides, urge on the floundering cattle so that there shall be no pause in their progress.

And so it goes on continually all the way across, with hoarse gee-haws and whoa-haws enlivened with many shrill yip-hi-his. The current is swift and strong in the deeper places, sometimes taking the smaller cattle off their feet until they are pulled back into line by the others. We were about two hours crossing one wagon with doubled-up team; so there were many re-crossings to take over the fifty separate wagons of the whole outfit.

In the midst of all this hurly-burly came a band of about fifty Cheyenne Indians, making the crossing at the same time—big braves on little horses, squaws leading the pack ponies, dogs and papooses perched on top, and other juveniles paddling along in nature's garb only. Both sides of the river were lined up with corralled wagon trains, and the banks were crowded with groups of drivers, soldiers and Indians interested in the proceedings.

At sunset about half of our outfit had been crossed over. I was on the farther side, clothed only in a very wet shirt, all the rest of my clothing and personal articles being in my other wagon across the river. I did not fancy the idea of returning, as a thunderstorm was impending and it was rapidly growing darker. The mess wagon was over however; I was ravenously hungry, having had nothing since early morning, and decided to remain. I chopped up a wagon tongue and a broken ox yoke for a fire, and helped get supper for our mess, and afterwards bunked in with one of the boys with a buffalo robe for cover. But the storm was right on our heels; we had not dropped off into dreamland when it burst upon us with terrific fury. For a time we feared our wagon would be capsized or the gale carry away its cover. First came hail that pounded the wagon sheets like a cannonade, and rain followed in torrents. Thunder and flashes of lightning were incessant, and apparently right overhead. But it was soon over, as generally happens when the violence is the greatest.

The next day we finished crossing without mishaps, and no particular damage from water, as we shifted the loads in the wagons so that sugar, flour, etc., were on top. Resuming our journey, we took a northwesterly course over to the North Platte, passing on the way several bands of Indians traveling eastward. They fraternized with some of our boys when we were in camp and afforded considerable amusement.

Our route up the North Platte was without particular interest. The scenery along the river is quite fantastic—as you may see from my sketches. Courthouse Rock,

LARAMIE PEAK. Circa 1940. Ink and wash on card.

The peak is seen from the north, the highest point in the Black Hills of Wyoming (now known as the Laramie Range). Jackson described tough times passing around these mountains. Courtesy Brigham Young University.

Chimney Rock, and Scotts Bluff, as they are called,[3] are merely hard shales and clays weathered into many curious and fantastic shapes resembling tall chimneys and castles with domes and minarets, all having a most picturesque variety of outline.

Fort Laramie appears to be the best built fort we have seen so far.[4] It looks like a large settlement from a distance. We drove right through without stopping, so that I had little opportunity to look around. Our course after this was over rough, mountainous country, touching the river only a few times, up to the crossing at Platte Bridge.[5] The afternoon of the day we passed Laramie we were until three o'clock in the morning in pulling up over a long, steep, and sandy hill. At Big Bitter Cottonwood we caught up with a Mormon immigrant train, passing by their corral as they were getting breakfast. There were some three or four hundred men, women, and children in the outfit, mostly English, with some Danes and Norwegians and all of the peasant class—that is, farmers. Each little family group had its own fire, making a lively and interesting scene, particularly at night, when their corral resembles a military bivouac.

Forty miles from Laramie we came to the place where the Powder River Road branched off for Montana.[6] Because of Indian troubles, the military authorities prohibited the passage of trains in groups of less than 300 wagons. Most of us drivers wanted to go that way and supposed all along that we would, but our wagon boss decided on the safer but longer route. It was 425 miles to Virginia City by the new line and by the old way about 850. It was better for us that we did not go that way, as but few trains succeeded in getting through at all.

We had some hard pulling and tough times in passing around the Black Hills.[7] It is a rough, wild country, in which we were frequently forced to drive late at night to make camp. On some of those steep, rocky hills it was a wonder we did not smash everything to pieces. Dust was a great nuisance. The soil is a red earth that pulverizes into a fine dust. Under the feet of our three hundred oxen it rose in such clouds that it was difficult to see or even to breathe.

Just before we reached Platte Bridge the Indians had been playing the deuce with some of the telegraph stations. The one at Deer Creek was burned just after we had passed it;[8] we could see the smoke and flames quite clearly. Later we passed several army wagons loaded with soldiers tearing down the road at breakneck speed, bound for the scene of action. We crossed the bridge August 18—quite an imposing bridge for this country, with the added distinction of being the only one over the Platte River. It is substantially built of logs on some thirty or more piers and seemed to be about a quarter of a mile long. The tolls were five dollars per wagon.

Leaving the bridge, we passed over a rough country, with some steep hills. This was in the heart of the hostile Indian country, and we heard many stories of the depredations that had recently occurred. They did not trouble us much, but we had to keep a strong guard out every night. Roads were good, and along the Sweetwater we found good grazing for the cattle and plenty of buffalo chips for the cooks' fires. Wood in any shape was a scarce article—nothing but sagebrush and willows, except far up in the hills, where there were a few pines beyond reach. Coyotes and wolves were numerous and gave us a serenade every night; sometimes I thought their howling and barking rather musical when coming out of the still night air. Antelopes, sage hens, and rabbits abounded, and we had many a chase after this small game, with a hit occasionally, which made an agreeable addition to our bill of fare.

Almost before we were aware of it we had passed the continental divide over South Pass. There were no features indicating a pass, as generally understood—only

~

"A little more than three weeks before our arrival—the 25th of July, to be exact, the [Platte River] Bridge had been the scene of a tragical [*sic*] encounter of the troops with a large band of Indians under Red Cloud, who had massacred a small detachment sent out to assist an incoming train—the train later being entirely annihilated by these same Indians—all this taking place within sight of the rest of the troops at the post. Platte Bridge is now to be Casper, in honor of Casper [Caspar] Collins, the young lieutenant who led the forlorn hope against the Indians" (Jackson 1923, 22).

~

Tension and frustrations over living and working conditions rose among the bullwhackers. Sugar rations ran out, and some of the men, Jackson's friends Rock and Gray included, pilfered it from the wagons. Ed Owens announced that all shortages would be charged against wages at the end of the trip. This angered Rock and Gray, who stormed out of camp. "[W]hen we reached the Sweetwater Station, Rock and Gray, who had gone on ahead with the Doolittle wagons, were already at work on a new job. Laughingly they told us they were now 'telegraphers.' But actually they were cutting and carrying hay for the telegraph company's horses, at $1.50 a day and their board" (Jackson [1940] 1994, 129).

~

Wagon train. November 26–December 9, 1866.
Ink wash sketch.

This sketch, discussed in Jackson's diary (Jackson 1866–1867), depicts how the bullwhackers attempted to vary their diet of bacon, flour, and coffee. Courtesy National Park Service/Scotts Bluff National Monument.

a broad expanse of rolling hills with two solitary buttes to the south, and the Wind River Mountains to the north, whose snow-clad summits were first seen from a point on the Sweetwater sixty miles distant. We found the air decidedly chilly in crossing the pass. On the 30th of August we had snow and hail, and the wind that came with it went through my rather inadequate clothing, chilling me to the marrow in my bones.

From here to Hams Fork, where I left the train, we traveled along with the Mormon immigrant train that I have mentioned.[9] A great many of their horses and cattle had been run off by Indians and nearly all who were able to do so were walking. As long as we were near each other, many of the immigrants, especially the more attractive women, rode on our wagons.

At Hams Fork the road divided, to the right for Montana and to the left for Salt Lake City. As our train was now bound for Montana and I had made up my mind to go to Salt Lake, Bill Maddern joined me in leaving the train, thereby forfeiting all pay due up to that time. To tide over the interval until another train came along going our way, we undertook a job of hauling hay for the stage stations of the "Overland."

From early morn to late at night seven days a week we worked at loading, hauling, and stacking hay, sleeping out in the open at nights. At one time came a heavy fall of snow and we awoke in the morning with an uncomfortably warm blanket of snow over us. I lost one of my sketchbooks here, containing many of my best sketches. Lost my coat also, at another time, with my diary in one of the pockets. Fortunately it was found and brought back to me.

I found it pretty hard work at first to load and stack hay, but after getting broken into it I could handle a fork as well as any of those who were brought up on that kind of work. We hauled forty tons to one station ten miles from the hay fields and the same quantity to another station twenty-five miles away. The contractor got $35 a ton and paid $12 a ton for cutting; we got a dollar a day for the rest of the work.

After three weeks of this kind of work, a freighting outfit of a dozen wagons came along bound for Salt Lake. It was short two drivers, and we took the job at a dollar a day. I had a six-yoke team and an immense wagon with a load of 8000 pounds. We got along all right until we crossed the Wasatch Mountains just before entering Salt Lake Valley. A snowstorm caught us there, which made bad work for all, particularly for me. As we left the Weber Valley to cross the range, it began raining. We lay over a day on account of it, and as it looked like clearing the next morning, we hauled out and started for the summit.

The roads, newly graded, were deep in mud and slippery, making hard work for the cattle to pull their loads. Before we got to the summit, many of the teams gave out and then it began snowing. We camped over night in Parleys Park with part of the outfit, and the next day renewed our efforts to take the remaining wagons to the top of the pass. In the meantime, it began snowing again and turned very cold. With doubled teams we managed to take up all but two of the wagons, mine and another, which were so deep in the mud that they had to be unloaded. They were left over night and by morning were frozen in so hard that it took nearly another day to dig them out.

The only footwear that I had at this time was a pair of moccasins without stockings. They withstood this kind of service but a short time and I was soon running around practically barefoot. The roads were deep in mud, while alongside the snow

∽

Eight bullwhackers, including Jackson, decided to depart from the train if it did not go to Salt Lake. As the train began to roll out on Friday morning Jackson finally got up the courage to discuss the subject with Ed, the wagonmaster. "When I broached the matter there was the devil to pay at once. [He] stopped the train & wanted to know what in hell this meant. Now was the time for the rest of the boys to come forward & speak up, but just at that time they had some other business on hand & couldn't be there. Bill Maddern was the only one who came in time. Told Ed that I hired on to go to Salt Lake & was going there come what would. Bill ditto. Ed & Frank K. [Ed's assistant] were both rip tearing mad, swearing by everything above and below that we should not & that we should either go with the train or they would fix us so that there would be no danger of us ever reaching Salt Lake. Such talk didn't scare us very much & we finally after much cussing and swearing all around carried our point. So the train gradually dwindled off out of sight & there Bill Maddern and I sat—two of the most forlorn & disconsolate looking mortals as one ever saw" (Jackson [1866–1867a] n.d., September 7, 1866). Eventually the men made it to an Overland stage station on their way to Bridger, where they took an interim job of hauling hay at $1.00 per day.

∽

W.H.J. AS HE REACHED SALT LAKE CITY IN THE FALL OF 1866. Circa 1920–1930. Hand-tinted colorized glass lantern-slide.

Upon arriving in Salt Lake City as a bullwhacker "my coat was the same yellow-black hand-me-down I had got in Detroit; my trousers were so patched and torn that I wore two pairs to avoid arrest for indecent exposure; my second-hand boots were squashed down and without heels; my hat was recognizable as a head covering only when I had it on. To complete the picture of a classic ragamuffin I now owned a curling tawny beard" (Jackson [1940] 1994, 138–39). Courtesy National Park Service/Scotts Bluff National Monument.

but thinly covered the roughness. I kept on with the driving until late in the evening; and then as it was my turn to help in herding the cattle until the night herders had their supper, I drove them two or three miles down the canyon to where there was feed. Running over the snow-covered ground benumbed my feet so that they were devoid of all feeling. I got back to camp about nine o'clock, pretty well played out; drank some cold coffee and bunked in. I didn't get out of that wagon again for three days; my feet were so sore and swollen from being frostbitten that it was impossible to bear my weight upon them.

The drive down Parleys Canyon was a hard one for me. The road was rocky and rough with many sharp turns and steep pitches. We were two days getting out into the open country, and all that time I was lying on top of bags of sugar and flour and tossed around like corn in a popper. At one of the halts to repair damages I had a chance to get my head outside the wagon cover and make a sketch of the canyon in one of its deepest places. The last day into Salt Lake City my feet were healed enough for me to walk and drive my team.

The city is situated on a gentle slope at the foot of the mountains, while the valley itself stretches off as far as the eye can reach to the west and south and is surrounded by snow-capped mountains. The lake is just discernible to the northwest with its mountain islands. The city, from a distance, looks like a great garden. Every house outside the business center, with hardly an exception, is surrounded with fruit trees and flowers. Peaches are ripening, and abound in great quantities. One of our drivers told someone in the crowd that came out to watch us pass that this was a Church train; that is, one bringing supplies for the Mormon merchants. The word was passed along and quickly other children came out from their homes with baskets and aprons filled with peaches, apples, and other fruits, which were given to the drivers without stint.

Most of the residential houses are built of adobes (sun-dried bricks) with a few log houses here and there, but on the main business street there are as fine store fronts as can be seen anywhere. The streets are wide and have streams of clear mountain water running along both sides. The Mormons are building a great Temple, the foundations of which are hardly completed as yet, but they indicate an imposing edifice. Some of the official church buildings are quite pretentious, particularly Brigham

Young's residence. There seem to be many "Gentiles" here, some of whom are prominent and influential in business affairs.

The weather was unpleasant when we first arrived; a wet snow with muddy streets made it disagreeable getting about. It cleared up afterwards and was as fine and balmy as one could wish, and it is said that it will continue so for some time. We are keeping house and getting along very well and with but little expense. Our mainstay is bread and potatoes with meat occasionally. It costs three of us about $5 a week besides room rent.

Today I received my first letter since passing Fort Laramie. I learned that other letters had been sent to Virginia City. I had written there to have them forwarded here but have received none as yet. But I must close; the length of this letter must have wearied you and you will probably thank me not to make them so long in the future. Hoping that this as well as my previous letters will reach you safely, I am, as ever

Your loving son,
WILLIAM

⁓

"Byers, the owner [of the wagon train that Jackson traveled with to Salt Lake City], came down to pay us off. There was a good deal of haggling about 'extras' and 'deductions' all around; but I think the low point of the bargaining came when Byers docked my wages two dollars to make up for time lost after I had frozen my feet in his service. In my whole life I can recall no single mean act quite the equal of that one....I was 114 days on the road from the Missouri River. 71 days were with the first outfit, 20 days with the haying contractors and 23 days on the final drive to Salt Lake City. The entire proceeds from my adventure was 21 dollars, plus experience, that I got from Byers" (Jackson 1923, 36–37).

⁓

Chapter Four
Trailing California Mustangs

After six weeks at the Birch farm the boys headed west with Ed Webb's wagon train for California. The fare was $30, for which they were assigned a Schuller wagon with a bed of straw inside. The train was empty except for passengers. It made good time, leaving Salt Lake on December 23, 1866, and arriving in Los Angeles on January 31, 1867 (Jackson 1866–1867).

"At Twenty Mile Ranch . . . Bill and I were welcomed for another free meal. After dinner and an exchange of ideas with our hosts, old Mr. and Mrs. Ward and their son Nels and his wife, we offered to go to work. Ward said he could use one of us, and Maddern at once withdrew in my favor, insisting that he would rather take his chances on getting work at the mines. When he left the next morning, I gave him a cheap watch I had managed to hang on to since Salt Lake—if he got hard up he could sell it; if not he could return it some day. Bill and I exchanged letters for a while; but I never saw him again" (Jackson [1940] 1994, 153–54).

December 1866–August 1867

Bill Maddern and I stayed two months in Salt Lake City, most of the time working for one of the Mormons who lived down on Mill Creek, and then we joined a mule freight outfit going to California. Bill, by the way, was a brother of the well-known actress, Minnie Maddern. Leaving Salt Lake City at Christmas time, we made our way over the California trail down through Utah and across the southern part of Nevada into the deserts and rich valleys of California. Thus the "wanderlust" which had seized upon me when I cut loose from Vermont finally landed me on the shores of the Pacific.

It was about the first of February when we reached Los Angeles, which at this time was largely Mexican in general appearance. Approaching it by way of Cajon Pass,[1] and pausing for a moment on the brow of a low hill overlooking Los Angeles River, we obtained a picturesque view—a long line of low, tile-roofed, adobe buildings interspersed with groves of palms and orange trees. A few modern structures showed more prominently out of the general level; the courthouse with its cupola and one or two churches were among the most conspicuous buildings. Off to the right was the old mission, reminiscent of the days when Father Junipero and his followers laid the foundations for this city with its environs,[2] which today has become the photographic capital of the world. The same elements that were later to make for its extraordinary development—clear skies, mountains, ocean, various peoples—were all present.

We intended to continue from this point to San Francisco, and hoped to travel by one of the small boats that occasionally put in at the neighboring port of San Pedro.[3] We just missed one, however, and before another came along we had spent our last dollar.

Joining another comrade in the same predicament, Bill and I shouldered our bundles and started out afoot towards the Golden Gate city.[4] We managed to get

SAN FERNANDO CAÑON. February 12, 1867.
Pencil drawing.

February 12 was a long day for the two foot-travelers. It commenced at sunrise with a walk to a spring to indulge in . . . "a big drink of water to fill up. Started out again on our pilgrimage. . . . After crossing a desert like valley for some 15 miles we came to the old mission of San Fernando where we replenished our commissary by the purchase of a few crackers for a quarter. Our route there took us up into the hills again passing some five or six solitary ranches at one of which we made a trade with a Mexican woman, who could not talk English, for a cake of Dutch cheese for 'two bits'—everything seems to be 'two bits'—and then went down under the hill where we were protected from the driving wind that has been blowing all day and made a noon day meal of what we had. Continuing our journey and following a narrow canyon to the hills we came to a house where an eastern woman lived where we stopped and had quite a long chat with her. Got two or three pounds of crackers for a quarter and a little farther on at the tollgate got a few matches. From there the road ascended quite rapidly and at the summit the grade is cut down perpendicularly through the rock at a depth of from 40 or 50 feet and just wide enough for one team to pass." The boys continued on until late in the day. They finally made a "dry camp" after traveling about thirty miles by foot with only the morning drink. They were told water was about four miles ahead but "the four miles turned out to be 6 or 7" the next day (Jackson [1866–1867a] n.d., February 12, 1867). Courtesy Colorado Historical Society.

enough to eat through the generosity of ranchers along the road, and found our nights' lodgings under the trees. After we had gone about a hundred miles, we parted company, each one taking some temporary employment we happened to find on the way. My opportunity came at a stage station at the foot of Tehachapi Pass, where a helper was wanted.[5]

By the end of March I had had enough of playing the part of hostler and general roustabout for the stage station and was impatient to move on again. I had meanwhile given up the idea of going to San Francisco; in fact, I was getting pretty tired of this kind of life. With something of a longing to get back to "the States" once more, I threw my bundle into a passing freight wagon, and was soon in Los Angeles again.

With a few gold coins in my pocket, some of which went to make me outwardly more presentable, I put up at the United States Hotel, where I spent a brief period of leisure, as long as my money lasted. Here Spanish was heard more frequently than English, and it was a motley group of vaqueros, miners, and shopkeepers that crowded the barrooms and lined the long tables at mealtimes.

LOS ANGELES. IN 1867. Oil painting.

For a few days we drove our mustangs into town every night, to be corralled in its outskirts. Modern Hollywood, capital of the moving pictures, lies among the Cahuenga Hills in the distance at right. Courtesy Seaver Center for Western History Research, Los Angeles County Museum of Natural History.

My desire to get back east was now growing stronger. Meeting old man Webb, one of the owners of the freight train with which I had traveled from Salt Lake, I explained my circumstances and expressed my wishes frankly. He advised me to get in with one of the outfits that were driving horses across the plains to eastern markets, and mentioned Jim Begole, who was gathering a band of California broncos for that purpose. Jim was one of my bullwhacker comrades who had come down from Salt Lake with us. "Better see Jim," Webb suggested.

I promptly set out to find Jim, who was working the range five or six miles out of town. After trudging along on foot and getting on wrong roads, meeting only Mexicans who did not *sabe Americano,* I finally by good luck stumbled on Begole's camp, a solitary wagon beside a slough, attended by an obliging young man.

"Yes, this is Jim's camp," he said, "but he is away hunting lost horses. I will try to find him for you."

He jumped on a pony that was near at hand and was soon out of sight among the bands of horses grazing over the meadows in the distance. Fortunately Jim was not far away, and he left his work long enough to tell me that we must wait until evening to talk business. I then found out that he was not yet sure he would go east with these horses, but if he did he promised to do his best to have me go with him. Jim at the time was only a vaquero working for Sam McGannigan, the boss of the outfit.[6]

For two weeks, while Sam and his vaqueros were rounding up a herd of mustangs and half-breed Morgans, I was kept in suspense. One day someone told me that Sam had a band of horses corralled in the lower part of town, and I went down to investigate. To my surprise, he ordered me to mount one of the saddle horses and help drive the whole band across the river and herd them wherever good feed could be found. My companion for the day was a young Mexican, who could speak very little English, a fortunate thing, as I wished to pick up some Spanish. Even before the day was over I was able to *"sabe Mexicano un poco,"* as he said, in the vernacular of the country.

Although Sam said everything was about ready for our start east, it was two weeks before we got away. The business of swapping and dickering for other horses, and the shoeing of the lively broncos for the hot desert and mountain trails took much time and was trying work. On my second day on the job I had to hold the horses the vaqueros had roped while they put hackamores (rope halters) on them before shoeing. As a result, I was dragged all over the corral with much damage to clothes, knuckles, and shins.

The shoeing process was hard on both men and horses. After being lassoed, the fractious animal was thrown and had his feet tied together in a bunch crosswise, sawbuck fashion, so that the shoer could get in his work. The bronco naturally kicked at such treatment, and the shoeing was haphazard. The horses that were thought to have sound hoofs were not shod, but many of them became lame later. Some of those that were shod cast shoes, so that we had to repeat the shoeing process nearly every day while traveling.

My chief occupation while we remained in California was herding horses on the hills about Los Angeles. These days were full of hard work and worry. Our horses had been gathered from so many places that they did not hang together well. We were troubled also by other horses grazing near. One day a black stallion came out from another band and attempted to run off some mares from our herd. At this, a stallion of ours immediately gave battle. The two, snorting defiance, with heads high and manes and tails streaming out, closed in on each other. They circled around as if sparring for an opening, then reared to a clinch, savagely biting each other's necks, and occasionally broke away, to back up in a fusillade of kicking. They repeated these

CATCHING UP HORSES IN CALIFORNIA. April 1867. Ink and pencil drawing.

While waiting for the drive to begin "little jobs . . . kept coming. . . . They knocked the knees out of my trousers and the toes out of my boots. They took pieces out of my hide. And they paid me nothing at all—except the $5 Sam advanced me to get out of hock at the United States Hotel. But they got me a place. On April 30, we loaded up McGannigan's wagon . . . and prepared to leave for the market in Omaha 2,000 miles away" (Jackson [1940] 1994, 157). Courtesy National Park Service/Scotts Bluff National Monument.

rounds till the invader was finally driven off. It was a more thrilling scene than those of similar horse combats that have been made into exciting moving pictures in these recent years.

Our horses had to be herded closely day and night. The night work was difficult, because with the thick spring fogs we often could not see the ground from the saddle. The only thing to do at such times was to keep within hearing of the bell, for horses generally are quite faithful in staying close to the bell mare. The horses were nervous on these foggy nights and ready to stampede at the most trivial happening. The mere snapping of a twig might send them off into separate groups headed for their former ranges. Something of the kind happened one night, giving Jim and Sam a chase down below Santa Ana before the horses were rounded up. Another reason for keeping our band closely guarded was the danger that thieves might run off some of the horses at night or in one of the stampedes. We did not feel safe from raiders until we were well on our way over the mountains and desert.

The day came finally when we were ready to take the trail eastward. We had in round numbers one hundred and fifty horses, with four of us—Sam, the owner, and Jim, John, and myself—to take care of them. John usually drove the camp wagon, though the rest of us occasionally took turns at that job. Four days out we were joined by another outfit headed by a man named Keller, with two men and about one hundred horses, bound for the same destination as ourselves. It was mutual protection for us to make the risky trip together.

On the day Keller joined us I had an experience that came near ending the journey for me right there. I was riding a half-broken, bald-faced bay horse, when my cinch happened to slip back too far. I dismounted to adjust the saddle and tighten up, but had hardly touched the ground when the bronco with a snort made a sudden jump sidewise, jerking the rope from my hand and snapping off the bridle rein. The next thing I knew he was away out in the sagebrush, trailing the saddle at his heels till it was just about demolished. Two or three of the boys gave chase and finally one of them succeeded in roping the runaway.

After picking up as many pieces of the saddle as I could find, I rode into camp on another horse, feeling pretty sore and aware that Sam was displeased. That evening he remarked that he thought it would be unsafe for me to go through with the drive, that the horses were mainly broncos with more or less of the devil in them, and that there was no telling what might happen to me—I might get my neck broken. He ended by suggesting that he thought it would be to my interest as well as his own that I should go no farther. All of this I accepted without protest and began at once to think of some other way to get east.

The next morning, however, Sam came over to me and said that he disliked to put me to any inconvenience, and that if I would do my best to handle the stock safely, I might go along—which I was quite ready to promise. I had some satisfaction in knowing I was not the only one in trouble. John went to sleep on night herd and let his saddle horse get away, causing us two or three hours' delay. The next night Sam himself, while on night duty, thought he saw a bear and took a shot at it. This started the horses; and we were aroused by Sam shouting, "Stampede!" as he was rushing towards our camp. Jim and I got up out of our blankets just in time to head them off from running over us.

Every day brought a new experience. When we neared the Mojave River, the horses, feverish with thirst, smelled the water and stampeded towards it. It was a tight race to keep up with them. My horse, as wild as the rest, kept me up in the thick of the herd half the time, almost smothered with desert dust. I had little control over him and was glad when, with the whole bunch, we plunged into the stream together.

A day or so later we were overtaken by some men from Los Angeles looking for stolen horses; they searched our band, but found none. We followed the Mojave River for several days until it sank into the sands. Burned ranches along the road showed that raiding Mojaves had been there since I had passed this way a few months previously.

In crossing the three hundred miles of desert that lay between the Mojave River and the Mormon settlements on the Rio Virgin in southern Utah, we had a trying time. Much of the driving we did at night, as the sun was so intensely hot by day that the horses could hardly endure it. Day herding during this time was especially hard, for the animals were restless from thirst and the intense heat and wandered everywhere. Fifty miles from where we left the Mojave River we reached Bitter Springs—well named from the warm and brackish water we found there. We tried

~

Kellar [Keller, who had previously joined the drive with his stock] left the drive over an argument about wife, Mrs. Jim Kellar, "who was very young and barely intelligent enough to distinguish bright objects" (Jackson [1940] 1994, 159). "From the first Sam, boss of our outfit, had cast lecherous eyes upon her and it was not long before he had dominated her to such an extent that he usurped the old man's place and prerogatives whenever the occasion permitted, which frequently occurred on account of the night herding business. The excitement now was not due to the discovery of this condition but to the boldness of the principal parties, the apparent obliviousness of the old man, and the incriminance of detection and its results, for he is supposed to be a bad man with a gun" (Jackson [1866–1867a] n.d., May 15, 1867).

"Kellar and I were on herd the night of the twenty-sixth, when, abruptly, the old man announced that he was going back to camp and 'get a decent night's rest.' Here was the crisis at last. Would I fire my pistol and give Sam warning? I compromised. I fired twice, as arranged, but 'in the ground so they could not be heard very far.'

"In the morning, when I returned to camp, there was no Sam, and Kellar was cutting out his horses from the rest of the band. So something had happened!

"The boys told me that Sam had not heard my muffled pistol shots, and that he was caught by Kellar *flagrante delicto*. But all the looked for gun play did not materialize, only an exchange of genealogical references. . . . That was about the saddest end to weeks of suspense that anyone could imagine. All the boys felt cheated, and I have wondered ever since about the wild, wild West where men were said to shoot each other at the drop of a hat" (Jackson [1940] 1994, 164).

~

SALT LAKE–LOS ANGELES TRAIL: COTTONWOOD SPRS.
May 19, 1867. Pencil sketch.

"Got a bright early start & drove over to Cottonwood [Springs] by noon. Camped in good water and had plenty of water. Some 3 or 4 Indians around camp in P.M. Got all of them to fix up my bow" (Jackson 1866–1867). The Salt Lake–Los Angeles Trail was a difficult and dangerous wagon road. Distance between water holes averaged thirty miles. In the year 1851 Mormon colonists left Utah using the trail and founded San Bernardino, California. Courtesy National Park Service/Scotts Bluff National Monument.

to water the horses by taking them up a few at a time, but they were so frantic for water that we could not control them, with the result that the springs were soon nothing but a thick mud puddle.

Driving the animals out to where there was some grass, we tried to hold them till we started on our night drive to the next spring. Some of us attempted to get a little sleep, preparatory for the work ahead, but the air was so stifling, so suffocating, that there was no rest for man or beast. It was sheer punishment that we suffered from the sun's fierce rays, which, reflecting from sand and rocks, burned our eyes and lips and parched our throats. Despite the aridity of the country, however, desert shrubs and plants in full blossom that May month made a sight to gladden the heart of any lover of the beautiful in nature. There were grander, if not more beautiful, sights ahead of us when we came into the valley of the Rio Virgin and the Painted Desert region of southern Utah; but before we reached these picturesque scenes, much trouble lay in store for us.

It was a long pull to the top of the plateau lying between the Muddy, a stream in Nevada, and the valley of the Rio Virgin, in Utah. The descent of Virgin Hill was almost like jumping off into space, so steep was the road.[7] Then there was the crossing and re-crossing of the river, at that time of the year a swift, turbid-red stream with treacherous quicksands. To add to our apprehensions, thunderstorms were impending with indications of a cloudburst, and there was real danger that we might be caught in one of the deluges that sometimes swept down those narrow valleys. Though we escaped this peril, we had to make twenty or more difficult crossings of the river, where it zigzagged from bluff to bluff across the narrow valley. Jim usually rode ahead to sound out the fords before the wagons started in. Two or three times his horse went down, rolling over with him in the swift current. Dan, one of Keller's men, had the hardest luck of all. While Dan was trying to help Keller get his wagon out of the quicksands, his horse plunged into a deep hole, and both Dan and the animal were rolled along for a hundred yards or more before making a landing.

We managed at last to get out of the narrow valley with its twisting river and camped up on a high bench between Beaverdam and Santa Clara.[8] It was supposed to be a dry camp, but the rain that poured down that night made a very wet one.

The next day we passed through the little Mormon town of Santa Clara, where we found the people keen to swap horses with us. As a result of the trading, we got rid of some of our footsore animals and acquired better travelers. Piute Indians of a peaceable sort followed us for some distance, trying to trade for our horses. The next town we struck was St. George, a quiet little place of adobe and log houses. This was the capital of Utah's "Dixie," as the people there like to call this extreme southwestern corner of the state. For the next three weeks we continued our journeying northward through the valleys of Utah, stopping to trade in each of the Mormon settlements along the route. The swollen streams and the wet weather also served to delay our progress.

June had almost gone before we left Salt Lake Valley over the same overland route by which I had entered it some months previously when with frozen feet I was bumped down Parleys Canyon in a freight wagon. Our band of horses, despite the trading, was but slightly smaller than when we left California. The men all stayed with our outfit, except Johnnie, the good-natured butt of the party, who left us for his home at Egan, Nevada. By this time our horses had become so welded together that it was difficult to separate them. This made easier going for a time; but there were other difficulties to be faced in making the journey across mountains and plains. The dangers from predatory bands of Indians increased as we went east. The crossing of the swift, swollen streams still gave us serious difficulty, for our horses seemed averse to taking to the water.

Blacks Fork was the first of the streams we found provided with a ferryboat—a flat scow, running on a rope trolley. Only a few of our most tractable horses could be driven or even dragged aboard the boat. Swimming was less expensive and more expeditious; so we ferried only our wagon and team horses and then attempted to swim the rest of the animals. Joining forces with some emigrants who had a bunch of cattle, we rushed the horses and cattle together into the water. The cattle crossed all right, but our horses drifted down the middle of the stream and came back to the side from which they had started. After two other attempts we managed to get all but fifteen or twenty across; but these refractory ones could not be persuaded to take either the boat or the stream until we had finally brought the rest of the other horses back again. Then with a rush and a hurrah we crowded the whole band into

CLIMBING OUT OF THE VALLEY OF THE RIO VIRGIN, UTAH. n.d. Ink wash drawing.

"In making the descent of the Virgen [Virgin] Hill I had a great time. My little white pony was so awfully restless & impatient & I had so short a rope that it was impossible to hold him, as I had to get off and walk down. He pulled me along, crowded me off the rocks, hit me a belt or two & went off on his own hook. Caught him again & mounted him to keep him. Got everything down safely & camped on the bank of the river. Herded the stock all night on the flats on salt grass. John and Harry on [herd]. Very windy and cold night" (Jackson 1866–1867, May 24, 1867). Courtesy National Park Service/Scotts Bluff National Monument.

SWIMMING THE HORSES. n.d. Pencil sketch.

Driving mustangs from Los Angeles to Omaha was Jackson's ticket to get back east in the spring and summer of 1867. Jackson is depicted on this difficult crossing of the Green River on July 9. Courtesy National *Park Service*/Scotts Bluff National Monument.

the water again and succeeded at last in getting all of them across. Our only loss was one saddle horse, which, led behind the ferryboat, got entangled in the ropes and was drowned. It was altogether a scene of action that would have made a stirring moving picture had such things been possible in those days.

Another thrilling adventure came to us on the Green River in Wyoming. We had here a stronger, deeper stream to cross. It was harder to get the cattle and horses to take to the turbid, chilly water, where the opposite shore seemed so far away. We rushed the whole mixed herd, as before, into the stream, but this time the cattle as well as the horses drifted down midstream and all came back. After several exasperating failures to get the herd over, it was suggested that if someone rode a horse ahead, the rest of the animals would follow. Jim asked me to try it, but said that if I did not care to do so he would.

This seemed to put the obligation on me, and I agreed to undertake it. Stripping to a single garment and mounting old Bally bareback, I plunged into the river and struck for the opposite shore, while everybody on shore crowded the horses in right after me, the cattle being left behind this time. As soon as I struck deep water, my horse rolled over backwards, submerging me completely. He started to return as the others were doing, and all I could do was to swim back among the floundering mass as best I could. Twice more I tried Bally with the same disheartening result; then I changed to old Whitey. My first attempt on him resulted as before, but on a second trial Whitey swam entirely across with me. None of the band, however, followed our lead all the way over.

Despairing of swimming the horses, Sam began ferrying late in the afternoon. All but six or eight were driven by one means or another on the ferry, and the few obstreperous ones were roped, thrown down, and dragged on. The cattle were left until the next morning, when all hands re-crossed the river. We rounded up the cattle, rushed them into the river, and, up to our necks in the water kept after them until the last straggler was on the way to the farther shore.

These desperately hard experiences were repeated with some variations when we struck the North Platte a few days later. From there on we had less trouble crossing streams; but we met other hardships and vexatious experiences on our drive to the Missouri. The trouble that came with some young fellows who joined our outfit at Fort Bridger and turned out to be in league with horse thieves; our plagues of mosquitoes that sent the horses and men half crazy; Sam's drunken spree that held us two days at Medicine Bow; the Indian scares on the way—these and other more or less exciting experiences can be only suggested here. We finally managed to get through the Laramie Mountains and down to the plains. The last part of the way, through the region where Indian dangers threatened, we were given an escort of a sergeant and two troopers from Fort Sanders.[9]

During these last days of companionship on the road a spirit of rivalry sprang up among the horsemen of the different outfits that had joined for mutual protection. We had several races between favorite steeds. Wagers of from ten to fifty dollars were laid on the various events. One race between a gray mare of the emigrant outfit and a big sorrel horse belonging to Sam was particularly exciting. The evening before the race, the boys curried, rubbed, and blanketed the two animals—probably to their astonishment—with as much care as if they were to run in a Kentucky Derby. A racecourse of three hundred yards was laid out on a level bench back of the camp, the sagebrush being cleared away for the prescribed distance. All the outfits stayed to see the race, and everybody placed some wager on the result. Jim played the part of jockey for our side, and one of the emigrants rode the gray mare. It was a tight race, creating intense enthusiasm as the horses came through with the mare barely a neck ahead of Sam's racer.[10]

Farther along the trail we began to strike the construction camps of the advancing Union Pacific Railroad. Up in the Laramie Mountains we had come across the tie cutters; now we found the graders. Soldiers were in evidence everywhere, guarding the graders from Indian attacks and the supply stores from robbers of all sorts. Small detachments of Pawnee Indian scouts in full cavalry uniform were patrolling the road. Some of them traveled along with us at times, through curiosity more than anything else, for they were eager to learn about our enterprise, and asked many questions as to where we came from and where we were going with our horses. They were full of boasting of their exploits with the Sioux and the Cheyennes, telling of the scalps they had taken from these enemies.

Our drive ended at Julesburg, at that time the terminus of the new railroad and at the height of its wild notoriety. Here our tired horses, which through losses and trading along the route had dwindled down to about half the original number that had left Los Angeles, were put on board boxcars for a thirty-six hour ride to Omaha. Getting the unruly animals into these cars was the hardest job we had tackled on all the difficult drive. Many of them had to be tied up and bundled into the cars like so much dead freight. It was a sorry-looking bunch of horses that came out at the end of the long journey. Thus I returned to the Missouri, not far from the place where I had left it a little more than a year previously.

Chapter Five

Photographing along the Union Pacific Route

August 1867–September 1869

Having no desire to return to former scenes and associations, I decided that Omaha, on the borderland between the East and the West, was a good place to begin life anew. The day after going into camp on the mosquito-infested bottom lands above town I told Sam I was ready to quit. This raised the question of how much pay I was to get for the time I had been on the drive. It is true that I had joined the party without stipulation as to pay, being intent only on some way to return east; but barring a few breaking-in incidents, I felt I had given equal service with the others and it was right that I should expect some remuneration.

Sam was grouchy, as well as closefisted, and said that the best he could do for me was twenty dollars. In view of the fact that this venture turned out very well, for Sam sold his horses at profitable figures, I felt some dissatisfaction, but I accepted the money. It was surprising how much, after all, I did with that twenty-dollar greenback, for I re-clothed myself from head to foot, quite respectably, though after the barber had been paid, there was not even a two-bit piece to provide for the future. Fresh clothes certainly made a great difference in my feelings of self-respect.

I got busy at once among the photographers in Omaha, learning about the prospects for getting into business again. There were two apparently prosperous galleries in the city at the time. One belonged to a man named Eaton, who was interested but gave no definite encouragement. Hamilton, the other photographer, was also interested, but to some purpose. After we had talked matters over, he made two propositions: one, that I should take over an idle gallery of his and run it on shares; the other, that he would employ me on weekly salary to do color work for him. Needless to say, I took the second proposition, particularly as it was accompanied with a guarantee of credit at the Douglas House for my first week's board.

PHOTOGRAPHING INDIANS OF NEBRASKA. 1868. Gelatin bromide print.

My first traveling dark room, prepared for photographing among the Pawnee and Omaha Indians in 1868. It was "a frame box on a buggy chassis, completely outfitted with water tank, sink, developing pan and other gear essential to a wet-plate photographer. Soon my one-horse studio (which at first scared the daylights out of all the livestock) ceased to be considered "bad medicine," and I was welcomed equally before the tepees of the Poncas and the earth houses of the Pawnees (Jackson [1940] 1994, 173–74). Courtesy National Park Service/Scotts Bluff National Monument.

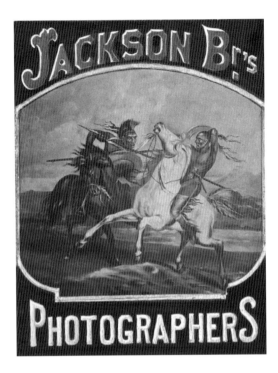

JACKSON BR.'s PHOTOGRAPHERS. 1867.
Ink wash and tempera on albumin print.

"This sign swung out from the corner of Douglas &
15th St., Omaha" is written on the reverse side of the
artwork. Courtesy Brigham Young University.

After a pleasant night with the boys, none of whom I ever saw again, I packed my bag, left the horse camp, and settled in town. Hamilton and I got along well together. I buckled down to my best work; and though the sudden transition from outdoor to indoor activities was trying at first, I was so much encouraged by my success that I forgot the difficulties. My letters home about the country and its opportunities resulted in bringing my brother Edward out to Omaha. Having negotiated the matter with Hamilton, we took over his two galleries and a little later added Eaton's. We were soon doing business as JACKSON BROTHERS, PHOTOGRAPHERS.

Thus it was that in the early spring months of 1868 I found myself established as a professional photographer. My brother was office manager and with the assistance of another man carried on the routine portraiture work. This left me free to take up landscape photography, or viewing, as it was generally termed. The indoor work and the details of getting our new business under way soon began to get irksome. I longed to get into the open again; and now that I was becoming fairly expert in the use of the camera, I saw an opportunity to do this in a really profitable way.

Omaha was at this time booming with construction activities connected with the Union Pacific Railroad. As headquarters for that great transcontinental enterprise, it was the center of stirring events. The papers were full of exciting news about the progress of the railroad. Their columns were filled daily with stories of the marvelous speed of the track laying, accounts of Indian attacks on the men at work, and descriptions of the numerous parties, military, civic, and official, on their trips along the newly constructed line. It is not strange, therefore, that, having been so recently over much of the same ground afoot and on horseback, I was eager to be on the road again and with my camera make a record of what was happening.

There were other picturesque things also to lure me a field. Several Indian reservations—Pawnees, Omahas, Winnebagoes, and Poncas on the north, Otoes and Osages on the south—were within a hundred miles of Omaha. Many friendly Indians of these tribes I had met in the city. I had even prevailed upon some of them to come into the gallery and pose for their pictures. It was no unusual sight to have the reception room filled with groups of blanketed squaws, papooses, and bucks, willing for a small recompense to brave the "bad medicine" of the camera. The result was many interesting portraits of the red men; but I was anxious to photograph them in their native settings.

A traveling outfit had to be devised to enable me to take photographs of the out-lying scenes. Picture taking in those days was not the simple matter of today, with our prepared films and plates and hand cameras. The pioneer photographer of that time had to be something of a chemist as well as an artist, and a mechanic also. He had to carry with him a kind of laboratory with many chemicals, trays, glasses, and other apparatus, for each plate must be prepared on the spot for every exposure. To make pictures in the field away from the usual conveniences of the gallery was simply a matter of having a traveling gallery. Just as many things were required, but they had to occupy less space.

My first outfit for field work was for home use, that is, for the city and its imme-diate neighborhood. It was a dark room on wheels, built on the back part of the run-ning gears of a light buggy, minus the springs, and was drawn by a single horse. Inside it was fitted with a sink, a tank for water, and other conveniences for picture making. This was a handy, if primitive, outfit, and with it I traveled over much of the prairie country north of Omaha, principally to get the Indian in his own home. The Pawnees, the most interesting of all, were living in permanent villages of earthen lodges, but there were also many tepees, so it was not hard to find good photographic subjects.

Greater attractions, however, lay at the end of the rails. Omaha, as I have said, was alive with the railroad-building race. The Union Pacific and the Central Pacif-ic—one from the east, the other from the west—were intent on winning as much of the route as possible.[1] The Central had crossed the Sierras and was rushing its con-struction over the Nevada deserts, while the Union Pacific was crowding its con-struction forces across mountainous Wyoming in a desperate endeavor to reach the valley of the Great Salt Lake before the Central got to this objective. From the Union Pacific directorate came imperative orders that Ogden, Utah, at least must be won, possibly the Humboldt River. With every mile gained there was the tempting prize of $64,000 in government bonds and 12,800 acres of the public domain.

With all this excitement, it is little wonder that men of every type and clime came to participate in the great game of putting the first iron horse across our continent.

LA-ROO-CHUCK-A-LA-SHAR (SUN CHIEF). 1868. Black-and-white collodion glass negative.

"A son of Peta-la-sha-ra and head chief of the Chowee band; also a leader in the councils. Height, 5.9; head, 22; chest, 36 1/2″ (Jackson [1877] 1978, 65). Once Jackson had perfected a means to do fieldwork photography, he did numerous ethnographic field studies. Pawnee Indi-ans were among his most poignant subjects. Jackson's studio business "paid well enough, but it was hardly exciting. Every once in a while I could increase the tempo by going off for three or four days as 'missionary to the Indians'" (Jackson [1940] 1994, 173). Courtesy National Anthropological Archives.

Pawnee, Jackson Bros. 1868. Albumin print.

Jackson took many portraits of Native Americans in his Omaha studio. Later a large number of these became part of the Hayden Survey collection. Later they were added to the National Anthropological Archives of the Smithsonian Institution. This one survives as an example that did not become part of that collection. Courtesy National Park Service/Scotts Bluff National Monument.

When we came east with our broncos, we had met the motley forces—sons of the soil, mingling with "tenderfeet" from the States, immigrants from Europe, Chinese and Japanese, all in the hurly-burly of the construction. With them came the gamblers and or denizens of the underworld, following the advancing rails to prey upon the workers as these tired men sought entertainment in the wild, temporary camps that sprang up like mushrooms at various points along the road.

In recent years men have recorded in books and in moving pictures the story of the building of the old Union Pacific. Some suggestion of the wild times of the 60's may be caught from such productions, but they can hardly portray the stirring reality of those rough-and-ready days. Crime there was, of course, fights and killings, and battles with the Indians, who resented the intrusion of the whites upon their domain. But despite all these exciting incidents, the main story, and the most thrilling one, was the building of the great transcontinental railroad over plains and mountains and deserts, along historic trails and through scenes of amazing grandeur. This it was that lured me out again over the old route I had traveled as a bullwhacker and as a vaquero. I was eager to get in picture form some of these scenes and some suggestion of the activities connected with the mighty national enterprise.

Opportunities for going out on the road soon came, mainly through requests from travelers who wanted to be photographed in various groupings at the end of the track. It was of course impracticable to use my outfit on wheels in this work. A further reduction in equipment had to be made. For the portable dark room I used a box measuring thirty by fifteen by twelve inches. By careful conservation of space, the necessary chemicals and apparatus were stowed in this box. It was convertible into a dark room by attaching to it a folding frame covered with a hood of black and yellow calico, with a baglike opening for the head and shoulders. The arms were left free for the usual operations, which I generally performed in a kneeling position. This arrangement, modified somewhat through experience, was my standard equipment for wet-plate operations. I varied it later by using a small tent.

By this time the Union Pacific line had crossed the continental divide, and the contractors were making the dirt fly in the Bitter Creek region.[2] Ten thousand workers with hundreds of teams were building the grade across the high plateaus of Wyoming, while a thousand track layers with their teams were following close on the graders' heels. A further contingent of some three or four hundred teams was carrying supplies to this army of railroad builders. Besides these, thronging every construction camp, were those forces of destruction—gamblers, saloon keepers, and others, preying day and night on the tired men who had to live in these camps. Despite the nightly carousals, filled with drinking, gaming, fighting, and killing, most of the workers kept themselves away from the debauchery and went on with tireless energy digging, blasting, cutting, hauling, and finally laying the iron rails to link the ends of a continent.

It was a fascinating picture of intense action, this track-laying process that day after day was putting the iron way farther into the West. With machine-like precision the various operations were performed. The tie haulers kept their loads of ties moving along the grade; the gang of tie layers quickly unloaded the ties and strung them far ahead. Following these, a truck car drawn by a horse came over the advancing track, bringing the rails. A dozen strong men dropped the rails in pairs on the ties. In an instant the rails were lined up, spaced, and secured by a spike or two, and the loaded car rolled forward over them to repeat the process. When emptied, it was unceremoniously thrown over to one side and another car took its place. Hundreds of workers followed behind, completing the spiking, the alignment, and the ballasting. So the work went on day after day with increasing speed until one day the maximum of seven and a half miles of track was laid between the rising and the setting of the sun. It may not seem a great achievement in these days of powerful machinery, but it was indeed a notable one for those pioneer times.

Equally intense were the activities along the route of the Central Pacific as it laid its tracks eastward from the Pacific coast. On May 10, 1869, the two lines met at Promontory Point,[3] at the northern end of the Great Salt Lake. The Union Pacific had won the race to the Salt Lake Valley. It had gone about ninety miles beyond Ogden, which afterwards became known as the Junction City.[4] This ninety miles is now mostly cut off by the shorter route, which goes directly across the lake on trestle work, instead of northward from Ogden around the lake.

There was a great celebration when the Union Pacific and the Central Pacific met. Noted officials from East and West gathered at Promontory Point to commemorate, with fitting ceremonies, this linking of the ends of our nation with its first

~

While in Cheyenne on June 24, "Hull and I began working the streets . . . . [It was] mentioned that the ladies at Madame Cleveland's were pretty solvent, what with the railroad, the near-by Fort D. A. Russell, and this and that, and [it was] suggested that we look into the matter" (Jackson [1940] 1994, 177).

"Hull and I thought we would go around and see if we couldn't get a job out of them. Talked it up a while but they seemed indifferent. I called for a bottle of wine, and soon after they began to show considerable interest in having a picture taken. Had another bottle, and then they were hot and heavy for some large pictures to frame and began to count up how many they should want. So we left promising that if the mother permitted we should surely be on hand to make some pictures" (Jackson 1869, June 24).

Two days later they ". . . went over to Madame Cleveland's to make the group of the girls with the house. Weather was just hazy enough to soften the light down for an outdoor group" (Ibid., June 26). After the pictures were completed we "had to go around to Madame Cleveland's [to deliver the photographs] & was much surprised to see Dr. Ferdinand V. Hayden come in with some military friends. He acted like a cat in a strange garret" (Ibid., June 28). The possibility of Jackson working for the United States Geological Survey as its photographer had not yet been discussed with Hayden. This was the first meeting between the two.

~

transcontinental railroad. Before an audience of hundreds of rugged men who had done the work, speeches were made, and a spike of gold and another of silver were driven to secure the last rail. Two engines were driven close together and the rival leaders of the great enterprise, standing on the engines, clasped hands in friendly congratulations over the mighty achievement.

Much to my regret, I could not be present, with my photographic outfit, at this significant ceremony. Other photographers were there, however, and their work has been cleverly copied in the motion picture, "The Iron Horse." At the time the last spike was driven, I was much more interested in another matter, for I had recently married a young lady of Omaha and was on my honeymoon trip down the Missouri River.

I had done some photographic work along the railroad line in 1868, and during the following winter I had been busy planning to go out on the road again to photograph the scenery along the whole length of the Union Pacific from Omaha to Salt Lake City. With a companion named Hull, I left Omaha in June of 1869. We had contrived a good portable outfit and had our railroad passes for the whole season. Our intention was to go through to the end of the road and work back eastward, but finding some commercial opportunities in Cheyenne, we decided to drop off there and give our new equipment a workout trial before attempting more important subjects.

The town of Cheyenne was then two years old. The town site had been selected in June 1867, by General Dodge, on whose shoulders rested the chief responsibility for the building of the Union Pacific. He had also located the military post, Fort D. A. Russell, which was built a few miles from Cheyenne.[5] At that time General Dodge was conducting a distinguished party of army and railroad officials, among them General Rawlins, Secretary of War.[6] They were on a tour of inspection, investigating the conditions under which the road was being built. The Indian problem was brought forcibly to their attention when they witnessed an attack of the red men on a party of graders. It resulted in the starting of a graveyard as one of the first acts in the settlement of the frontier town. This cemetery grew rather rapidly in the next few years.

Cheyenne sprang up almost overnight. Men poured into this new railroad center from Julesburg, and immediately there was a mixed population of saloon keepers, gamblers, and their riff-raff followers, together with a host of migratory merchants, restaurant keepers, hotel men, barbers, smiths, clerks, and other working folk. By the time the first train pulled into Cheyenne on November 13, 1867, there was a big delegation of citizens with a brass band to give it a rousing welcome. The boom days of the city passed, however, with the advancing of the road; and Cheyenne soon settled down to a fairly orderly existence as an important division terminal, keeping of course some of its "wild and wooly" days.

The six days we spent in the town were enough to demonstrate that our photographic outfit was practicable and that we could make it pay our way. They were busy days. Every available moment was spent in making negatives, taking pictures, and printing them. Albumin paper was silvered by floating it in a bath of silver nitrate, and fumed with ammonia when dry; this work we did at night. The printed paper was then put through several washing, toning, and fixing operations, and dried, trimmed, and mounted. Naturally we were elated, after all this work, when fine pictures resulted, and were correspondingly depressed when the finished product turned out poorly. Photography in those pioneer times was still largely in the experimental stage.

Before leaving Cheyenne, we bought a tent, thus adding considerably to our already burdensome equipment. But a tent we must have, for we expected to live in the open most of the time when working along the more remote regions of the road.

Passing through Echo and Weber canyons, I was more than ever impressed with the scenic possibilities for the photographer in those picturesque mountain defiles. After coming out into the Salt Lake Valley, we rode through Ogden, and northward along the majestic Wasatch Range, and thence westward to Corinne.[7] This settlement was made up largely of canvas houses and tents, and it was a lively place at this time, being a shipping point for the Montana mining towns. From Corinne we went on to Blue Creek, where half a dozen tents were pitched on the salt flats bordering the lake.[8] Then our train began the ascent to Promontory Point, crawling up the heavy grade at a snail's pace to the summit at Promontory station. Here the Central Pacific train was waiting to make connection for California.

This temporary junction point was in the midst of a sagebrush plain. The station consisted of a row of canvas-covered rooms; the town itself was made up of tents

Corinne, Utah. July 1–8, 1869.
Copy of modern print from wet plate negative.

"We worked Corinne for just one week and while it did not add much to our personal comfort and enjoyment, we were quite successful financially. . . . The weather was hot and sultry. A fine impalpable dust covered everything with a mantel of gray. . . . The light had a yellowish-hazy cast, which, with the extreme heat, made successful photography very difficult. . . . Our best work was done early in the morning. . . . The oppressive heat begat a continual thirst. Bear River water was worse than nothing, having a brackish flavor that was not pleasant, but made fairly palatable with 'portable lemonade.' . . . Cockroaches and ants were all too numerous, particularly at night, when they would crawl into our hair and ears as we slept" (Jackson [1867–1869] n.d., 7, 8). Courtesy U.S. Geological Survey.

PROMONTORY POINT, UTAH. June 31–July 1, 1869.
Copy of modern print from wet plate negative.

The flag marks the point where the Union Pacific and Central Pacific lines were joined on May 10, 1869. This photograph was taken two months later. Jackson's original description reads ". . . the spot where the tracklayers met and laid the 'last rail' . . ." (Jackson [1875] 1978, 9). Arundel Hull, Jackson's assistant, may have taken this photograph as both photographers were working side by side. Courtesy U.S. Geological Survey.

of varying sizes. Hull and I had reached our destination, so we stood by during a busy half hour while the transfer was made from one train to the other. When the field was clear, we set up our dark box and got to work making negatives of "the last rail," the place where the gold spike and the silver spike had been driven about six weeks previously. We did not see those precious, historical spikes, however, as they had been immediately replaced by iron ones.

Returning from Promontory Point, we lingered a full month in the Salt Lake Valley, most of the time at Uinta. From our camp there we made side trips to Salt Lake City and up into Weber Canyon to photograph the Devils Gate and other scenic wonders of the gorge.[9] Nearly all of this first month's work was sold immediately, chiefly for running expenses. Little went into our permanent series of views of general interest, intended for sale in Omaha and elsewhere.

There were two stage lines running from Uinta to Salt Lake City at the time. We took top seats on the big Concord coach of the Wells Fargo line, which carried the mail. The ride proved very pleasant, as we passed through farming settlements set in the midst of an abundant, ripening harvest. The air was thick with smoky haze, probably due to forest fires, so that we saw little of the lake, merely having glimpses when we passed within a short distance of its shore, white with salt. We put up at the old Salt Lake House, and that night went to the historic Salt Lake Theater, built by Brigham Young, where we saw Annie Ward in a comedy.

Among the people I met next day was Charles R. Savage of the firm of Savage and Ottinger, the Mormon photographers.[10] Mr. Savage, one of the earlier pioneers in the valley, was a skillful photographer with a fine appreciation of scenic features, and he turned out some of the best landscape work of the times. He was one of the photographers at the "Laying of the Last Rail," and I had an interesting half-hour's chat with him about this as well as his other experiences in outdoor photography.

A little later we made the trip from our camp at Uinta to the Devils Gate region in Weber Canyon. Leaving our surplus materials in care of the station keeper, we put our outfit aboard a work train that took us up the canyon. We were almost wholly dependent on these work trains to pick us up and drop us wherever we wished. In return for these favors, we kept the crews supplied with pictures.

While traveling west to Promontory Point, Utah, Jackson and Hull witnessed a scene of vigilante justice. "Arriving at Wasatch [Utah] at 7:30 the following morning the first thing we saw was a Negro hanging from a telegraph pole alongside the R.R. track. It was said he had stolen a large sum of money—had a mock trial—with hands tied behind him he was ordered to run for his life; a crowd then commenced to shooting and he was soon brought down and then strung up on the telegraph pole and left there until well along in the day" (Jackson [1867–1869] n.d., 5).

MAIN STREET, SALT LAKE CITY. September 10, 1868. Copy of modern print from wet plate negative.

Jackson and Hull had one hurried day to photograph in and around Salt Lake City. They had a lot of difficulty with afternoon light conditions. Jackson's description leads to fire haze or blowing dust as possible causes: "The light was bad indeed, a smoky yellow haziness that was very unfavorable." It took careful "nursing" of the plates to produce satisfactory results (Jackson 1869, September 10). Courtesy U.S. Geological Survey.

The Weber River at Devils Gate makes an ox-bow bend, which is spanned by two high bridges only a short distance apart. At that time the men were still working on these bridges. We settled ourselves in a little nook in the rock, nearly under one of the bridges. It was just wide enough to hold our tent and yet leave room between

THE 1,000-MILE TREE. August 3, 1869. Albumin print.

"... a solitary pine in Wilhelmina Pass, or the narrows of Weber Cañon, marking the 1000th mile west of Omaha" (Jackson [1875] 1978, 9). "Got the section men [working on the tracks] to take us aboard, & we put down with all our traps at the 1000 mile tree.... In P.M. made views of the tree & of the section men. Couldn't find any place level or smooth enough to pitch our tent on, so we took a shovel the section men left & scooped out a place in the side of the hill & slept on our tent instead of under it" (Jackson 1869, August 3). Courtesy National Park Service/Scotts Bluff National Monument.

us and the river for the passing of teams along the narrow wagon road. At first the rushing waters kept us awake at night, but this music of the mountain stream soon became a soothing lullaby.

Our pictures of the craggy scenes about the Devils Gate turned out the best we had yet made. Everything seems always to work better when the scenery itself is satisfyingly attractive in every respect.

After three days of photographing the various scenes of interest there, I decided one Sunday morning to climb the high cliffs that towered above our camp, to ease my curiosity as to what lay beyond. It was a hard scramble, mostly over slide rock and through scrub oak, among which I had to fight my way; but after much laborious work I finally reached the summit, some three thousand feet above the valley. The splendid scene from that vantage point was well worth the climb. Spread out before me, a hundred miles or more from north to south, lay the Salt Lake Valley. The great briny lake itself, like a glistening mirror, broken in places by its mountainous islands, formed part of the vast panorama. I lingered only long enough to pick out familiar objects in the distance, and made the descent in a fraction of the time it took to go up.

Weber and Echo canyons offered many striking subjects for our photographic work. With the help of trainmen, section hands, and station keepers, we managed to transfer our apparatus from one place to another. Our collection of pictures included such points of interest as the Devils Slide, the Thousand Mile Tree, the Witches Rocks, the Pulpit, and the castle-like formations in Echo Canyon.[11]

It was all rather hard work but full of interest. We came into contact with all sorts of folk, but they were kindly disposed and helpful. At Castle Rock we boarded for a few days with the section hands, a rough-and-ready jumble of men of different nationalities. One night the foreman of the bridge builders came walking by our camp on his way to Wasatch and decided to spend the night with us. Hull made an extra lot of flapjacks for supper, and we three spent the evening around the fire swapping yarns.

With a group of men we went over to Bear River to catch some of the fine trout that abounded in the stream. There we fell in with Indian Bill, a squaw man. Bill had his tepee near the river, a short distance from where we pitched camp. He came over

GREEN RIVER BUTTE. 1869.
Copy of modern print from wet plate negative.

Jackson's photographic work was abruptly halted at the end of September. "[My] immediate presence in Omaha [was requested] to straighten out some business matters. . . . I do not remember whether this ended my work for the year, or that I returned later for the Green River subjects, with the further possibility that I left [my assistant] Hull to finish up" (Jackson [1867–1869] n.d., 24). Courtesy U.S. Geological Survey.

~

Arundel Hull had spent the previous two years photographing many of the same scenes that he and Jackson photographed in the summer of 1869. Unfortunately, little of Arundel's work has survived. Some of it has been credited to other photographers. Nina Hull Miller, Hull's daughter and author of *Shutters West* (1962), claims the photo titled *Promontory Point, Utah* (page 48) is a Hull photograph. Jackson admits to a lapse of memory as to whether he or Hull took other photographs late in the season (see the notation with the Green River Butte photo above). The confusion is understandable as the men traveled together and undoubtedly assisted each other in their photographic endeavors. During this period it was also acceptable to claim a photograph as one's own if it was purchased or if an assistant took it. Which photographer actually took this view may never accurately be determined.

~

and spent the time till nearly midnight relating the experiences of his life. Bill had forgotten where he came from; his first recollections were of his life among the Indians at Fort Bridger, when he was very young. He had lived with old Washakie's band nearly all the time and spoke the Shoshone language like a native.

As a photographic venture this side trip was a failure. It was an experiment in the preparation of a new kind of dry plate, and the few exposures we made turned out badly. These days, however, were filled with interesting experiences and good fishing, and we came back with two horses packed with trout. We also had some good sport shooting ducks and sage hens, which were numerous in that part of the country.

This side trip closed my outdoor work for that year.[12] Business affairs in Omaha required my immediate attention, so I took the first eastbound train, leaving Hull to pack up and return at his leisure.

Chapter Six

Across Wyoming with Hayden

July 1870–September 1870

The driving of the golden spike was a signal for a new rush for the settlement of the West. Now that there was railroad transportation, the vast plains, the Rocky Mountains with their rich treasures, and the valleys of the Rockies and the Sierras were brought within easier, surer reach of the farmer, the stockman, and the miner. It was essential that more definite information about these regions be made available. The government, awake to this need, responded by sending out trained men in various groups to make surveys and to write reports for publication.

One of these exploring expeditions, the United States Geological Survey of the Territories, was under the direction of Dr. F. V. Hayden.[1] During July in 1870 Dr. Hayden dropped off at Omaha on his way to join his party, then encamped near Cheyenne awaiting his arrival. He called at my studio during his stay in Omaha, partly for acquaintance' sake, for we had met the previous year while he was making his Nebraska survey. He wanted to obtain some of my photographs, being particularly interested in those of the Green River formations in Wyoming. The Doctor, examining these, became interested in the work I had been doing along the railroad, and grew enthusiastic over the scenic features of the region of his present survey—along the old Oregon Trail across Wyoming and back by the Overland Stage route.[2] He pointed out the rare opportunity there was for a photographer, traveling with his party, to make views of great value.

These suggestions met with a quick response, and Dr. Hayden finally proposed that I join his party. He explained that his appropriation was too small to enable him to offer me more than my traveling and outfitting expenses, but I could keep for my own use all negatives made; he wanted merely to have the photographs available for future use. He felt that photographs would aid him greatly in furthering the object of his explorations, which was to familiarize people with the nature and the resources of the regions visited.

As an adventure, the proposition appealed to me strongly, but I did not at first see how I could profitably undertake it. My brother had given up the photographic business and gone into farming, and I had just opened a new gallery. The longer we talked it over, however, the more attractive the Doctor's proposition appeared. Finally, with my wife's consent, I agreed to go with him for the two or three months he planned to be out.

There was just a week in which to get ready to join the party at Cheyenne. My usual equipment of cameras was not adapted to the work before me, so telegrams were rushed to eastern houses, where the necessary supplies could be obtained. Within six days I had assembled everything, and after another day spent in packing, I was off for Cheyenne in a Pullman.

The eighteen hours' run—now made in about half that time—gave me ample opportunity for reflections on my experiences up and down this old Platte Valley. First, I had traversed it as a bullwhacker; then as a horseman trailing mustangs; next as an itinerant photographer, lugging my boxes from station to station. Now I was riding in a palatial car, photographer still, but with the prestige of employment in the business of the government.

I found the party at Camp Carling [Carlin], the quartermaster's depot for Fort D. A. Russell near Cheyenne. There were twelve members of the Survey, occupying four wall tents, and eight employees engaged as teamsters and cooks. The cook's outfit struck me as being the very acme of camp luxury. Dr. Hayden was in Denver when I arrived, but his chief assistant and camp manager, Stevenson—or Jim as everyone called him—took me in hand and soon I was on friendly terms with all. My being a photographer doubtless helped to get me into the good graces of the boys, as this was a new departure in the operations of the Survey, and all were eager for photographs showing their camp life to send back home.

Our chief, Dr. Hayden, was a graduate of Oberlin College. Prior to the Civil War he had participated in several military-scientific expeditions into the Upper Missouri regions. He was a tireless collector, sometimes working alone in hostile Indian country. He was never known to carry firearms. The Sioux gave him the name,

The Camp of the United States Geological Survey. August 11–12, 1870. Modern print from wet plate negative.

Hayden's men gathered at Fort D. A. Russell, near Cheyenne, Wyoming. This was "the rendezvous camp where the Survey was organized and equipped for field service" (Jackson [1875] 1978, 11). Courtesy U.S. Geological Survey.

DR. HAYDEN AND HIS FAVORITE HORSE PATSY.
Circa 1872. Albumin print.

Dr. Hayden was the leader of the United States
Geological Surveys from 1867 to 1878. Courtesy
National Park Service/Yellowstone National Park.

"The-man-who-picks-up-the-rocks-running." The story is related that "at one time, when engaged in the exploration of the Laramie beds of the Upper Missouri, he was pursued and finally overtaken by a band of hostile Indians. Finding him armed only with a hammer, and carrying a bag of fossils, which they emptied out and examined with much surprise and curiosity, they concluded that he was insane and let him alone."

Dr. Hayden served through the Civil War as a surgeon in the federal army, and afterward became a professor of geology in the University of Pennsylvania. This position he retained until 1872. It was during this period that he planned and started his Geological Survey of the Territories, laying the foundation for the United States Geological Survey as it exists today.

The week at Camp Carling was one of busy preparation. It was no easy task to get my dark box and other equipment into working order and carefully packed. The baggage and supplies of the expedition were carried in four wagons, each drawn by a four-mule team. When we were on the march, the members of the expedition, all mounted roamed far and wide, coming back to the wagons only at the end of the day when camp had been made. With my camera and working equipment, I had to follow the mounted party in all its wanderings.

Most of my supplies were carried in an ambulance that accompanied the wagons, but I was given a crop-eared mule to carry my working kit. The little animal was at once named Hypo, a short form of the high-sounding name of a chemical used in photography.[3] From the quartermaster I obtained a pair of parfleches, used commonly by Indians and trappers for carrying their goods on pack horses. They are large folding envelopes of rawhide, usually decorated with painted designs. They are laced up in front with leather thongs and are provided with loops at the back to hang from the crossbars of the pack-saddle. In one of these I carried my dark box with the bath holder; in the other a box of equal size containing my camera, glass plates, and chemicals for the day's work. On top, in the space between the boxes, was placed the tripod and a small keg of water to be used for plate washing when I was away from a water supply. When fast riding was the order, the whole pack was lashed securely with a cinch rope.

After getting my outfit in order, I joined the other men in drawing our mounts and the commissary supplies. Our entire traveling equipment, on order from the Secretary of War, was provided by the quartermaster at Fort D. A. Russell. The horses were condemned cavalry mounts, but in the main they were fine looking, serviceable animals. With them we drew McClellan saddles and also arms and ammunition for those who had none. I had my own Henry rifle and a Remington pistol. It was required, by the general commanding this department, that every member of the Survey be fully armed, as the Indians were occasionally hostile in the region through which we were to travel.

My first photographic work was a tryout of camera, dark box, and chemicals on several camp views. These I had the local photographer print at once for distribution. Then I had to go up to headquarters and make a few groups of the officers.

Meanwhile, Dr. Hayden had returned from Denver, bringing as his guest to accompany the expedition, Sanford Robinson Gifford, the well-known landscape painter.[4]

On the morning of August 7, 1870, we broke camp, starting off in a cold sleety rain. As photographic work under such conditions was impossible, my outfit was carried in one of the wagons instead of on Hypo's back. Our first day's journey was a short one, just a good breaking-in experience for everybody. We pitched camp on Lodge Pole Creek, about sixteen miles from the starting point.

The next morning came with a cloudless sky and everyone primed for the work ahead. The packing of my photographic outfit on Hypo was the outstanding event. There were no experienced packers in the party at this time; but Jim was an old campaigner, and with the assistance of the wagon boss, he managed the operation. Fortunately the little mule ended his bucking protests with the first cinching of the packsaddle, so he gave no further trouble in completing the loading.

The wagons, with the teamsters and cooks, went ahead along the appointed route and were directed to make camp at the end of the day's drive. The members of the surveying party rode off in groups on their particular missions. With Dr. Hayden leading, our group of six followed up Lodge Pole Creek to near its sources in the Laramie Range. While in the hills, I unpacked my outfit several times to photograph the rock formations the Doctor indicated. This of course delayed the party, and it was

MY FIRST PACKING OUTFIT WITH THE GEOLOGICAL SURVEY. 1870. Albumin print.

Hypo carried the pair of parafleches containing cameras, plates, dark box, and chemicals, with tripod and water keg on top. In the first edition of *The Pioneer Photographer* the horse and figure with the whip on the right had been eliminated. This may have been the actual print used in the first edition, as a light pencil line on the photograph shows where it was cropped. Courtesy National Park Service/Scotts Bluff National Monument.

W. H. Jackson on Independence Rock. Circa 1950.
Lithographic print of hand-tinted print.

This Jackson rendering was created from his 1870
photograph "East from Independence Rock" (Jackson,
[1875] 1978, 14). According to the information residing
with the artwork, the scene shows Jackson carving his
initials in the rock. However, Jackson's diary indicates
that the wagon train did not stop as they passed the
rock, and moreover there were no females
accompanying the caravan and in any event Jackson
certainly did not wear white shirt and vest while
bullwacking. The original sketch was later duplicated,
hand tinted, and titled by Clarence Jackson, William's
son, as a part of a series for Harold Warp. Clarence
extensively promoted and wrote about his father's
accomplishments. Unfortunately, some of the
information he passed on was either embellished or
inaccurate. Courtesy Harold Warp Pioneer Village
Foundation.

quite late when we called the day's work done. We expected to find camp soon after
getting down out of the hills, so we rode along cheerfully watching for a glimpse of
white tents of campfire smoke that promised a good supper. Impatient to get on, the
Doctor with all the others galloped on ahead, much faster than myself and helper
could go with the pack. Leading the mule with a halter strap, we followed at a walk
or at best a jog trot, for we did not yet have confidence enough in our packing to
turn Hypo loose and to trot along with us.

The sun went down as we jogged wearily along. Twilight came and then the stars,
but still no signs of camp. Nine, ten, eleven o'clock passed without our finding it.
There was no possibility of our missing it, so we kept on, confident that it could not
be far away.

It was curious how keen our sense of hearing became, made more acute probably by our hopes. Out of the deathly silence that prevailed, there came in imagination

many familiar sounds—the tinkling of the bell on the bell mare, the neighing of a horse, voices calling—all most tantalizing. With midnight our patience gave out completely, and we vented our accumulated wrath on those in charge of the wagons. With smooth roads over an open country, they had evidently gone as far as they could, with no regard for those who were making the long side trips.

Since early morning we had covered at least sixty miles. It was too hard a grind on both men and animals for the first day out. At half past twelve we turned aside by some willows, took off the pack and the saddles, and lay down for a supperless sleep during what was left of the night. This was not long, for daylight in that upland country comes early. Up at dawn, we found the missing camp less than two miles ahead and got there in time for breakfast.

That day we made a short drive of only twelve miles down the Chugwater, passing a military camp on the way. After photographing some picturesque sandstone bluffs that border the stream, and traveling some distance beyond, I discovered the loss of a lens. Gifford rode back with me five miles to the place where I thought I had left it, but we found no lens there. Dr. Hayden used the occasion for a serious talk, quite properly, about the need of greater care in the future. To lose essential articles in the wilds would defeat the purpose of the expedition. Fortunately, after supper, I found the missing lens in one of the compartments of my box. The trouble gave us all a needed lesson at the outset of our trip.

The days that followed each brought their interesting incidents. New scenes to photograph appeared at every turn of the road. We chose those of distinctive interest, from a scenic as well as geological standpoint. Our object primarily was to gather such pictures as would reflect the notable features of the regions we were exploring; and then on my own account, I desired to get rare stereoscopic views and other views for the trade.

We soon reached the big game country, where we were able to lay in a supply of fresh meat from time to time, as we needed it. Elk and antelope were especially abundant, and occasionally we came in sight of buffalo in small bands, also mountain sheep. Near the head of La Bonte Creek, one of our men killed an elk. We packed it on my horse, none of the other animals being willing to take such a load. When we met the other members of our party later, we used pocket knives and geologists'

THE EMIGRANT'S GRAVE. August 29, 1870.
Copy of modern print from wet plate negative.

"Scattered along the dreary 1,200 miles from the crossing of the Missouri to the promised land of the Mormon are little mounds of earth covered with slabs of rock, and sometimes with a plain piece of board at the head, with a simple inscription, and occasionally, when near some ranch, surrounded by a fence" (Jackson [1875] 1978, 15). Different information came to light in subsequent years. In a letter to Jackson, Robert Ellison reports "that the grave of the soldier which you photographed in 1870 . . . is reported by the Adjutant General of Ohio as being one of their soldiers who was killed on December 10, 1862" (Robert Spurrier Ellison Papers n.d.; Ellison to Jackson, June 6, 1927). The soldier was Private Bennett Tribbett, who died of appendicitis on December 14, 1862. Mr. Sanford R. Gifford, a guest artist with the 1870 Survey, is peering at the grave marker. The Survey camp is in the distance. Courtesy U.S. Geological Survey.

hammers to cut up the meat, and four of us took a quarter each and set out for camp. A little later Raphael, a hunter whom we added to our party at Fort Fetterman,[5] killed a mountain sheep, or bighorn, which was carefully skinned for preservation. The meat again was divided for easier carrying into camp.

We crossed the North Platte near the present site of Casper, named for young Lieutenant Caspar Collins, who a few years before had been killed in an encounter with Indians near this place.[6] Our camp that night was made at Red Buttes, over the big hill beyond Casper. There we had a bit of excitement for a few minutes when someone suddenly raised the cry "Get your guns!" followed by another shouting "Indians!" The cause of the uproar was the appearance of a bear in the bushes near by.

As we approached the Sweetwater, we noticed signs of buffalo. As Gifford and I were cutting across the country through the sagebrush, we saw one in the distance. Making a cautious approach, we began shooting at rather long range, but the old bull in alarm dashed off, leaving a trail of dust behind him. We took up the chase with random firing, which probably had no other effect than to make him run faster. He could make better time than our horses through the sagebrush, so we gave up the chase. Soon after this, we sighted a herd of thirty or forty. Again we tried to advance cautiously, but they got the scent and were on the run before we could get near enough for a shot.

Later we discovered three more buffalo in the distance. This time we tried a more careful approach by making a wider detour to windward. Coming to Horse Creek, Gifford and I stopped to rest our horses and lunch. Resuming the chase, we got one of the buffaloes separated from the others, and riding up within short pistol range, we soon brought him down. Early in the day our horses had been hard to control in the presence of the buffalo, but later they were readily guided up to within a few feet of the shaggy brutes. The riding was hard, however, as there was much jumping of sagebrush. Other members of our party succeeded in dispatching the other two buffaloes.

A busy time followed. The skins were removed and the heads and principal bones were carefully prepared so that they could be sent later to the Smithsonian Institution in Washington for mounting. The meat was saved for our own use. Nearly everyone took part in the process, using pocket knives when no others were available. When all was done, one of the wagons was brought up to carry the meat, bones, and hides to camp, where such further treatment as was necessary could be given.

Camp had been made at Independence Rock, a well-known landmark on the old Overland Trail.[7] The rock had been given this name, it is said, from the fact that an early pioneering party had camped there on the Fourth of July. It is an immense rounded mass of granite, rising above the level valley floor near the Sweetwater River. It is nearly two hundred feet high at one end and about fifteen hundred yards in circumference. On one side the slope is so gradual that we led Hypo to the top with my photographic outfit on his back. The rock is particularly interesting on account of the great number of names inscribed on it. Many of these are names of early explorers and of well-known army officers and civilians, dating back to the days of the California gold rush or even earlier.

We lay over at this historic spot a day to enable the geologists to extend their observations and to give me an opportunity to make as many views as possible. The day was cold and windy, and conditions were unfavorable for my getting all the views desired; but the next morning was clear and still, so that I was able to finish up my work there before starting out on the day's drive.

From this point we followed the old Oregon-Mormon Trail along the winding Sweetwater up and over the famous South Pass. It had been the great highway of a nation in the years just passed, before the advent of the transcontinental railroad. Along it had trudged thousands upon thousands of trappers, explorers, settlers, and gold seekers. They had left a trail worn deep in the gravel, sand, and rocks, which we followed for many days. The old trail was not new to me, for I had walked along many miles of it.

Many points of historic and scenic interest were passed. First came the Devils Gate, the great gorge through which the Sweetwater pours; and then Split Rock. On farther at Three Crossings we found one of the few remaining Overland stage and telegraph stations. All these stations were abandoned when the stage line was moved farther south on account of Indian troubles. Near the station was a soldier's grave, typical of many other graves we found along the trail, mute evidence of the tragic cost of the conquest of the great West.

We saw no more buffalo, but great bands of antelope hovered continually in the distance. Some of these shy animals our hunters succeeded in getting by adroit stalking. Sage hens flew past us frequently and were easily bagged, the young ones making

WASHAKIE, CHIEF OF THE SHOSHONES. September 3, 1870. Copy of modern print from wet plate negative.

He is seen with some of his head men and their families, in camp near South Pass. He stands somewhat blurred by movement in the center with his hat in hand. "About him are gathered all the chief men of the camp. . . . They were . . . on their way to the Wind River Valley to hunt buffalo for the winter's supply of food and clothing. Although the village had the appearance of being a permanent abiding-place, yet the following morning, before the sun was an hour high, there was not a tent in sight, and the last pack-pony with trailing lodge-poles had passed out of sight over the hills to the eastward" (Jackson [1877] 1978, 76). Courtesy National Park Service/Yellowstone National Park.

very good eating. Coyotes were still as numerous as I had found them in '66, and kept up their yelling serenades as usual, especially in the early morning. They kept always at a respectful distance.

From St. Marys Station we rose rapidly to the summit of South Pass, some seven thousand feet above sea level. Here was the parting of the Atlantic and Pacific waters. When we arrived at Atlantic City, a mining camp at the crest of the divide, we had come up about one thousand feet from the place where we left the Sweetwater. Three miles from Atlantic City we came to Camp Stambaugh, a military post, where we pitched our camp. The officers of the post gave us a cordial reception, entertaining us at a lunch and otherwise doing the honors in a hospitable way.[8]

The presence of Chief Washakie and his band of Shoshone Indians at this place was most fortunate,[9] for Dr. Hayden was anxious to have as many photographs as possible of the Indians. About seventy lodges of the Shoshone band had been pitched not far away. Ordinarily there might have been serious objections on the part of the superstitious red men, but with the help of the officers of the camp and their interpreters, the way was made easy by first getting old Washakie to pose for his portrait, then grouping him with his head chiefs. After this, we had free run of the Indian camp, making as many views as we cared to have.

After a two-day side trip into the foothills of the Wind River Mountains, we resumed our journey to Pacific Springs.[10] When saddling my horse the next morning, I found he was quite lame from a small stone that had become wedged under one of his shoes, so it was not advisable to ride him for a while. As Hypo was not being used at this time for side trip work, I transferred my saddle to him. He was a frisky little mule and had cut up some lively capers under the pack, but was considered fairly well broken. For a while everything went well, but out on the road something happened that made him bolt and run. Then he began bucking and kept it up until the cinch loosened, the saddle turned, and I was thrown over his head, getting so hard a fall that I had to ride in the ambulance the rest of the day.

Still following the Oregon-Mormon trail, we went on down the Little Sandy and the Big Sandy, tributaries of the Green River. Reaching the Green, we forded it and traveled on to Granger, where for the first time in thirty days we came into communication again with the railroad and telegraph line. Here we heard the rather exciting news of the termination of the Franco-German War. Standing on the busy little station platform and watching the trains filled with passengers carrying newspapers of recent dates, I could hardly realize that just four years before I had plodded a lonely road along this very way, hauling hay for the old stage station, still there a few rods distant.[11]

We were now in the heart of the Bad Lands of southwestern Wyoming. Twelve miles farther on we came to Church Buttes, a remarkable formation in the Bad Lands and a famous landmark along the old trail.[12] While Gifford and I were making pictures of the interesting scenes, the geologists under the lead of Dr. Hayden were digging for fossils. They collected a wagon load of ancient turtles, shellfish, and other creatures that lived in the great inland sea that once covered this section of the country. For my part, I made seventeen negatives during the day, something of a record for wet plate work, considering the many changes of location I had to make in getting the different views.

BADLANDS—BLACKS FORK. September 9–11, 1870. Albumin print.

"This formation is known as the Mauvaises Terres, or Bad Lands, and consists of a vast deposit of soft sedimentary sandstones and marly clays in perfectly horizontal strata, containing within their beds some very remarkable paleontological remains. . . . This is also the land of 'moss-agate.' They are found everywhere. . . . It looks like some ruined city of the gods, blasted, bare, desolate, but grand beyond a mortal's telling" (Jackson [1875] 1978, 16). Courtesy Andrew Smith Gallery.

JACKSON CAÑON. September 1870.
Copy of modern print from wet plate negative.

"I certainly never experienced the proud satisfaction of having a place named for me. That came after I discovered a little canyon near Casper. (When permanent settlers moved in they gave 'my' canyon another name. In 1925, however, the citizens of Casper restored the honor of which I had been unintentionally deprived, and Jackson Canyon is now so marked on the maps)" (Jackson [1940] 1994, 191). Present-day Geological Survey notations add "...now known as Sheep Canyon...at northwest end of Casper Mountain" (William Henry Jackson Photograph Collection [1869–1878, and 1883] n.d., #279). Courtesy U.S. Geological Survey.

Our next camp was at Fort Bridger, the historic post which had been planted on Blacks Fork, at the place where the Oregon Trail and the Mormon Trail divided. These two famous trails, which came together at Fort Laramie, had been one all the way across Wyoming to Fort Bridger. The fort was built in 1843 by Bridger, the well-known trapper and scout. Later it was taken over as a military post by Colonel Albert Sidney Johnston.[13] Judge W. A. Carter, who had come with Johnston, was still at the fort in the capacity of post trader.[14] With true southern hospitality, he and his gracious daughters brightened our stay at the post by entertaining us at their home.

At this camp I undertook a general overhauling of my working outfit. My dark box was almost beyond repair, so I got an order to have the post carpenter make a new one. One of the boys made a quick round trip to Salt Lake City for some of the required materials and additional supplies. Mr. Gifford also went there before leaving us for the East. We were sorry to have him go, for he had been a constant companion on all our photographic side trips.

From Fort Bridger we made up a small party for a trip into the Uinta Mountains to the South, with Judge Carter as guide. Early in the afternoon of the day we left the fort, September sixteenth, it began to snow. This, added to a wind, which drove the sleet into our faces, made it very disagreeable, riding. We reached an old sawmill about four, pitched camp there, and built a rousing fire to get everyone dried out. Beaman and I worked until after midnight completing the preparation on my new dark box so as to be ready for business the next day.

The following morning the party made an early start for the high mountains, while I remained behind to put the finishing touches on my outfit and to photograph the old mill. Then, following the others, I made my way up and over one of the long ridges coming down from the main Uinta Range. There were many beautiful vistas, including grassy meadows and little lakes, with glimpses of the distant snow-clad peaks.

At the end of an old wood road our camp for the second night was pitched in a grove of aspens. It was named Camp Jackson in my honor, for it was customary to name the more picturesque camps after some member of the Survey. Over in Wyoming near Casper a canyon I discovered had been named Jackson Canyon. As this name appeared only in a government report, the settlers who came later knew nothing of it and adopted another name. When I visited the canyon again in 1927, the local Historical Society made the occasion a christening event and with some formality rededicated it under the original name.[15]

At camp Jackson all were up at the break of day to make an early start for the higher elevations. We chopped and blazed our way for three miles through the aspens and jack pines, then came out into a long meadow-like park that led up to Photograph Ridge. It was given this name because of the commanding view it afforded of the heart of the Uinta Mountain range, but more particularly from the number of photographs made from this point. The panorama of snow-clad peaks seen from this vantage point is one of the finest mountain views in the Rockies.

We passed through several snow flurries on the way up through the timber, and out on this exposed ridge above the timber line we caught the full force of the storms that occasionally rage over it. Clouds were continually gathering and sweeping over us, then breaking to let the sun shine out warm and bright for a few moments. It would have taken a moving picture camera to get the most splendid effect of it all. During the sunny intervals we managed to get several negatives. Finding no running water at this high elevation, we caught falling snowflakes on a black rubber blanket, and when the sun shone out there was sufficient warmth to melt enough snow for the developing and fixing solutions. Our final washings were deferred till later. This pioneer photography was a much more complex problem than photography is in these days of kodaks and films.

Our other experiences in the high Uintas were all interesting, but difficult at times. Judge Carter led us to a nameless lake of great beauty near the top of the mountain. It was a long, hard expedition, lasting until long after dark. Most of the time we were at an altitude of eleven thousand to twelve thousand feet, but the splendid scenes of the lake and of the Uintas were ample compensation for the day's effort.

A good joke at the expense of the cook gives concrete evidence of the height we reached during those days. John had obtained some potatoes, and he planned to surprise us with them at the evening meal. After boiling the potatoes for the usual time, he found them still as hard as when he put them into the kettle. Saying nothing, he concluded to have them for breakfast; so replenishing the fire, he watched the potatoes boiling away merrily until after midnight. Still the potatoes were hard. Then in disgust he banked the fire about them and turned in. When morning came, the

FROM PHOTOGRAPH RIDGE. September 18, 1870. Copy of modern print from wet plate negative.

At the head of Blacks Fork a commanding view of the heart of the Uinta Mountains opened up. "From a point looking west, deep down into the valleys, with their silvery streams finding their way down from the lofty, cone like, snow-capped summits. [This photograph was] made just upon the upper limit of arborescent vegetation; showing in the foreground how the thrifty pines of the plains below, up here, have a hard struggle for existence, being dwarfed down to low, trailing shrubs, spread out along the ground, and always toward the east, indicating the winds upon these mountains are mostly from the west" (Jackson [1875] 1978, 17). Courtesy U.S. Geological Survey.

THE FLAMING GORGE, GREEN RIVER. September 8–9, 1870. Copy of modern print from wet plate negative.

It is so named from the bright red sandstones. This was the first of the great canyons encountered by Major Powell when he set out in a boat to explore the canyons of the Colorado River in 1870. This view "at the mouth of the Henry's Fork, is of great beauty, and . . . derives its principal charm from the vivid coloring. The waters of the river are of purest emerald, with banks and sandbars of glistening white. The perpendicular bluff to the left is nearly 1,500 feet above the level of the river, and of a bright red and yellow. When illuminated by full sunlight, it readily suggests the title given to it. It is the entrance or gateway to still greater wonders and grandeurs of the famous Red Cañon, that cuts its way to a depth of 3,000 feet between this point and its entrance into Brown's Hole" (Jackson [1875] 1978, 18). This placid stretch of river now lies inundated at the bottom of the Flaming Gorge Reservoir near the Utah-Wyoming border. Courtesy U.S. Geological Survey.

"spuds" were still uncooked, and John had to fall back on the dependable frying pan to complete his work. From this incident he got the nickname of Potato John, which he carried for the many years he remained with the Survey. He had learned from the experience at least one good lesson: the higher the altitude, the lower the temperature of boiling water.

Returning to our main camp at Fort Bridger, we made another side trip into the Uintas about the headwaters of Blacks Fork, and then the expedition moved down Henrys Fork to the Green River to the vicinity of the Flaming Gorge. From here on a three-day side trip we reached Browns Hole, a winter grazing ground for cattle.[16] While we were encamped there, we saw some thousands of them being driven in from ranges farther east.

After these trips we returned to Green River City and then followed the old Overland Stage route across southern Wyoming towards the east. I did little photographing on this return trip, as it was quite cold most of the time and there was little of pictorial interest along drab Bitter Creek and over the Red Desert.

At Fort Sanders our party was disbanded for the season. Some went to Camp Carling to turn over the outfit to the quartermaster; others went directly home. Stevenson and I, with the ambulance, two good mules, and a driver, went down to Denver and the Pikes Peak region. We made frequent stops along the foothills for photography, and finally completing our season's work at Manitou Soda Springs, which were still the same as when only nomadic red men sought their sparkling waters.

Returning to Denver I went directly to Washington over the Kansas Pacific Railroad, just completed for through traffic. We left Denver in the evening, and when we awoke the next morning the train was running through vast herds of buffalo that covered the plains on either side as far as the eye could reach. They were always in sight during nearly the whole day's run, and occasionally the train slowed up when the buffaloes lingered too long on the right of way. In the baggage car forward a few men engaged in the questionable sport—if such an act can be termed sport—of shooting into the thick of the herd with rifles, with no other result than making victims for the wolf and the coyote.

This trip to Washington, before returning to my home in Omaha, was for a final conference with Dr. Hayden, the outcome of which is shown in the following chapter.

NATURALISTS AT WORK. 1870 or 1871.
Copy of modern print from wet plate negative.

The scientists are preparing the day's collection of the
bird life of the country. James Stevenson, Survey
manager, is sitting at the left and Potato John Raymond,
cook, is in the foreground. To the right of Stevenson are
Dr. Charles Turnbull, physician and assistant, Henry
Elliott, artist, and John Beaman, topographer and
meteorologist (William Henry Jackson Photograph
Collection [1869–1878, and 1883] n.d., WHJ #896).
Courtesy U.S. Geological Survey.

Chapter Seven

First Photographing of the Yellowstone

September 1870–February 1872

When I agreed to accompany Dr. Hayden's Geological Survey of Wyoming in 1870 as photographer, I gave little thought to what might follow, except that I expected to return with a collection of negatives that would be of some value to my view business. At the end of the season, however, the photographic work proved to be so satisfactory in every way that Dr. Hayden decided it must be one of the regular branches of the Survey's operations, and at our final conference in Washington I was made its official photographer. This was very much to my liking. I looked forward with satisfaction to having the Survey take over all the negatives I had made and also to the transfer of my residence to Washington.

The six months following my return to Omaha were fully occupied with winding up my business, making prints for the use of the Survey, and preparing for the next season's field work.[1] On the Wyoming Survey I used a whole plate, or 6 ½ by 8 ½, camera. For the coming season I adopted an 8 by 10 camera and also retained the stereoscopic size because of its general popularity. For emergencies I included in my outfit the 1870 camera, and a useful purpose it served later, as we shall see. As Dr. Hayden wanted quick publication, we took along the necessary supplies for making prints in the field, such as albumin paper, silver baths, and toning solutions.

The general plan had been to continue the work of 1870 by extending it into adjacent territory. Before this plan took shape, however, public attention was directed to the wonders of the Yellowstone through lectures and magazine articles. A lecture in Washington by Mr. N. P. Langford, which Dr. Hayden attended, made him decide on the Yellowstone as the field of his operations for 1871.

Up to this time this region was more or less of a mythical wonderland. John Colter, of the Lewis and Clark exploring party, is credited with being the first white man to pass through the region that is now the Yellowstone National Park. He discovered parts of it during the early years of the nineteenth century. From his description of the spouting hot springs, the boiling mud pots, and other wonders, it had been given the name of Colter's Hell.[2] Bridger, the trapper, scout, and guide was undoubtedly familiar with its wonders, but his stories seemed incredible and were not taken seriously.

The Raynolds Expedition, which Dr. Hayden accompanied in 1859, attempted to reach the headwaters of the Yellowstone from the south, but being too early in the season, failed to penetrate the snow-clad barriers.[3] Then along in the early sixties the Montana gold craze sent a few adventurous prospectors through this region and they saw much of the wonders that are now well known. In 1866, when I was traveling over the Oregon Trail in the vicinity of South Pass, old frontiersmen told me of the great lake, the waterfalls, and the geysers not far away to the north, and I remember that at the time I had a longing to go there.

It was not until 1869 that an expedition was organized for the sole purpose of proving the truth of what had been told of this region. The Folsom-Cook party of Montana in that year made the rounds of some of the important features of what is now the Yellowstone Park.[4] Their report led to an expedition in 1870 under the leadership of General H. D. Washburn.[5] Mr. Langford of Montana, who became the first superintendent of the Park, was a member and its chief historian. His articles in *Scribner's Monthly*[6] and speeches from the lecture platform created intense and widespread interest throughout the country, and led, as I have said, to a more thorough exploration of that region by Dr. Hayden.

It was with tremendous enthusiasm that we prepared for the invasion of this new wonderland. Additions were made to the regular staff, increasing its numbers to twenty. Seven of them had been out with previous expeditions. A topographer was now included, as the little known regions must be accurately mapped.[7] Then there were botanists, entomologists, and others interested in its flora and fauna, who supplemented the work of the geologists.

Among the newcomers were half a dozen youths, sons or protégés of men prominent in the official or political life of Washington, who were assigned various duties as collectors in natural history and as all-round assistants. To these boys, however,

~

For making immediate prints Jackson had the capacity to produce a ferrotype—an earlier type of photographic print done on a metal plate. "By this time I had my first gadget for 'speed' work—a drop shutter, actuated by a rubber band, that enabled me to shoot action at high noon with a one-tenth second exposure. But most of my pictures were stills at five seconds and upward. When speed was no consideration I always stopped my lens down to get maximum depth and definition" (Jackson [1940] 1994, 197).

~

the whole business at first was very much of a lark, and the affairs concerning their horses, guns, fishing tackle, and other equipment were of greater importance than the duties assigned to them. From among them I got a regular assistant, who became an efficient helper as well as a congenial companion.[8]

Accompanying us as an honored guest, we had the famous artist, Thomas Moran.[9] He entered into the spirit of the work most heartily, dividing his time impartially between his own color sketching and assisting in the selection of camera subjects. Moran has been the greatest painter of the Yellowstone, and it was his wonderful coloring, in pictures of canyon and hot springs, that made the convincing argument for their preservation for the benefit of all posterity. His first large painting of the falls and the canyon was bought by the government and is in the Capitol at Washington. A more important canvas of the same subject now hangs on the wall of the National Art Gallery. I never tire of looking at this marvelous representation of one of nature's greatest handiworks.

The first week in June found me in camp with other members of the Survey at Ogden, Utah, the most convenient point from which to begin our journey northwards. Army headquarters at Cheyenne were again drawn upon for our road equipment: horses, mules, and wagons, as well as commissary supplies, which were all sent to Ogden by rail. Some of the employees of former years, cooks and teamsters, also came along; there were fifteen of them, making our whole number thirty-five. Five wall tents assured good temporary sleeping accommodations; and seven wagons, two of them lighter ambulances for run-around work, provided transportation, for baggage, such as chairs, tables, trunks, and bulky canned goods, all of which had to be left behind when we took to the trails with our pack outfits.

There were a few days of busy preparation, during which the new cameras and lenses were tried out in making camp views and photographs of waterfalls and canyons in the neighborhood. My working outfit for the road was about the same as the year before, but instead of the parfleches I had sole leather cases, which were handier for loading and unloading in the frequent requirements of picture making. Another convenience was rubber bags for carrying water instead of the cumbersome keg.

Breaking camp June tenth, we strung out along the road in an imposing array of twenty-one horsemen and seven big army wagons, most of them drawn by four

U.S. GEOLOGICAL SURVEY. PLATE 75 a.

Thos. Sinclair & Son, Lith.

FRANKLIN BUTTE AND NORTH END OF CACHE VALLEY.

FRANKLIN BUTTE AND THE NORTH END OF CACHE VALLEY. 1878. Lithographic print.

The camp of the Geological Survey in 1871 in Cache Valley, Utah. In prehistoric times this valley was covered by an arm of Lake Bonneville. The line of the terrace across the middle of the picture represents the shore of this ancient lake. As the Survey years progressed, many of Jackson's photographs were transformed into engravings to illustrate Hayden's annual reports. The technology to publish photographs had not yet been fully developed. Courtesy Wayne Johnson, Historian.

mules each. Everyone was glad to leave the sun-scorched bench where our tents had been pitched. We had a long journey ahead of nearly five hundred miles before reaching even the borderland of real exploration. The first few days we rode through a succession of picturesque Mormon settlements in the midst of gardens and fruit trees, out into Cache Valley, which was once upon a time flooded by an arm of the great Lake Bonneville of ancient times.

From Cache Valley we passed over the divide to the Portneuf, with its curious lava flows, and to Fort Hall, a cantonment recently built some forty miles eastward from the site of the historic Fort Hall, which had been the rendezvous of trappers and Oregon emigrants.[10] From here we crossed the Snake River at Taylors Bridge[11] and then traveled wearily over the sandy plains of Idaho. Near the notorious Hole in the Wall stage station,[12] we had hazy views of the far-away Tetons, the famous Trois Tetons of the days of the pioneer trapper and fur trader,[13] who contested with the wily Blackfeet for the right to trap beavers. We were soon to know these famous peaks more intimately.

A SUCCESSFUL FISHERMAN. July 20, 1871.
Albumin print on stereoscope card.

Thomas Moran, the painter of the Yellowstone,
accompanied the 1871 expedition. That he was an expert
fisherman is shown by this string of trout. Moran was
"of slight and frail physique and did not seem to endure
the strenuous life of the wilderness. He had never
camped out before except for a night's bivouac on the
shore of Lake Superior. . . . Moran had never ridden a
horse before, and while getting accustomed to the
experience, was quite unabashed in using his camp
pillow to protect his rather spare anatomy from the hard
lines of a McClellan saddle. . . . But he made the
adventure with fine courage and quickly adapted
himself to the new and unfamiliar conditions and, as it
turned out later, none was more untiring on the trail, or
less mindful of unaccustomed food or hard bed under a
little shelter tent, than he was" (Jackson 1936, 152).
Courtesy National Park Service/Grand Teton
National Park.

Crossing another divide, this time from the waters of the Pacific to those of the
Atlantic watershed, we soon reached Virginia City, Montana. This had recently been
the liveliest mining camp in all the West, the rush to it rivaling for a time the stampede
of '49 to the California gold diggings. In Alder Gulch, near by, which had yielded
many millions in golden nuggets, we found a few Chinamen gathering the little that
was left from more prosperous times.

And then, four weeks from the time we left the Ogden camp, our train rolled into
Fort Ellis,[14] the outpost to the Yellowstone region, where we made our preparations
for the journey beyond. At about the same time another party arrived at the fort, sent
out by the War Department to make a topographical survey for the purpose of recon-
structing its maps. Captain Barlow and Captain Head [Heap] of the Engineer Corps
were in charge of this party.[15]

The officers at Fort Ellis entered into all the preparations with the greatest zest
and interest, partly perhaps because General Sheridan had authorized the detail of a
small company of cavalry to escort the expeditions. Before we left this hospitable post
the officers arranged a side trip into the hills about twelve miles distant, to a picturesque lake among the mountains.[16] Here, in addition to enjoying some remarkable

Boteler's [Bottler's] *Ranch.* July 17, 1871. Albumin print in Jackson Album.

This view shows "a log cabin of the pioneer stamp, owned by three brothers, who have earned a wide reputation for whole-souled, hearty hospitality.... Here wagons and extra baggage [and a small party of men] were left, for beyond this point was nothing but a narrow trail (1871), accessible only to the sure footed mule or hardy Cayuse" (Jackson [1875] 1978, 24), a wild western range horse. The men, left to right are: an unidentified man; two of the Bottler brothers; Albert Peale, mineralogist; and Clifford Negley, Survey assistant (Merrill 1999, 122). The ranch was located some twenty-seven miles north of Gardiner, Montana. At the time it was used as a place to launch expeditions into the Yellowstone region. Courtesy National Park Service/Yellowstone National Park.

scenery, we had excellent fishing. After pitching camp for the night by the shore, we soon had a long string of fine trout for supper. The beauty of the little lake, reflecting perfectly the surrounding forest as twilight approached, made a delightful picture.

Moran, an expert fisherman and also a past master in alfresco cooking, promised us a better dish than the frying pan afforded. Scraping aside the coals and ashes of the camp fire, he dug a hole in the hot earth and in it placed the fish, previously cleaned and wrapped in wet brown paper; then covering them with earth and hot coals, he allowed them to remain until cooked. It was not an attractive mess as it came from the extemporized oven, but when the charred paper was removed, we had as dainty a bit of steaming white flesh as the most exacting taste could wish for.

The wagons could be taken some thirty miles beyond Fort Ellis to Boteler's ranch on the Yellowstone,[17] where we had to change from wagon to pack transportation. Boteler's ranch, the base of supplies for the Survey while afield with the

FAMILY GROUP. September 13, 1871. Albumin print.

"In 1871, while returning from the exploration of the Yellowstone region, and while encamped near the head of the Medicine Lodge Creek, [Idaho,] the camp of a family of the Sheep-eater band of Bannacks [sic] was accidentally discovered near by, almost completely hidden in a grove of willows. Their tent or tepee [sic] is made of a few boughs of willow, about which is thrown an old canvas picked up in some of the settlements. The present of a handful of sugar and some coffee reconciled them to having their photographs taken. . . The Sheep-eaters are a band of Bannacks, running in the mountains north of the Kamas prairies, and are so shy and timid that they are but rarely seen" (Jackson, [1877] 1978, 70-71). Courtesy National Park Service/Yellowstone National Park.

pack train, included a log cabin of ample proportions. It was built on a high bench well back from the Yellowstone. Here three brothers, Hollanders, kept bachelor hall. They were running a hay, cattle, and dairy ranch with attempts at crop raising. Jolly and generous good fellows, they permitted us to take their place by storm and make great inroads on their dairy products. It was a feast for the gods, to sit at their rude tables before a large bowl of rich creamy milk and a loaf of bread of their own baking, which was as good as the cream—and that was the highest praise one could give it.

The transfer from wagons to pack train kept everyone busy for the three days we were at the ranch, particularly those in charge of the pack outfit. Shep Madera and Tom Cooper, two first-class packers whom we had picked up in Virginia City,[18] with the assistance of our other employees tackled the thankless job of reducing all camp equipage and commissary supplies, as well as the personal "war bags" of the men, to the limited capacity of pack mules. Shep, as the boss of these operations, soon brought order out of confusion. One wall tent was allowed as headquarters for the Doctor, but for everyone else shelter tents were provided—dog tents we called them in the army. These were small enough to be carried in a knapsack. Commissary supplies were limited to the fundamentals of flour, bacon, and coffee with some dried fruits. Two hunters were engaged to go along with us; their sole duty was to provide fresh meat for the camps.[19]

We set up our printing outfit at this place. My assistant and I had our hands full in trying to meet the demands for pictures, especially camp views and personal groupings, which were wanted by nearly everyone in the party to send back east. Dr. Hayden and Stevenson, particularly, made good use of these among their political associates and other friends in Washington.

Finally, on the morning of July 20, our train strung out along the trail. The horsemen were leading and the pack train, with the mules groaning under their unaccustomed loads, brought up the rear. Our military escort had gone ahead. Indeed, we saw little of the troop at any time; they made their camps apart and came and went independently of our movements. There was no real need of an escort as a protection from Indians, as they seldom passed through this region and those whom we were likely to meet, the Bannocks, were not at this time hostile. The escort was more of a junket for the soldiers than anything else; it was probably so regarded, for it was soon withdrawn to Fort Ellis, leaving only a small detail for the benefit of Captain Barlow of the Engineers and his party.

Everyone was keyed up to the highest degree of expectation as we followed the narrow trail along the Yellowstone to the mysterious regions beyond. Not one in the party had ever been there. Much had already been said and printed, but the impression that the half had not been told gave zest to each day's journey. The Mammoth Hot Springs had been overlooked by previous explorers.[20] Could not we make other discoveries also of equal importance? Around our evening camp fires the adventures of the day and the anticipations of the morrow were related with the usual embellishments supplied by lively imaginations.

From the first I was frequently separated from the main party in its march from one camp to another. All along the way we came upon interesting scenes that must be photographed. The train could not be halted while I was doing this, so I dropped out of line with my assistant and the pack mule. Sometimes we did not come up with the party again until long after camp had been made.

When we first came on to the Yellowstone, I lingered for some time to make a view of the valley, with the river meandering through it, from a spot where the trail passed over a high rocky ledge. Then came a canyon,[21] where Moran indulged in his favorite pastime of fishing while I looked up my viewpoints. Another halt was made to portray the freaks of Cinnabar Mountain; and then coming to Gardiner [Gardner] River, we followed the advance party over the hills to the foot of the great white terraces of the Mammoth Hot Springs.

Here was the first really important work for both scientists and picture men—a subject never before described or photographed. I have maintained that the first photographs of the Yellowstone region were, with two exceptions, those of the Hayden Survey of 1871. Captain Barlow had a photographer with his party, Thomas Hine of Chicago,[22] whom I knew well, a man who had a fine reputation as a landscape artist. He returned to Chicago with his negatives just in time to have them destroyed in the great fire. There was also a local photographer, Crissman of Bozeman, Montana,[23] who was permitted by Dr. Hayden to accompany the Survey over a part of its route. Thus there were three photographers working in the Yellowstone country in '71; but prints were never made from Barlow's negatives, and Crissman's had only

MAMMOTH HOT SPRINGS. July 21, 1871.
Albumin print.

John Crissman's photograph shows Thomas Moran, the painter, studying the beautiful coloring of the terraces at Mammoth. The springs had been previously discovered but nothing had yet been published about them. Crissman, a photographer from Bozeman, Montana, accompanied the 1871 and 1872 expeditions through portions of Yellowstone, and some of his images were retained by the Hayden Survey for both years. While Jackson is commonly credited for all of the photographs in the catalogue *Miscellaneous Publications No. 5* (Jackson [1875] 1978), Crissman is acknowledged as the photographer for some but not all of his Yellowstone images in the catalogue. Courtesy National Park Service/Yellowstone National Park.

a limited, local use. The photographs that I made, therefore, were the only ones used that year for publicity illustration and general distribution.

The significance of our work was pointed out by H. M. Chittenden in the first edition of his Guide to the Yellowstone,[24] "The chief value of these explorations," he wrote, "was not in the line of original discovery, but in the large collection of accurate data concerning the entire region. The photographs were of immense value. Description might exaggerate, but the camera told the truth; and in this case the truth was more remarkable than exaggeration. Unfortunately for Captain Barlow's collection, the great Chicago fire almost destroyed it. . . . The report and collection of photographs and specimens by Dr. Hayden were therefore the principal results of this season's work, and they played a decisive part in the events of the winter of 1871–2"—that is, in the creation of the Yellowstone National Park.

I now had before me novel and marvelously fine subjects for my camera. The delicate tracery in the deposits about the hot spring pools and terraces afforded an endless variety of detail for picture making. Setting up my dark box in the shade of a cedar tree at the foot of the great terrace, I made exposures all over the formation from this base of operations. The subjects were near enough so that I could run to and from the dark box without getting my plate too dry to develop satisfactorily. The water flowing from the springs had a temperature ranging from the boiling point at the source to about 120 degrees in the little channels passing near my dark box. I used this hot water entirely for the final washing of the plates, and found it advantageous because of the quick drying afterwards.

We followed a rugged trail over rough country to Baronett's Bridge,[25] said to be the only bridge over the Yellowstone throughout its entire length. Then we went on to Tower Falls, where Tower Creek runs a tortuous course between fantastic pinnacles of conglomerate rock and makes a final leap of one hundred and thirty-two feet into a deep ravine. To get any comprehensive view of the falls, it was necessary to go to the bottom of the ravine below, a descent of about two hundred feet, through steep sides covered with a thick growth of small timber and brush. Rather than take the dark box down to the bottom, I worked from the top. Backing my plate with wet blotting paper, and wrapping the holder in a wet towel and the dark cloth, I scrambled and slid down to the rocky bed of the stream, with plate holder and camera in hand. After taking the picture, I had a slow, laborious climb back again, and reached the top out of breath in a wringing perspiration. Four round trips gave me the desired number of negatives, a full half day's work, making a stiff price in labor for the one subject.

Passing over the divide to the right of Mt. Washburn, we had our first view of Yellowstone Lake, reflecting its mountain background; and farther away, barely discernible through the summer haze, the Teton Range appeared above the distant horizon. It was a glorious view, giving in one broad sweep of the eye nearly all of the wonderland we were soon to enter.

Descending rapidly, we made camp on Cascade Creek, a small stream entering the Yellowstone between the Upper and Lower Falls. Two very busy days were spent in exploration for the best points of view. Working enthusiasm was keyed to the highest pitch by the grandeur of the canyon and the falls, the greatest scenic features of the Yellowstone. We were up with the sun each morning, everyone making discovery of some new or more wonderful viewpoint, and then choosing the best for each particular aspect of river, canyon, or falls. It was a most entrancing thought—that we were in the presence of one of the grandest views in the world and one that never before had been photographed.

I have mentioned Crissman, the Bozeman photographer who accompanied our party. He was a good-natured and companionable man, who quickly made friends with everyone of the Survey. He was getting along finely until one day at the falls something happened that came near putting him out of business. Working along with us, almost side by side, he planted his camera for a view of the Lower Fall on the very brink of the canyon at Artist's Point. After making an exposure, he left the camera there, while he went back into the edge of the woods to develop his plate. He went out again with another plate, but soon came sauntering back to us and said in a quiet, resigned way, "Well, boys, my whole outfit has gone to hell a-fluking."

Sure enough, when we rushed out to see what had happened, we found a vacant place where the camera had stood. Over the edge the scattered fragments could be traced down a slide for several hundred feet, sent there by a vagrant wind. Bellows and splintered wood and the tripod legs could be seen among the rocks, with the dark cloth hanging from a bush projecting from the side of the canyon wall. It was hopeless to

TOWER FALLS. July 26, 1871. Albumin print in Jackson Album.

This "near view from near the base" (Jackson [1875] 1978, 26) of the falls was taken with Thomas Moran's assistance. Moran developed a lifelong friendship with Jackson during his Survey travels in the Yellowstone region. He spent much of his time assisting Jackson with photographic chores. Courtesy National Park Service/Yellowstone National Park.

THE LOWER FALLS OF THE YELLOWSTONE. July 28–30, 1871.
Albumin print.

The falls are 308 feet in height. At "the brink of the Lower
Falls, the [Yellowstone River] is contracted to a width of 100
feet, and then plunges over the precipice a solid, unbroken
mass, falling . . . into the spray filled chasm, enlivened with
rainbows, and glittering like a shower of diamonds" (Jackson
[1875] 1978, 27). Courtesy National Park Service/Scotts Bluff
National Monument.

think of recovering anything, which probably accounted for Crissman's seeming res-
ignation to his loss. But he was not to be entirely put out of business; my 1870 camera, brought along as a duplicate outfit, now came into good use. He was provided
with this and the necessary equipment for continuing his work.

We had to hurry on, for the main body of the expedition had gone to the lake and
we must follow. Enough time was taken, however, to get several views. One of the
most charming was the broad expanse of river and valley lying between the falls and
the lake. That valley was afterwards named Hayden Valley in honor of our leader.

Joining the rest of the party at the outlet, we began the entire circuit of the lake
through the trackless forests surrounding it. The usual procedure in these daily
marches was for the pack train with the cook and other camp hands to go ahead in
the appointed direction and make camp at the end of an average day of travel—six
to eight hours. The scientists—such as the geologists, topographers, and naturalists
interested in botany, bugs, and such things—each followed their special line of investigation. They often digressed far from the line of travel and depended mainly upon
picking up the trail of the pack train to find camp at the end of their day's work. Ordinarily this worked all right, although it sometimes happened that the packers went
much farther than expected in order to find a suitable camping place, and consequently the belated ones might be long after dark getting in. An incident of this kind
in my own experience the first day of our travel around the lake is an example of what
happened once in a while.

We had a fine day for photographing and it was well along in the afternoon by
the time we had put away the last plate, packed up, and swung into our saddles to
locate camp. We were following the shore line of the lake, sometimes on the beach but
more frequently through the dense forest that came right down to the water. The
western side of the lake is almost entirely covered with a dense pine forest, where
windfalls at frequent intervals made traveling slow and difficult. While daylight lasted, it was comparatively easy to find the trail of the preceding party, even where they
left only a faint trace. Expecting every moment to get a glimpse of camp through the
trees, we patiently jogged along until twilight deepened into positive darkness. Then
abandoning all attempts to follow the trail, and pushing ahead into the dark forest,
we soon became entangled among jack pines so thick that it seemed impossible to

worm the pack mule through them. Having come through, we found ourselves involved in a maze of fallen trees that for the moment barred any further progress.

The night dragged on interminably. We knew we could not miss the camp, for it must be on the shore and we were never far from it. Just about the time we had resigned ourselves to tying up for the rest of the night, the alert senses of our animals detected the camp and made it known by glad brays and whinnyings, which were answered from out of the darkness by their camp mates. It was midnight as we entered the silent camp. Quietly we unpacked and unsaddled, and after foraging among the pots and kettles for a bit of grub, found our bed rolls and with little ceremony rolled up in our blankets and were soon sound asleep.

From the Thumb or extreme western arm of the lake, we went over to Firehole River. We had little knowledge of direction or distances. We knew only that somewhere to the west across an intervening divide the Madison River had its sources and on one of its tributaries was the geyser basin that we were seeking. In the absence of definite information, there was some uncertainty as to location and names of rivers and lakes by which we were to be guided; and indeed later surveys showed that many of our conjectures were wrong. Our party of three, however, found its way to the Firehole with no more than the usual trouble in traveling through trackless forests in a mountainous region. We struck the Upper Geyser Basin at its head. There was not much photographing on this trip as my time was limited. The main party was about to undertake the continuation of the circuit of the lake, and if we were not to be left alone in the wilderness, we must rejoin them. But if the geysers were slighted on this expedition, another one a year later was to do them full justice.

Returning to the main camp on the lake, we found that Lieutenant G. C. Doane,[26] who with a sergeant and four men accompanied the Washburn expedition in 1870, had come out to join our party. As the Lieutenant had been around the lake, his familiarity with the country and its landmarks helped to make easier our course through the dense forests interspersed with grassy glades, marshes, or lily covered lakes. But previous experience or sense of direction was not always to be relied upon when traveling through thick timber with many detours to escape entanglement in windfalls or thickets of dense pines. At one place, with the Lieutenant leading, we made our way up a gentle draw through the woods until we came out on a low divide and then

CRATER OF CASTLE GEYSER. August 8, 1871. Albumen print in Jackson Album.

"Here we see the peculiar crystallization of the silica in large globular masses, like spongiform corals, and running off into the usual exquisite bead-work to the laminated base. . . . On the right, close to its base, is a small but very active and turbulent little geyser, probably an offshoot from the greater one. In the center of the view, and the most striking object in it, is the beautiful hot spring, with elegantly-carved boarder and water of the clearest turquoise blue. . . . The water is of almost unnatural clearness, and the varying depth gives a most beautiful gradation of color" (Jackson [1875] 1978, 31). An almost identical image taken a year later shows a Survey member climbing the cone. Courtesy National Park Service/Yellowstone National Park.

Collecting photographs of Native Americans, which depicted their dress and customs, was an important addition to the Survey's exploratory tasks. Naturally, Jackson became involved in this process. Hayden collected views by many other photographers as well. In 1877 he released *Miscellaneous Publications No. 9; Descriptive Catalogue of Photographs of North American Indians*, by W. H. Jackson, Photographer of the Survey. In Hayden's "Prefatory Note" (Jackson [1877] 1978, IV–V) he hints that other photographers were involved in creating the photographs but credits only Jackson and William Blackmore, the eminent British anthropologist who donated his collection to the Survey. By not crediting the photographers, Jackson and Hayden inadvertently created a major flaw in the catalogue. Jackson received credit for taking many photographs that were taken by others. For a number of the views, the photographers have since been properly identified; many remain without proper credit. Neither Jackson nor Hayden did much in the post-Survey years to correct the catalogue omissions.

began our descent on the other side. Continuing on our course, with no outlook and everything as alike as two peas, after five or six miles our leaders were nonplussed by striking into a freshly made trail, so recent as to suggest another large party in our immediate neighborhood. As this was unthinkable, the conviction was forced upon us that we had doubled upon our own trail!

One of the most difficult passages in completing the circuit of the lake was the fording of the Upper Yellowstone River. Along the river and its tributaries there was a continuous succession of beaver dams and boggy meadows, among which, for a time, it seemed almost impossible to find a crossing. Floundering through, however, and gaining the opposite side, we soon came out on the eastern side of the lake with clear open spaces, a bold, rocky shore line, and back of all the prominent peaks of the Yellowstone Range, afterwards named the Absarokas.

There had been but little photography done in traveling around the lake, but out here in the open we got busy again. From the Signal Hills panoramas of the lake were made, and then the prominent peaks of the mountains near by were photographed. One of them had been ascended by Doane and Langford the year before; and now Doane, accompanied by Stevenson, again made the ascent of the peak which has been named for him. Two other peaks of the same group now bear the names of Langford and Stevenson.

Although this was the most attractive part of the lake, we were glad to move on. It was the middle of August; the nights were cold, with frequent heavy frosts. Supplies were nearly exhausted also and the hunters had been unsuccessful in bringing in game. Someone did shoot an old goose as it was wending its way southward; but many hours of boiling merely turned its flesh to the consistency of rubber, and it finally was put up as a target for pistol practice to see the bullets bounce off!

The best part of our work having been done, we now passed rapidly over to the East Fork, and thence out to our base at Boteler's. Loading the wagons again, we began the tedious five-hundred-mile ride to the railroad at Evanston, where everything was shipped back to Fort D. A. Russell.

On the homeward journey Dr. Hayden wished me to make a special photographic trip to the Pawnee and Omaha villages in Nebraska. The Pawnees were then living in their ancient earth-covered lodges on the Loup Fork about one hundred miles west from Omaha. It was understood that they were soon to be removed to another reservation, and then the villages would disappear before the oncoming wave of occupation by settlers. As these were among the last of their kind in the Upper Missouri country, and their like would never be seen again, the Doctor was very much interested in having them photographed. It was about this time that he began the collection of Indian photographs, which numbered some two thousand subjects when finally turned over to the Bureau of Ethnology in Washington.

From the Pawnee villages we journeyed across country in a buckboard to the Omaha Reservation on the banks of the Missouri. The Indians there had progressed much farther in the ways of the white man, but with the cooperation of the agent we got some fine pictures of typical "old-timers" among them. But on all sides school-houses and small cottages were being built on plots of ground which had been apportioned to them. Photographs from these negatives, which I sent to the agent's family in acknowledgment of their assistance and hospitality, led to a lifelong intimacy.

In Washington the Survey headquarters were located in a building on Pennsylvania Avenue, where photographic workrooms were fitted up for my use. There were many requests, official and otherwise, for photographs of the newly explored regions, and I had a busy time indeed in meeting the demand. But all these activities and many plans for the future were suddenly interrupted by the passing away of my dear wife, only a little while before my departure for the West.

~

William Jackson's wife, Mollie, went to Nyack, New York, to spend her "confinement" with Jackson's parents while pregnant. "In February, when her baby was born, Mollie died. Our child, a daughter, survived only a short while. These are matters about which, even now, I can write no more" (Jackson [1940] 1994, 204–5). The work for the 1872 season began almost immediately.

~

Chapter Eight

Photographing the Grand Teton

June 1872–September 1872

The 11″ × 14″ camera was added for obtaining larger pictures, as easily produced enlargements were still in the future. "Since it was impossible to prepare and develop the bigger plates in my portable dark box, I now had to set up a dark tent every time I wanted to make a picture. This little tent had a cover of gray-white canvass; but inside it was lined with orange calico to cut out the actinic rays" (Jackson [1940] 1994, 205). "The work of this season [included] forty-five 11 by 14 views, the very first plates of this size ever to be made in the Rocky Mountains" (Jackson [1875] 1978, 35).

The reports of our '71 Yellowstone expedition, together with the photographs that were widely distributed, played an important part in the setting aside of this wonderland as a National Park. The widespread interest in this magnificent region, now for the first time portrayed in the photographs and in the splendid paintings by Moran, was mainly responsible for the continuing of the Survey the next year over the same region.

Two parties were organized to explore this territory more thoroughly and more widely. One under Dr. Hayden was to go directly over our 1871 route; another larger one under Stevenson was to approach the Park from the southwest. I was assigned to the division under Stevenson. There were about forty of us all together, including our guest, Mr. Langford, recently appointed superintendent of the Park. Our route, as before, was from Ogden, Utah, to Fort Hall. From there we were to proceed to the Three Tetons for the survey of that region; and then, traveling northward, we were to reach the Park by what is now known as the West Entrance.

This side trip to the Tetons was really secondary to the main object of the expedition, but by this time the Yellowstone had lost something of its novelty, and the Tetons, never before photographed, now became of the first importance, so far as I was concerned.[1]

There was little done photographically, until we reached the Teton Basin at the western base of the Teton Range. The basin in earlier days had been called Pierre's Hole, after Pierre, an Iroquois Indian trapper. It was a famous rendezvous for the old-time fur trappers. Our camp was made at the upper end of this basin on the Teton River [Teton Creek]. This was used only as a base for the scientists, who went out in small parties, each to cover its own special field.

For the ten days that the camp remained here I spent every daylight hour exploring canyons and traversing the snowy fields above timber line in search of views of the higher peaks. Dr. J. M. Coulter, the eminent botanist, was a member of the expedition and my companion on many of these trips. Two others and a packer to care for the animals made a party of five.[2] With our own supplies we went our separate way and seldom met the other divisions.

Between two branches of the Teton River there is a high tableland extending well above timber line and covered with fields of perpetual snow. This plateau leads directly up to the Grand Teton but is cut off from it by the deep gorge of Glacier Creek.[3]

With two pack mules, one to carry blankets and food, and the other, Old Molly, taking the photographic outfit as her regular job, we camped for three days at the verge of timber line on this plateau. From this point we extended our explorations for effective viewpoints. The traveling was not generally difficult, as the inclination of the rocky strata was such that it afforded a gradual rise with but few breaks. The worst places were bridged by snow banks, which were now packed hard enough to travel over.

In making our way to the extremity of the plateau for a close-up view of the Grand Teton, we came to a wall of rock over which a goat might have made its way, but which seemed impossible for a pack mule. On one side was a sheer precipice, but on the other a ledge supported a bank of hard snow, which offered a passage around the wall. The snow, however, lay at a dangerously steep angle and overhung a drop of several hundred feet.

It was with some misgivings that we contemplated this passage. Snow is treacherous. If one of the animals should happen to strike a soft spot and fall on that steep incline, there was a possibility of going over into the chasm below. However, as this was the only way to get a close-up view of the magnificent peaks, we decided to take the risk.

As a precaution, we first prepared a way by tramping out a trail and then leading over the saddle animals. Finally we followed with Old Molly and her precious pack, relying upon a firm hold on the halter strap to keep her from falling over the cliff if any mishap should occur. Fortunately none did. The returning passage did not seem so hazardous, as success inspired confidence in both men and animals.

A PRECARIOUS PASSAGE. Circa 1929. Ink wash sketch.

It was difficult and dangerous for the pack mule to reach the point for a close-up view of the Grand Teton. The men were arduously ascending Table Mountain where the stereograph entitled "Hayden's Peak or the Great Teton," (page 82) was created. Courtesy Brigham Young University.

HAYDEN'S PEAK OR THE GREAT TETON. Circa July 20, 1872. Albumin print on stereoscope card.

A close up of the Grand Teton from the Idaho side 13,747 [13,770] feet in height. It has been called the American Matterhorn and the most historic summit of the West. "Although not the highest, it is the grandest and most alpine-like peak in the West. No others can show such abrupt angles and bold outlines, where snow even can rest only in small patches on the ledges." (Jackson [1875] 1978, 35). It was taken from the summit of Table Mountain. Courtesy National Park Service/Grand Teton National Park.

ONE OF THE BIGHORNS OF THE TETON MOUNTAINS. Circa 1929. Ink wash, graphite, and tempera.

The animal was intensely interested in what was going on in the [dark] tent until the operator appeared. This incident occurred while photographing the main peaks from the crest of Table Mountain. Courtesy Brigham Young University.

From the point that was gained by this precarious passage we had a glorious near view of the Three Tetons with the Grand Teton, 13,747 [13,770] feet in height, directly in front of us.[4] We remained here the greater part of the day making negatives—11 × 14, 8 × 10, and stereoscopic, in panoramic as well as single compositions. It was a perfect day, clear and cold, but with enough warmth in the sun's rays to melt the snow in trickling rivulets on the southerly exposures, thus keeping up the water supply required for plate washing.

While my assistants were hunting for water, it happened that I was alone for some time, wrapped up in my tent preparing a plate for the next view. On emerging, I was astonished to see a magnificent mountain sheep—a buck with enormous horns—on the rocks within thirty feet, watching my movements with apparent fascination. For a few moments we gazed at each other, the buck motionless, but the spell was broken when I made a motion towards my rifle a few yards away, and he bounded out of sight.

The lonely tent and the mysterious sounds from within must have been of absorbing interest to this wild denizen of the hills. His presence there was evidence of the extreme isolation of this region, for it was, perhaps, one of the least frequented places in the Rocky Mountains. Sheep and bears were numerous all over the higher plateau, and elk, deer, and moose lived in the wooded seclusion of the canyons and hillsides. One of our over-night bivouacs was named the Moose Camp because of the killing of a young moose there by one of our party.

After getting the close-up views from the central plateau, with two assistants I crossed the canyon of the left fork of Teton River to another plateau for more comprehensive views of the entire range beyond.[5] The way was difficult and there was more snow to fight through to reach the vantage points for pictures, but these troubles were soon forgotten as the glorious panorama opened up before us.

Returning from the heights, we found a way to make quick work of the descent. As we were riding along a high ridge, we noticed long banks of snow, lying at a steep incline and extending down several hundred feet into the edge of timber below. It was too suggestive of a toboggan slide to be passed by without a trial. Unloading the boxes from Old Molly, I sent all the animals, in care of the packer, down by the longer and roundabout way. Using the two boxes as toboggans and selecting the most promising one of the snow slides, my assistant and I accomplished, in less than ten minutes, a cut-off in distance that took the packer nearly an hour to make in the regular way. But it was not all smooth sailing. Our extemporized toboggans would not ride straight all the way down. There were swerves ending in a mix-up, rider and box rolling over and over until the box could be recovered and the tobogganing resumed.

During the ten days we were out from the main camp we had no connection with it except through a messenger sent to renew our supply of flour, bacon, and coffee. We made our camps wherever night overtook us, or wherever it was most convenient for the work in hand, sometimes in a deep canyon by a roaring mountain torrent or on the higher levels among the snow banks. We lived in the open, without tents, depending entirely upon our tarpaulins to keep blankets dry at night when mountain storms broke loose.

On one occasion camp was made in a canyon at the foot of a cliff several hundred feet in height. With two assistants and the pack mule I left this camp one morning for the timber-line regions, where I found so much photographing to do that the sun

PHOTOGRAPHING IN HIGH PLACES. Circa July 10, 1872. Copy of modern print from wet plate negative.

"A common experience among the Tetons" (Jackson [1875] 1978, 42). William Henry Jackson fixes a glass plate negative, while photographic assistant Charlie Campbell looks on, standing directly below the Grand Teton. They are perched on the jagged ledge of a lesser summit now known today as Mary's Nipple. Jackson's oil painting (page 2) of this scene appears embossed on the front cover of the first edition of *The Pioneer Photographer*. Courtesy National Park Service/Scotts Bluff National Monument.

THE BIVOUAC ABOVE CAMP. Circa 1929.
Watercolor and pencil.

Jackson depicts the location where he and his assistants
spent an exposed, hungry, and uncomfortable evening
stranded by darkness on a rocky ledge. They could only
watch the inviting campfire of their Survey companions
below until dawn the next day. Courtesy National Park
Service/Grand Teton National Park.

was well down over the Idaho plains before we packed up and started for camp. We
tried to quicken the descent by taking advantage of short cuts and slides, but met with
many delays, so that it was already quite dark when we got down into thick timber.
It seemed to be only a question of going ahead until we came out into the bottom of
the canyon below camp; but again the unexpected happened. After sliding down a
particularly steep incline of sand and rock, we found ourselves on the verge of the cliff
directly above our camp. A big fire illuminated the surroundings, and the boys
grouped around it were preparing supper. The aroma of boiling coffee and frying
bacon floated up to us from the depths below.

Our shouts brought a response but no help. A survey of the situation convinced
us that it was not advisable to attempt, in the darkness, to try to get out of the pocket in which we found ourselves. This could easily have been done afoot, but the horses and the pack mule had to be considered; so there seemed to be no alternative but
to remain right where we were until daylight.

Taking off saddles and pack, we tied up the three animals securely and then sat
down on the edge of the cliff and watched what was doing in the camp below. For
three or four hours we had occasional interchanges of bantering suggestions back and
forth as the boys prepared and finished their meal, which did not exactly lessen our
cravings of hunger after a hard day's work of mountain climbing. As they leisurely
turned in for the night and the camp fire flickered out in a thin column of smoke,
we wrapped the saddle blankets around our shoulders and courted a few hours of rest
and forgetfulness until the gray dawn gradually lightened the sky back of the Grand
Teton. With returning daylight we soon found a way out of our difficulty and were
in camp in time for a hearty breakfast.

The Teton region at this time was a game paradise. Our various parties were kept
supplied with fresh meat without having to hunt for it, deer, moose, or mountain
sheep being nearly always in sight when needed. It was equally easy to get a mess of
trout from the streams near by. Bears were abundant also. The first day in the main
camp, two of the younger boys went fishing and unexpectedly happened on bruin.
This was larger game than they expected to meet, but they succeeded in killing the
bear with pistols only. One of the topographers, working on the plateau above timber line, counted eleven bears during a day's observations.

A few days before the party broke camp for the continuation of the trip north-ward, Stevenson and Langford decided to attempt the ascent of the Grand Teton. Several others started with them, but one after another dropped out until these two only were left to claim the honor of being the first to reach the summit of this grand old peak. Twenty-six years later, in 1898, Mr. W. O. Owen, state auditor of Wyoming, was one of a party of four, which made a successful ascent.[6]

Ever since that time the question as to who was really first on top has been debated, for Owen claimed that Stevenson and Langford never were on the true summit, mainly because they left no evidence of having been there. A rather warm discussion followed until finally, both Stevenson and Langford having long since passed out of the picture, Owen had the field all to himself and has secured official confirmation of the priority of his party of '98 by an act of the Wyoming legislature. It is unfortunate, however, for a perfect record, that it must always carry with it the shadow of a doubt. Great credit is due the Owen party for the discovery of a passage at a critical point, which makes the attainment of the summit a comparatively easy matter for experienced mountaineers. Quite a number of parties have made the ascent since that time.

Leaving the Teton region, we took a northerly course up Henrys Fork. Most of the time, however, we were crossing its tributaries and the high, wooded ridges between, keeping well away from the main stream, as it was deeply canyoned except for a short distance near its source. It was rough going and particularly hard on the pack train, which was still heavily loaded. To get out into the comparatively open country about Henrys Lake was a great relief.

Two or three days were spent here in surveying and photographing. Sawtell's ranch on the east side of the lake, the home of a group of hunters and fishermen, made a sociable rendezvous for us all.

After crossing Tahgee [Targhee] Pass (a continental divide separating the waters of the Snake River from the headwaters of the Missouri), I left the main outfit with a small party and struck out independently. Langford joined us and we relied on his knowledge of the country to pilot us through to the Lower Firehole. Trails were obscure and landmarks indefinite, so it was not altogether surprising that we went up the Gibbon Fork instead of the Firehole branch of the Madison River. We were

~

Nathaniel Langford wrote a detailed article for *Scribner's Monthly* (June 1873), which brought him and James Stevenson, Survey Manager, national notoriety as the first party to conquer the Grand Teton. However, the Survey duo left no trace on the summit, and their accounts were later found to be inaccurate. William O. Owen later claimed he was the first to scale the peak in 1898. William Jackson became entangled in the controversy. At first he truly believed that Langford and Stevenson had reached the summit of the technically difficult peak. With mounting evidence to the contrary he changed his mind within a few years. "A number of factors entering into the story make it improbable that Stevenson and Langford ever reached the summit. For a time I was inclined to take their word for it, but when Wilson, one of the topographers of the Survey, and its best mountaineer, who had been among the first to ascend Mt. Rainier, failed in his attempt to ascend the Grand Teton in '77, I then felt quite sure that this honor had been reserved for the later claimants" (Jackson 1929a, 190).

~

INTERIOR OF SAWTELL'S RANCH AT HENRYS LAKE, IDAHO.
August 1872. Copy of modern print from wet plate negative.

The ranch-men [Sawtell and Wurtz] are in front at right and left with J. M. Coulter [botanist] and N. P. Langford [guest of the expedition, and later, first Superintendent of Yellowstone National Park] sitting next. "The ranch is located "at the northern end of Henry's Lake. Messers Sawtell and Wurtz, the pioneers of this region, have built themselves very comfortable quarters by the side of a very fine, large spring. They catch large quantities of fish from the lake, for which they find a ready market in Virginia City and the mining towns. Large game of all kinds is abundant" (Jackson [1875] 1978, 42). Courtesy U.S. Geological Survey.

~

Many photographs taken in Jackson Hole by William Jackson are reported as having been taken in 1872. No photographs taken in Jackson Hole were created until 1878 or later. None of Jackson's records indicate he crossed the Teton Range to the east in 1872. He delineated his routes for both 1872 and 1878 on a Grand Teton National Park map. It clearly shows that he did not venture into Jackson Hole until 1878 (Grand Teton National Park, 1931). In an address prepared for the dedication of Grand Teton National Park he reiterates this, saying, "I saw the Tetons from the east for the first time in 1878" (Jackson 1929a, 190). Other members of the Hayden Survey did venture into Jackson Hole from Yellowstone in 1872.

~

hopelessly at sea as to our locality until finally we ran up against a waterfall—known later as Gibbons Falls—which definitely proved, according to Langford, that we were not on the Firehole River.[7]

Night approaching, we camped where we were on a small flat among the trees. There was no room to graze the animals and we had to tie them up closely. This resulted in the loss of Patsy, Dr. Hayden's favorite riding horse, lent to one of the party for this trip. Patsy had been given too much rope and, getting entangled in it, was strangled during the night.

The next morning I climbed a tall pine on the hill above camp, from which I saw the columns of steam rising from the hot springs of the Firehole. With the general direction thus given, we were soon "out of the woods."

It had been previously arranged that the different divisions of the Survey were to meet in the Lower Fire Hole Basin about the middle of August. Although traveling

Group of all the members of the survey.
August 15, 1872. Albumin print.

This 8″ × 10″ group photograph was "taken in Fire Hole
Basin the day after the simultaneous arrival of all the
different divisions" (Jackson [1875] 1978, 46). In the
11″ × 14″ version of the photograph the figures are
numbered for identification. Its caption reads, "A
simultaneous meeting of all of the divisions on the 15th
of August, including sixty-two persons in all" (Jackson
[1875] 1978, 36). Courtesy National Park Service/Scotts
Bluff National Monument.

widely divergent routes, all arrived at the appointed rendezvous almost simultaneously. Dr. Hayden's party, coming in by way of Fort Ellis, arrived first. Stevenson,
who had left his division to make a detour around by Virginia City for supplies, came
next; then the Teton division arrived; and finally my party—all within a few hours
of one another on the sixteenth of August. When assembled, there were about sixty
men and more than one hundred horses and mules.

A spirit of jovial good-fellowship dominated the gathering. It had, in a way,
something of the nature of a trappers' rendezvous of half a century earlier. As a matter of course, much photographing of the members of the party was in order; and
they were all lined up for this purpose, both collectively and individually.

This meeting, primarily, was for the purpose of comparing notes as to what had
been done and mapping out a program for the continuance of the work within the

OLD FAITHFUL IN ERUPTION. August 1872.
Copy of modern print from wet plate negative.

Due to the brevity of his visit in 1871 Jackson never photographed Old Faithful as it erupted. The negatives he produced in 1872 were not of superior quality. It took until 1883 for Jackson to get what he considered good negatives of the geyser. Courtesy U.S. Geological Survey.

Park. Another object was to send out, by the pack train that brought in supplies, all of the accumulated specimens as well as the negatives made thus far. It was not wise to subject these to the risks of packing transportation any farther than absolutely necessary. Within a few days all the parties had departed, each on its special mission of investigation or discovery.

For the rest of the season our photographic group continued to work separately from the other divisions. With a small party, we spent a week going over the two geyser basins in detail, using 11 × 14 plates mainly in portraying the wonderfully beautiful tracery and ornamentation around the various geyser craters and hot spring pools.[8]

We then turned our attention to the mountainous country along the western boundary of the Park. Dr. Hayden, who also rode over this country, said in his report: "The central portion of the range, in which the different branches of the East Gallatin have their origin, is composed mostly of basalt and breccia.[9] These have been worn into the most fanciful architectural forms. Mr. Jackson, the photographer of the Survey, penetrated this region for the first time last summer and obtained from it some most marvelously beautiful views of the scenery. I doubt whether there is any other portion of the West where all the elements of landscape beauty are more happily combined."

We had a wonderfully fine time among the rocks, waterfalls, and cascades, but in getting out of the country, we ran into one of the rockiest and most difficult trails that we had ever traveled over. For ten miles along the lower canyon of the Gallatin rock slides of immense boulders frequently extended from far up the mountain down into the bed of the river. Our trail ran across this jumble of rocks, following the water closely, and a stumbling, sprawling time our riding and pack animals made of it as they picked their way along.

One of the pack mules carrying the 11 × 14 camera as part of its load was apparently so disgusted with the trail—or the pretense of one—that it deliberately turned aside and jumped into the river. It went entirely under at first, but ears and head soon appeared. Then, sustained for the moment by the buoyancy of the pack before it became saturated with water, the mule was whirled along in the surging current until swept into an eddy. From the swirling waters it was dragged ashore by a rope cleverly thrown by one of the packers.

The problem now was to get the animal out on terra firma. There was no sloping sandy beach to climb up on. It was more like a mill race with walls of rock. In any case, nothing could be done while the mule was encumbered by a heavy pack. It was necessary for someone to get down into the water and release the diamond hitch that held the pack in place. Even when relieved of its load, the dejected and repentant mule had to be pulled up on the bank by main force. After this experience, it was apparently satisfied with the trail and made no more "side trips."

With another trip to the Yellowstone River and a few more pictures in the vicinity of Fort Ellis, we ended our photographic work for the season. As all the other members of the Survey came in, our government equipment was turned in at the fort, and the expedition disbanded.

The return to Ogden was made by stagecoach starting from Virginia City, a ride of five hundred and fifty miles, usually made in five days. With so many of us returning

GIBBON FALLS. Circa 1872–73. Ink wash sketch.

As Jackson and John M. Coulter [botanist] were out exploring the Yellowstone back country for good photographic subjects, they discovered these previously undocumented falls. The men were on the Gibbon River about five miles east of present-day Madison Junction. The Gibbon River was named in 1872 by the Hayden Survey in honor of Gen. John Gibbon, who was exploring with troops in the same area (Whittlesey 1988). Courtesy National Park Service/Yellowstone National Park.

BANNACK INDIANS. August–September 1872.
Copy of modern print from wet plate negative.

This photograph was taken near Virginia City, Montana, shortly before Mr. Jackson returned with other Survey members to Ogden, Utah, at the end of the 1872 season. Courtesy U.S. Geological Survey.

in a body, in addition to the regular travel, the capacity of the two six-horse Concord coaches was rather overtaxed. I was on the lead coach carrying twenty-two passengers, making a crowded interior with ten on top or outside. Five or six men sat on the seats with the driver, but the rest of us had to roost on the deck behind. I took the latter place by choice, as there was an opportunity to spread blankets and lie down.

The one hundred and twenty hours of continuous travel was interrupted only by short stops for meals and for changing horses. We who were on top thought we had the advantage over the others, for we had some freedom of movement, instead of being cramped into almost immovable positions in the interior. The nights were cold and the days hot, particularly on the Snake River plains, where long stretches of heavy sand made the traveling very slow and tiresome.

The coach following ours had an experience, which we happily escaped. In the neighborhood of the Hole in the Wall,[10] above Market Lake, it was held up by a band of "Road Agents" and everyone was relieved of money, watches, and other jewelry, besides the usual loot taken from the express boxes. Fortunately our boys had not been paid off, most of them having only enough cash in pocket to take them to Ogden. The young men, particularly those out for the first time, seemed to think that the hold-up conferred quite a distinction, as it was an experience that made the other boys rather envious.

I returned to Washington fairly well pleased with what had been accomplished. For one thing, I had successfully employed a larger plate for field work than had been used heretofore. Though the number of photographs was not large, judged by modern facilities for production, yet they were good enough to receive general commendation.

Chapter Nine

Among the Colorado Rockies

May 1873–July 1873

The difficulties we met trying to get pictures of the lofty Tetons were but an introduction to further mountain adventures. Previously I had done some photographic work in the rugged canyons and among the foothills near Denver, just enough to give me a desire to see more of what lay beyond. Now this desire was to be satisfied with a real campaign among the Colorado Rockies. One reason why this Colorado campaign was undertaken in 1873 was the increasing hostilities of the Indians, especially in the Wyoming and Montana regions. These troubles with the red men, which later culminated in the Custer tragedy, caused the transfer of our Survey work to regions farther south.

Colorado had but recently emerged from the "Pikes Peak or Bust" days,[1] and was still largely uncharted territory from the scientific point of view. Dr. Hayden, in laying his plans before the Secretary of the Interior, wrote: "There is probably no portion of our continent, at the present time, which promises to yield more useful results, both of a practical and of a scientific character. This region seems to be unoccupied, at this time, as far as I am aware, by any other survey under the Government, and the prospect of its rapid development within the next five years, by some of the most important railroads in the West, renders it very desirable that its resources be made known to the world at as early a date as possible."

With new people on the Survey came new plans for organization. It was divided into three principal divisions, each consisting of from five to eight men, with a proportionate pack train. To each division was assigned a definite section of the territory for its operations. In addition, I was to be a free lance, working over the territory of all the others, and having charge of a regulation outfit of two packers and a cook. To my party was added, for this trip, Coulter, the botanist, who was out with

In 1873 Jackson was given the responsibility of being photographic chief. "G. [James Gardner, topographer] took me aside & gave me some idea of what was required of me. I was to command a party to consist of about eight including two packers and one cook. [We] are to operate entirely independent of all of the others. They assigned me at once a wall tent, but for this camp only and 'dog tents' for field use. A complete mess outfit and a fine one too" (Jackson 1873, May 18).

"I felt like a general in command of an army. . . . There was another reason for me to be in high spirits. Two years before, while taking pictures on the Omaha Indian Reservation, I had been entertained by Dr. Edward Painter, of Baltimore, then the agent in charge, Mrs. Painter, and their daughter, Emilie. . . . When my wife died, I received a letter that was far more than a perfunctory expression of sympathy, with the result that I called on the Painters the next time I visited Omaha. After that letters went back and forth with a frequency that would seem remarkable — except for the fact that they were all between Emilie Painter and myself. Our lively correspondence became intimate, and shortly before I left for Colorado I asked Emilie to marry me. Even knowing the worst—that I was a traveling man—she accepted my proposal and set the wedding for October" (Jackson [1940] 1994, 210).

us the previous year; Lieutenant Carpenter, on leave of absence from his post, interested in entomology; and young [Seward] Cole, son of the California Senator, interested in ornithology. Tom Cooper and Bill Whan, my packers, were two of the best the Survey ever had; and John Raymond (Potato John, our cook) was a veteran of five or six previous expeditions. Bill was later called back to help Stevenson, and Harry Bishop took his place.

Taking the field early, I arrived in Denver on May fourteenth, not the first, but well ahead of most of the party. Camp had been made on Clear Creek about three miles out of the city, and outfitting preparations were under way. Besides the eight or ten who remained on the Survey from previous expeditions, there were many new faces, among them J. T. Gardner, recently from King's Survey of the 40th Parallel, chief topographer and organizer of the several divisions. He outlined my itinerary for the season as follows: "First to Longs Peak, thence south along the Snowy Range to Grays Peak, and from there work around by way of Pikes Peak to a rendezvous of all parties at Fairplay in South Park." Beyond that point instructions were less definite, but I was expected to cross the Sawatch Mountains and join in the exploration of the Elk Mountain country about the heads of the Grand River and the Gunnison. It should be noted here that the branch of the Colorado long known as the Grand River was in 1921 given the name of the main stream, the Colorado.

The Lieutenant was the last of my party to arrive. Dressed in well-worn buckskins, he looked the part of an experienced mountaineer. He had brought his own camping outfit and at once pitched his little "shelter" alongside of ours. Quiet and reserved in manner but a thoroughly good fellow, he proved an agreeable addition to our party.

By May twenty-fourth we were ready to pull out. As is usually the case with the first packing up, there was much confusion and worry. Some of the mules had never before been packed or they were naturally cantankerous. They did not take kindly to being saddled and cinched up into the semblance of a wasp, and they started bucking all over camp. Three mules were required for the grub and the cook's outfit; two were packed with the photographic outfit and materials. When we had loaded up the sixth and last mule to its capacity, there was enough left over for still another one; but as we were anxious to get out of camp, it was arranged that an extra pack mule would be sent later to overtake us next day.

At last, after several re-loadings of the obstreperous mules, we got started. Potato John, the cook, leading off on his bell mare, made a great stir and caused much amusement. John was not a graceful rider, and his mare, unaccustomed to a bell around her neck, became uneasy and cavorted all over camp, stumbling over tent ropes and scattering the boys in all directions. We looked "business," however, as we finally rode out, saddle bags filled to repletion, overcoats rolled behind, big revolvers on the hip, and rifles slung across the saddle in front. As we were the first of the divisions to break camp, the other boys gave us a hearty cheer as a send-off. Very soon we were out on the broad open plains, happy to be on the move.

For the first two or three miles there was trouble in plenty. Most of the loads were heavy, and some not properly balanced, so that they began to slip and turn, necessitating frequent stops to reload. During one of these halts Tom's horse broke away, throwing him into a bed of cactus plants, and then ran back to the main camp. One of the boys brought the horse out to us again, but it made so much delay that we covered only about ten miles this first day. It was after nine o'clock next morning when our extra mule reached us, and even with this additional pack we were still overloaded. Getting a late start, we took a bee line for Longs Peak, regardless of road or trails.

All went well until near noon, when a storm broke upon us so suddenly that it caught us unprepared. Being on a high terrace, or table-land, we got the full force of the driving rain accompanied with heavy hail, which none of the animals would face. All we could do was to turn our backs and wait for the fury to spend itself; it left us drenching wet, with the water running out of the tops of our boots. Early in the afternoon we camped at Valmont on Boulder Creek, where we had to corral and buy hay for our stock, because all the grass lands were fenced in. Nothing was open except on the benches or tablelands, where there was no nutritive grass, wood, or water.

The third day out from Denver we entered the foothills of the Rockies by way of St. Vrain Canyon. On the morning of the twenty-ninth, arriving on the divide between the Little and Big Thompson Creeks, we had our first glimpse of Estes Park—a most lovely view. Continuing on down, we went into camp at the lower end of the Park, where we had a fine view of Longs Peak. Just above us was a rustic cottage occupied by summer residents, a sight which surprised us as we supposed the Park to be entirely unoccupied. That evening after supper we called on the cottagers,

LONGS PEAK FROM ESTES PARK. May 28, 1873. Albumin print on Hayden Survey mount.

Longs Peak, 14,271 [14,256] feet high [was taken] from the lower end of Estes Park; now included in the Rocky Mountain National Park. "The park is about four by six miles in diameter, lying inside the foot-hill range and close under the main range. Being well sheltered and of easy access, it is proving to be a most excellent pasture for large herds of cattle. A few families have also settled here, and taken up permanent homesteads. It is quite a pleasure-resort, and as the only practicable route for ascending the peak leads up from this valley, it is destined to become a favorite stopping-place for health seeker and traveler. The Big Thompson, draining all this region, is an excellent trout-stream, and in season affords most excellent fishing" (Jackson [1875] 1978, 51). Courtesy American Heritage Center.

IN THE SNOW. June 15, 1873. Albumin print.

Jackson's diary reads as though this incident occurred on June 14 when the dreary weather canceled photography. They were attempting to photograph Red Rock Lake and the snowy peaks of the Front Range. "Packed up the outfit and went to the head of the gulch to get views of fine lake there. Avoided the snow until within 200 yards of the lake. There, it was too deep for the pack [animals] & after floundering about for a while took it on our own backs. Commenced to snow and hail at the same time, changing form into a drizzling rain— and so continued for two or three hours. Packed up & left our traps there & returned to camp" (Jackson 1873, June 14). Wet plate photography was not possible in the rain. The scene was photographed the following day as the men returned when better weather permitted photography. Courtesy National Park Service/Scotts Bluff National Monument.

Mr. and Mrs. Hubble and a comely young daughter, and spent an entertaining evening with them. They were immensely interested in our work.

It rained all night, but a clear morning gave promise of a big day's work before me. Ascending Prospect Mountain, I located a point of view and set up my camera and dark tent. Heavy clouds had filled the sky meanwhile and the wind began blowing so hard that there was no use in attempting any exposures, so I cached all my boxes under some rocks and returned to camp. We whiled away the stormy afternoon in our tents and ended the day delightfully with supper at the cottage. The next afternoon, having completed my photographing from Prospect Mountain, we set off for other fields.

We left the Park by way of the pass between Twin Sisters Mountain and Longs Peak[2] for the purpose of getting close-up views of the Snowy Range from about the headwaters of the Boulder [Creek]. The morning of June fifth found us near Bald Mountain. If I was to get anything, it must be from this vicinity. Sending the train around so as to keep it away from the snow, Bill and I took our pack mule in tow and struck out to prospect for vantage points from which good views of the entire mountain range could be taken.

For three or four hours we had the usual rough traveling incident to picking a way through "the forest primeval." This soon became unpleasantly monotonous. Crossing the numerous streams, swollen from the rapidly melting snows, our animals would flounder down steep banks into rocks, water, and ice and then scramble up over treacherous, snow-covered ground, with pitfalls into which rider or pack mule tumbled nearly out of sight.

Despite these difficulties, we got along fairly well until, as we gained in elevation, we encountered deeper snowdrifts. These at first we avoided by passing around them. They soon became so continuous that there was no other way than to flounder through. For a while we rather enjoyed the experience, whatever the mules may have thought of it. Through some of the deeper drifts we tramped out a trail ahead of the pack and saddle animals, but not with complete success. The snow was soft, and when they could not touch bottom they were helpless. Several times we had to unpack and roll the mule over to solid ground. This incessant struggle became so discouraging that we would have turned back if we had not had occasional glimpses through the trees, where the mountains seemed so near that we felt sure the crossing of one more ridge would open up the desired view.

Finally we came out upon a lake in a park-like opening,[3] back of which was an unobstructed, splendid view of the snow-capped Rockies from Longs Peak to James Peak. It was so satisfactory that we stopped right there. Thoroughly wet by our battling through the melting snows, we first built a fire to dry ourselves before undertaking the photographic work. Then setting to work, I made in two hours time a series of negatives that well repaid us for the hard labor in getting them.

When packing up for the return down the mountain, I missed my belt and pistol. Recalling that some distance back in the timber I had climbed a tree to get our bearings and had left the belt at the foot of the tree, I started Bill down hill with the pack, while I took the back trail into the timber. Fortunately I found the missing articles, and taking up Bill's trail, soon overtook him. The trip back to camp was about as hard as the upward climb, but as it was all down hill, we got along faster. Eventually, we came to a wagon road that took us into the little mining town of Ward,[4] and from there we pushed on ten miles to our camp on the north fork of the Boulder.

After a few more days of working around Boulder Creek and making views of Caribou,[5] a small mining camp among the snow banks, we struck off towards James Peak. The trail led up over wooded hills until it brought us among the gnarled and stunted trees peculiar to the timber-line region. There we lost the trail among the snow-drifts that surrounded us on all sides. They lay in long banks, frequently ten feet deep, but with intervening spaces of bare ground. Taking advantage of these bare places, we advanced fairly well, having to force a passage through only a few of the drifts.

As we got nearer the peak, our hopes of finding a camping place with grass for the animals began to wane. We happened, however, to come out on the brink of a steep hill, and there, nearly a thousand feet below, lay a valley with a stretch of meadow land through its center.[6] This was such a camp site as we were seeking.

Near by us was an old, deserted miner's cabin and from it a road had been graded to the bottom of the hill. Although abandoned for many years and obstructed by fallen timber, it facilitated our descent. We were soon in the midst of a "Deserted Village"—a group of log houses, hewed and designed with considerable regard for appearances.[7] Some of them had been left unfinished and others looked as if they had

THE SNOWY RANGE OF COLORADO. Circa 1920–1930. Glass lantern-slide.

A visit from Mt. Audubon to James Peak can be seen in the lantern slide. "In the foreground is one of the little snow-fed lakes [Red Rock Lake], so numerous throughout the mountains, and forming a pleasant variety to the monotony of numberless snow-white peaks. Although this view was made late [early] in June, it will be seen that the hill-sides are heavily draped in a mantle of snow, lying deep through all the forest. The difficulty in reaching even this altitude was very great, requiring most laborious plunging through the thick drifts" (Jackson [1875] 1978, 52). The original photograph was taken on June 5, 1873 (Jackson 1873, 9). Courtesy National Park Service/Rocky Mountain National Park.

THE TWIN PEAKS. June 18, 1873.
Copy of modern print from wet plate negative.

Grays and Torreys Peaks, Colorado, 14,274 [14, 270] and 14,267 feet in height. "From peak to peak the distance is nearly a mile, and through this saddle is a 'pass' from Georgetown to the mining-towns on the Blue River. . . . The combing crest of snow at the summit frequently lies all summer, and it then becomes necessary to tunnel under it, so that the pack animals may pass over. To the right of Torrey, away in the distance, across Middle Park, are the Blue River Mountains, their glittering snow-fields alone making them visible" (Jackson [1875] 1978, 54). Courtesy U.S. Geological Survey.

never been occupied. We found also the remains of three stamp mills—one of them in ashes. Scattered over the surrounding hillsides were many smaller and more primitive cabins, each with its accompanying prospect hole and dump of ore—mute witnesses of fruitless labor and of golden dreams that had come to naught. The mining camp had evidently been abandoned for many years. It had probably been started soon after the first discoveries of '59 or '60, but there was not the slightest clue—not even a name or a date on tree or log of a cabin—to indicate the name of the place or who had lived there.

In the afternoon four of us started afoot for James Peak. I was seeking photographic possibilities, and the others were out for adventure. It was comparatively easy going until we got to the deep snow, and for the most part this was hard enough to bear our weight. For one full hour we walked over a smooth expanse of pure white snow, its increasing depth being approximately indicated by the gradual disappearance of the timber-line trees beneath its surface, until finally they were covered completely. Coming out at last on a wind-swept ledge or crest, we had the whole grand panorama spread before us, from the near-by peaks at our back, over the undulating foothills to the eastward, where the distant plains merged imperceptibly into the sky.

Next morning I had Harry put our photographic apparatus on Old Maggie and with his assistance started out to make a permanent record of what we had seen the day before. As there was too much snow on the direct route, we went back on the trail two miles and then got on the windward side of a long spur that led directly up the main peak. It was almost entirely free of snow and made good traveling, except for a thick growth of stunted timber-line shrubs that were almost impenetrable for the pack mule and saddle horses. For four tedious hours we fought our way up through many difficulties and finally came out on the summit—corresponding to the point we had attained the day before.

Near at hand were James Peak and Parry Peak. Away to the north Arapahoe and Longs presented clear-cut outlines, while to the south the view culminated in the group including Gray and Torrey and Mt. Evans. It was a scene of such thrilling grandeur that I worked with enthusiasm to transfer it to my plates. The work was cut short by a rising storm of snow and sleet that sent us back down the mountain in much less time than it took to go up. The urgency of the situation tempted us into many precarious short cuts, which fortunately brought us into camp all right just in season for a hot dinner.

This was the time of good cheer, no matter what the experiences, good or bad, of the day. At "grub time" all was forgotten as we gathered around the canvas manta, spread on the ground as a tablecloth, and proceeded to do full justice to the bacon, rolls, and coffee, with such extras as John happened to find available. Everyone was brimming over with good-natured jollity, and the incidents of the day, pleasant or otherwise, were recalled and laughed over, with joking, banter, and repartee.

The next day, packing the photographic outfit on "Number 5" and with Harry to assist, I went up to the head of the gulch in which we were camped, to photograph a picturesque little lake discovered the first day of our prospecting. We kept out of snow fairly well until within two hundred yards of the lake, when it became too deep for the pack mule. After floundering around some time trying to get through, we gave it up and carried in the outfit on our shoulders. Before we could get ready for work, however, it began to snow and hail. As there was every prospect that the storm would continue for the rest of the day, we cached the boxes and returned to camp.

The following morning dawned wonderfully clear. Getting an early start, we made quick time out to the lake, completed our photographing, and were back in camp by noon. After lunch we packed up at once and started down the canyon. It was a rough trail that was hard on the pack animals, the loads riding poorly and requiring many re-packings. We were following Fall River but soon left it and crossed over to Clear Creek and camped three miles below Empire.[8]

The next day we took the cut-off trail leading over to Georgetown.[9] It was an interesting sight as the pack mules slowly picked their way down the narrow, tortuous trail. Looking back up the mountain side, along whose craggy side our train was winding, we felt as if the mules were about to tumble right down upon us. In passing through Georgetown, our outfit not only kicked up a big dust but caused a great commotion in the streets. The pack mules were continually starting off into every side street and alley, and when turned back, ran along the sidewalks and even attempted to enter the open doorways of the stores.

Passing on over Leavenworth Mountain, we camped up near Argentine Pass at an elevation of eleven thousand feet. Our objective was Grays Peak, and this was as

～

The Hayden Survey topographers made many detailed panoramic sketches from high vantage points. Jackson transferred the idea of their scroll-like drawings to the science of photography, creating some magnificent early panoramas. Although it was a natural step for the photographer to become involved in this process, it was also a tedious chore, as each glass plate was exposed and then developed separately. The camera had to be carefully rotated so that each negative fit into an uninterrupted sweep of the vista before the lens. At times the exposures and the cloud formations seem out of sync between the views because of the length of time it took to create each image. Temperature, cloud cover, wind, availability of water, and the condition of the chemicals influenced the varying amounts of time. Thus, it could take hours, depending on these factors, to complete a panorama. Jackson made a number of such panoramas during his decade with the Hayden Survey.

～

near as we could get with the train. After a quick lunch, all except the packers and the cook started out for some exploration climbing. We rode our horses up to seven hundred feet above camp and then went afoot to the summit of McClellan Mountain, seventeen hundred feet higher. From this point we could overlook the range of peaks of which Gray and Torrey were the central feature.

The clear-cut summits of the twin peaks were so inviting that Cole and I decided to climb the nearest one.[10] Up and down we went across two or three intervening peaks and came out on Gray, 14,274 [14,270] feet high. But at this time we did not really know one from the other. We knew only that Gray was the highest, and from where we stood, the opposite mountain, Torrey, seemed to be the higher one, though it is actually ten feet [three feet] less in height. So to be sure I had been on the right one, I ascended that also. Cole was satisfied with one peak.

Early the next morning, the light being favorable, we succeeded in leading our pack mule to the top of McClellan, where we put up the small dark tent. The best part of the day was occupied in photographing the peaks from that viewpoint. Our return to camp was made with the now familiar accompaniment of thunder and lightning, with hail, snow, and finally rain, which continued nearly all night.

From here we were to go to the Chicago Lakes under Mt. Evans. We started out with the intention of going directly there across the intervening hills and canyons, instead of through Georgetown, where tolls were expensive. The first summit was made easily enough, but we had before us a descent of some two thousand feet to the South Fork of Clear Creek, and a bad time we had of it in going down. The way lay over soft soil, and we started in by zigzagging, but some of the animals would not trail. The Lieutenant's horse fell and rolled over several times, fortunately landing on its feet against a tree. One of the pack mules carrying the mess kit tried to go straight down and acquired such momentum that it would have gone clear to the bottom if it hadn't come up against a big rock.

The mule's pack, going over its head piecemeal, was scattered all down the mountain. The big oven rolled finely; then came a keg of molasses, which made a lively chase after the oven; and the other things that did not roll so well were distributed along the same line. It was a task to reconstruct the pack.

Once at the bottom, we abandoned our first intention to take a direct trail. We had had convincing proof that the short way may be the longer, so we decided to follow the creek down into Georgetown and find a better trail to the lakes. There was more rough work ahead of us, however. At one place a bank of hard snow bridged the stream and we attempted to cross on it. Midway one of the pack mules broke through and almost completely disappeared. The animal was rescued all right, but it required strenuous work.

As we approached Georgetown, we were still obsessed with the idea of getting into town without going through the toll gate. Keeping well up on the mountain side, we followed for a time a fairly good wood road, but it soon left us among rocks and fallen timber. We were half way up, but the pack mules had become leg weary and were often falling and rolling over, with danger of serious injury; so we finally gave up the attempt. A quick descent was made, and we went into camp a mile below town, corralling our stock there for the night. Since we were in town, we decided it was best to have our animals re-shod for the rocky trails ahead. This gave us a late start in the morning, but by taking the zigzag trail over Griffith Mountain, we reached the Chicago Lakes at five o'clock. Camp was made at the upper border of timber line near the lower of the two lakes, with the grand amphitheater of cliffs and mountain summits in the background.

The following day being unfavorable for photography, Coulter and I climbed the mountain back of the lakes for a survey of the glorious surrounding region. Meanwhile, the boys in camp had some great sport. Trout were abundant but would not take any bait that could be devised. The outlet of the lakes ran through wide but shallow channels lined with sedgy grass. Beginning at the upper end near the lake, the boys chased the fish down these channels, and by spearing or netting they caught enough to make a delicious dinner for all.

With good weather conditions the next day, I completed my photographic work by ten o'clock. We were expected to make our way to the mouth of Platte Canyon, where someone from Denver was to meet us with aparejos to replace our old pack saddles. Arriving at the appointed place three days later, we found none of the improved packing outfits; and hurried rides back and forth to Denver revealed that

CHICAGO LAKE. June 23, 1873. Albumin print on stereoscope card.

"Lying at the foot of Mount Rosalie, the source of Chicago Creek, and the most picturesque lake in Colorado. . . . This lower lake contains many trout, not very large, but most delicious, the water in which they live coming direct from the pure snows above, and retaining an icy coldness all summer. . . . Not withstanding the difficulties [in getting here], many travelers visit this place, both for the rare scenery and for a mess of the best trout in the mountains" (Jackson [1875] 1978, 55). This is at the base of Mt. Evans, Mt. Rosalie being about three miles to the southeast. Courtesy National Park Service/Scotts Bluff National Monument.

none were to be had. In the meantime, taking Harry to help with the pack, I went up into the canyon to do some photographing. We struck such rough going that our pack mule deliberately bolted the trail and, plunging into the river, came near going through some rapids into deep water; but we caught the perverse animal in time. It was just the sort of experience we had the year before with one of the pack mules on the Gallatin River in Yellowstone Park. In each instance, the mule was carrying my photographic outfit.

On the fourth of July we struck out for the rendezvous at Fairplay.[11] Sending the train ahead, we made a brief stop at Manitou [Springs] to enjoy its effervescent waters, and then passed on through Ute Pass.

The seventy-two-mile trip across South Park to Fairplay we made in three drives. This was accomplished by breaking camp early in the morning, getting everyone up by starlight, long before the scorching sun appeared on the eastern horizon. John was always on time and sometimes ahead of time. With his cheerful fire lighting up the immediate surroundings and with the savory aroma of coffee pot and frying pan filling the air, the rest of us rolled up our bedding and arranged it conveniently for each mule load. Meanwhile, the two packers were out rounding up the animals and generally had them all tied up by the time breakfast was ready. This over, the riding horses were saddled first and then everyone did his bit in assisting the packers. Load after load was sorted out and placed upon the patiently waiting mules, the mess kit coming last, so as to give John time to clean up and put away his utensils.

After a final inspection to see that nothing had been overlooked, we swung into our saddles, and the scattered mules were rounded up with cheery "hoop-las." Then with the cook leading on the bell mare, the others followed in Indian file just as the rising sun cast its ruddy glow over sky and land. These early starts were delightfully cool and refreshing at first; but as soon as the sun was well above the mountain tops, its ardent rays began to scorch our backs, and for the rest of the drive we jogged along in a comatose condition, dozing and blinking from the effects of the hot sunlight. Our camps were usually made about noon, which allowed nearly eight hours of traveling, about as much as our mules could stand under their heavy packs. As we generally averaged three miles an hour, twenty-four miles was considered a good day's work.

The first day out from Ute Pass we rode over rolling, wooded hills, with alternating parks of aspens and pines, until we came upon the [South] Platte River.[12] The next day, after ten miles more of gently rolling country, we came out quite unexpectedly into a full view of almost the entire expanse of the South Park. It was too hazy for a clear view of all the distant peaks—Silver Heels, Lincoln, Quandary, and a continuous row of lesser heights; but they could be defined by the snow masses that glistened like plates of burnished silver.

The third day, with Fairplay almost in sight, we planned to make an early start. John was instructed to have all of us up for a three-thirty breakfast, and he was punctual—to a fault. While the stars overhead were shining bright in an almost black sky, we were roused from the depths of our soundest sleep. The appetizing aroma from coffee and bacon soon had effect, and the camp was astir again. It was only after we had finished breakfast and were looking for the first indications of approaching daylight, that one of the party casually looked at his watch to note the time. It was one o'clock! Hardly more than midnight! The joke on all of us was so amusing that we took it good-naturedly. We were too much awake to think of sleeping again, and as it was still too dark to travel, we passed the time in more leisurely preparations until the stars began to pale in the sky. Coulter and I then started off first, about half past three, and by forcing our horses to a rather fast gait, reached Fairplay before eight o'clock, just as the town was waking up and getting astir.

Wilson's and Gannett's divisions of the Survey came in the same day. We made our rendezvous camp together about three miles out of town. At the post office we found letters from Dr. Hayden and Stevenson, saying they would arrive there about the tenth with the supply train. The day was given over to having a good time with our comrades of the other divisions and joining, in a mild way, in the diversions of the town. It was a "wide-open" western mining camp and contained all the elements of a miners' paradise.

For the few days following everyone made a side trip somewhere.[13] The geologists, topographers, and the photographer took time to explore some particular section of the neighborhood. This included the whole Park Range from Hoosier Pass to Weston Pass, one of the best mining regions of Colorado in the early sixties.

COLUMNS IN MONUMENT PARK. 1874. Lithographic print.

The 11″×14″ photograph from which this lithograph was made is documented as "Eroded Sandstones In Monument Park. Situated upon a small tributary of Monument Creek, about nine miles north of Colorado City [Colorado Springs]. The Denver and Rio Grande Railroad, a narrow-gauge road, running south from Denver, passes across the lower end of the park. The most interesting groups, however, lie back two or three miles from it" (Jackson [1875] 1978, 55). Courtesy U.S. Geological Survey.

PIKES PEAK. July 4, 1873.
Copy of modern print from wet plate negative.

The mountain is seen looking over the walls of the
Garden of the Gods, elevation 14,110 feet and above
Colorado Springs at 8,102 elevation. "The Signal-Service
Bureau of the United States Army have established a
station upon the summit, and observers have taken up
their residence there, isolating themselves completely,
for a long dreary winter" (Jackson [1875] 1978, 56).
Courtesy U. S. Geological Survey.

Off to the southwest about twelve miles away rose Mt. Lincoln, the highest of the group of which it is the center. Making an early start one morning, from an overnight camp at its foot, we got into a well-traveled trail above timber line, which zigzagged to the summit, 14,284 [14,286] feet up in the air. There we had barely enough room to unpack and set up our dark tent. The Montezuma, a well-known silver mine, was located about one hundred feet below the crest, the necessary working room having been blasted out from the mountain side. Working rapidly to keep ahead of a threatened storm, I made the whole panorama on 11 × 14 plates. The view was splendid, taking in all of South Park, from Pikes Peak around to the Sawatch Mountains; but the great distances and the hazy atmosphere were not favorable to getting the best photographic results. This was long before the time when panchromatic plates and color screens were devised to procure perfect work in getting distant scenes with beautiful cloud effects.

We were frequently handicapped at this time by the weather. Mornings were usually clear, but nearly every afternoon black storm clouds gathered around the mountain summits and sent down spats of snow and hail or rain, cutting short the day's work and forcing a return to camp to get dried out.

Up to this time I had ridden a horse, but it was injured so badly at our Fairplay camp that I had to turn it in and get another mount. The only one to be had at the time was a little white mule, with white eyes, which was considered too capricious and unmanageable for packing and was running loose. Dolly had some bad tricks, acquired, I think, from previous ill usage; but these were soon overcome, and thereafter she served me so well that I would have no other while I continued with the Survey.

Chapter Ten
Around the Headwaters of the Arkansas

THE UPPER TWIN LAKE, COLORADO.

July 1873–August 1873

Our chief having arrived, we were given new assignments and instructions as to the completion of the season's work. By July eighteenth we were ready to go our separate ways again. The itinerary mapped out for me was to keep in touch with the Hayden-Gardner party, working my way across the Sawatch Range to the Elk Mountain region lying between the Gunnison and the Grand Rivers, and then to add a finishing touch to my campaign by photographing the Mountain of the Holy Cross. I was to get through and be back in Washington by September first.

My photographic division, packed heavily with new supplies, was the first to leave the Fairplay camp. Heading for the divide between South Park and the Arkansas River, we entered Weston Pass and then turned off up on the mountain until, darkness overtaking us, we camped near timber line. Packs came off in a jiffy and a fire was soon started for the cook. We had had only a light breakfast in the morning and were ravenous. Later, with the welcome shout of "grub pile," more wood was heaped on the fire, which lighted up the dark shadows fantastically as we pitched into the good things John had spread before us.

This detour from Weston Pass was made to give us an unobstructed view of the Sawatch Range, from Mt. Massive to the Collegiate Peaks. And a fine view it was, with the Arkansas River in the foreground, the Twin Lakes in the middle distance, and a background of the highest mountains in Colorado.

The first day we came upon this splendid panorama it was too windy and cloudy to do any photographing. While we waited for photographic weather, Gardner's party came up. In locating camp near us, they stirred up two or three bears and a live-ly chase resulted, but the scared bruins escaped. Photographic work was completed

THE UPPER TWIN LAKE, Colorado. 1874.
Lithographic print.

A careful inspection of this lithograph shows it to be a reproduction of a different photograph than the one seen on the next page. It came from Jackson's stereoscope negative of the same scene. The figures, the campfire, the moon and stars were added to depict camp life at dusk or dawn.

THE UPPER TWIN LAKE, COLORADO. July 26, 1873.
Copy of modern print from wet plate negative.

The lake is on the eastern slopes of the Sawatch
Mountains, Colorado. Elevation, 9300 feet. Near the
source of the Arkansas River. It is "well stocked
with trout, and, being surrounded by some of the
grandest scenery in the Territory, is destined to
become a favorite pleasure resort. A comfortable
house of entertainment is already established by
Messrs. Derry, who have boats and other facilities
for lake fishing" (Jackson [1875] 1978, 58).
Courtesy U.S. Geological Survey.

the next day by noon. Then, following the other party, we made a direct descent to
the valley, a sliding, scrambling drop of two or three thousand feet, pulling our riding animals down by their bridle reins. Luckily we found a good ford over the
Arkansas and then ambled on to the Twin Lakes.

We camped between the two lakes on land included in the Derry Ranch.[1] Old
man Derry wanted twenty-five cents a head for the grazing of our stock. We object-
ed, for there was nothing but sagebrush on the land. We hired a boat from him, however, in which nearly everyone went fishing. The result was a big catch of fine, large
lake trout. Hayden and Stevenson, riding by in the afternoon, were given all the fish
they could carry.

The Doctor's advice was that I should go down the Arkansas about fifteen miles
to the place where his party was in camp and photograph some views he wanted of
that region. Taking Harry and two packs, I made this side trip; and despite the bad
weather conditions, we got some good photographs of Mt. Harvard and of the great

lateral moraines along Clear Creek. On our return the third night, black clouds hung over us, and for the last few miles around the lower lake it was so dark that we could see the mules ahead only by the faint glimmer of light from the white mantas over the packs.

While waiting at this camp for a box of glass plates that had not arrived with the other supplies, I decided to climb Mt. Elbert, the highest peak of the Sawatch Range (14,420 feet) [14,433 feet]. Our plan was to get as near as possible to timber line during the afternoon, and then, with an early start the following morning, to reach the top and complete our work there before the usual storm clouds came up. We started out after luncheon, and about a thousand feet above the lakes got into a belt of young quaking aspens, so thick it was next to impossible to force the pack mules through it. Going into camp near by, we worked until dark cutting a trail through to open ground on the other side.

Up at daybreak next morning, we had breakfast over before sunrise. The cold night with a heavy frost had left our animals all "humped up," shivering, and fractious. We got the packs on all right and thought the mules would be in better condition when warmed up by the work before us. Starting into the thick brush, we were getting on finely when Mag, carrying my boxes, seemed to go to pieces all at once. In attempting to jump a log hardly more than knee high, she fell over backwards and went tumbling down the mountain until she became so wedged into a mass of young trees and fallen logs that she had to be chopped out with the ax. We managed finally to get her on her feet, but when we attempted to lead her over the same place without a load, the same thing happened again, only this time she rolled farther down into the timber and went through enough tribulation to kill a dozen mules. It took much longer to get her out this time and our precious hours were slipping away.

As Mag was pretty well used up, we put my pack on Gimlet, our most ambitious and reliable little pack mule. But he also fell at the same place and went through about the same performance as Mag had. Our saddle animals too were not acting right. They seemed to be very weak in their legs, so we concluded they were all "locoed" through eating a poisonous weed during the night. It was useless to try to go any farther, so we gave up the climb. Returning down the mountain, we stopped on a prominent point, from which I made a series of panoramic negatives of the lakes.

❧

Jackson alludes to Dr. Hayden's drive and impatience in trying to accomplish his Survey objectives. Some of Jackson's 1873 notes reflect this, occasionally in blunt terms. "Rained all night & thus did not get up 'till 8, & did not pack up for the road until 11. About 3 miles out met Bob White with a message from the Dr. to hurry as the 'golden opportunities' were passing &c [*sic*]—his usual impatience." (Jackson 1873, August 5). During another incident Jackson states, "Grub pretty short & I believe it had its effect on the Dr. Talked to me for about an hour, giving me quite a lecture trying to be severe, but not having any sufficient grounds to work on it, simmered down to a homily on what was to be done in the future" (Ibid., August 14).

❧

The expected box of glass plates had not arrived when we reached camp, so there was nothing to do but wait. With several days' delay in prospect, we moved up the canyon, deciding to use our few remaining plates in making a photographic panorama from the top of La Plata. Getting an early start on a clear, bright morning, Coulter, Harry, and I, with photographic outfit packed on Old Mag, began the ascent.

We struck first through the thick timber, but missing our intended course, came out considerably above a little valley that would have made easier traveling up to timber line. It was a terrifically hard time we had getting down again, our animals being knocked about badly before we got back on the easier trail. Then we had fair going up to about one thousand feet above timber. Here we unpacked, tied our horses and mule to the rocks, and ate our lunch. Dividing the apparatus into three convenient packs—the silver bath, the camera, and the box of plates forming the major part of each load respectively—we slung these over our shoulders and started up the two-thousand-foot climb to the summit. It was wearisome work, but by taking frequent short rests we made it in an hour and a half.

Storm clouds were already gathering around us on all sides. Occasional gusts came sweeping over the summit, sprinkling snow and hail that made us shiver with the cold. After getting the dark tent in order and well anchored down with rocks, I set up the camera and waited for openings between the flights of passing clouds for my exposures. By the exercise of much patience I finally got a set of six negatives embracing the entire panorama, but did not get through until five o'clock.

We made quick work of gathering our traps and descending the mountain to our waiting animals. On the way down I slipped on the rocks and, falling backwards, broke the bath holder I was carrying and lost all the solution it contained. The loss of the solution was a negligible matter, but the breaking of my bath holder was a more serious affair.

It was with equal expedition that we packed up and took the return trail in an endeavor to get out of the thick timber before darkness set in. But it was already after six and night overtook us in the deepest, densest part of the woods. For an hour and a half we were engaged in working our way in utter darkness through brush and trees and among rocks, where each animal had to be led separately by serpentine and corkscrew paths to get it through. When we finally came to Lake Creek at the bottom of the hill, we happened on a place where the banks were almost perpendicular. Down these we slid and tumbled into the ice-cold water of the rock-strewn stream, and then had to explore for some distance for a way out. About nine o'clock we came stumbling into our camp, pretty well used up; but John had supper waiting for us, and under its beneficent influence the fatigues and aches of the day faded away. We were soon afterwards snuggled in warm blankets and lost in refreshing sleep.

It was three days before Stevenson came up with my glass plates. Meanwhile I had busied myself in varnishing and packing up the accumulated negatives, and in attempting to repair the broken bath holder. Hard rubber is difficult to mend, and although seemingly successful at first, I eventually had to discard it and use a flat tray instead. It was inconvenient to manage in my small tent, but I got as good results as with the dipping bath.

From the Lake Creek camp we crossed the continental divide to the Pacific slope of the Rockies. For several days we followed an old Indian trail, made plainer by the preceding party. Up and down we went over steep and rugged hills, from the tributaries of the Gunnison to those of the Grand [River].² We picked up frequent notes on the way, advising us of the movements of the other party, and finally a messenger came from the Doctor with word to hurry up, as he feared we were "losing golden opportunities."

In passing over the high divide between East River and Rock Creek, we finally came on their camp. All of the party had gone on ahead and the packs were just about to leave; so when our train came up we followed them. Making the descent of a long, steep hill that taxed the security of our packs, we camped all together at the foot of the hill in a little valley covered with abundant grass. We were on Rock Creek, at the foot of Snowmass Mountain, and in the midst of magnificent scenery. The variety and profusion of wild flowers at this season was wonderful.

Of course, we got busy at once. The first views were of Snowmass Mountain from a little lake at its base.³ The trail we made in leading up to it was so steep that we had no use for riding animals, and we had a difficult time to get Old Mag to make it with the pack. The next day we moved up the creek to an open space near its source, and made a side camp preparatory to reaching as high a point as possible for a panoramic view of the principal peaks.

HAYDEN SURVEY PARTY AT ROCK CREEK.
August 8, 1873. Albumin print.

The scene is at the "foot of Snow Mass Mountain, Elk Mountains behind" (Jackson 1873, 30). The speckled appearance of this view could be due to various factors. When the chemicals used in preparing a photographic print were working well, stable prints were produced that have withstood the rigors of time. It is also possible that the negative may have been damaged or defective. If the chemicals used to produce the negative were not in balance, the same thing could occur to the negative. The photo is not catalogued in Jackson's photograph catalogue *Miscellaneous Publications No. 5* (Jackson [1875] 1978). For whatever reason, the negative survived long enough to make this print, despite the fact it was never catalogued. Courtesy Museum of New Mexico, Photo Archives.

Snow Mass Mountain and Elk Lake [Snowmass Lake].
August 13, 1873. Copy of modern print from wet plate
negative.

"The Elk Mountains lie west of the Sawatch range,
occupying a triangular space, bounded upon two faces by
the Grand [Colorado] and Gunnison Rivers, and upon the
other by the main range, enclosing an area of about 400
square miles. The center of the range (the peak in our view
being one of the highest points) is composed of granitic
rocks as a core, about which, upon every side, are tipped up
the sedimentary rocks into curiously-castellated mountains,
to an almost equal height. . . . The lake in the foreground is
about one hundred acres in extent, occupying an old
glacier-bed. Still nearer is an exposure of glacier-smoothed
granite, with a stranded bowlder [*sic*] resting upon it. The
height of Snow Mass Mountain is 13,961 [14,092] feet"
(Jackson [1875] 1978, 59). Jackson's diary is somewhat
confusing as he refers to Snow Mass by its older name,
White House Mountain. Courtesy U.S. Geological Survey.

In the morning Coulter, Tom, and I got an early start for the high ridge. It was
a stiff, hard climb, mostly over loose slide rock, and required constant urging to force
the mule over it. After about three hours of hard climbing we made it, but at the end
we were all so fagged that as soon as the pack was off the mule, we took a good half
hour's rest before going to work. We remained on the ridge until four o'clock.
Although it was quite cold and windy, with occasional spats of rain and hail, I was
able to secure a set of ten negatives—some of them very effective views, showing the
heart of the Elk Mountain group from an elevation of about thirteen thousand feet.

The next day our combined parties broke camp and started on the return over
the range. After they were well on their way, I went off, with Harry to assist, to photograph some cascades near by. While I was thus engaged, John came back with the
distressing information that Gimlet, carrying my boxes of negatives, had slipped his
pack while going up a big hill, and many of my plates were broken. Leaving Harry
to pack up, I hurried after and found the situation fully as bad as reported. The Doctor had been the first to discover the mishap. It was a serious matter and he evidently wanted to be severe with someone about it. At first he seemed inclined to regard
me as in some way responsible, but I was so distressed and showed it so plainly, that
he had nothing more to say.

It was explained that the mule, straying from the trail, had not been missed by
the packers. Having no attention, the saddle had turned on the vagrant animal; and
the boxes, becoming loose, had rolled down the mountain. They were built to with-
stand all kinds of rough usage; but the cover of the one with the 11 × 14 plates,
although secured with screws, had come off, and the plates were scattered over rocks
and brush for quite a distance down the hill. The box of small plates was not injured.
Gathering up the wreckage, I found that ten plates were hopelessly damaged and broken, chiefly those made from the mountain panoramas, including La Plata and Lincoln. It was decided on the spot to make good the loss by replacement, so I recalled
my part of the outfit and returned to the old camp. The rest of the day was spent
repairing damages as far as possible.

With Tom to help, I went up next morning to the lake under Snowmass Mountain and made those views over again; then to the falls and cascades below. All
replacements for this locality having been made, we got off on the trail by three

o'clock and ascended the big hill without mishap. As there was a fine view to be had from the top of this hill, which could not be made then because it was raining, I left the photographic outfit there and descended the other side a mile or so to camp.

The stock strayed away during the night, so we were late getting out next day. Walking back alone to where my traps were left I made my negatives, and Harry brought up the mule later. About mid-day we met the Doctor returning on the trail to see how we were getting on, and he remained with us until we rejoined the main party.

It was decided that we should go up White Rock Mountain for panoramic views from near its summit. In making this climb, we took some of Gardner's mules so as to give ours a much-needed rest. The Doctor and Gardner went with us. At eleven o'clock we reached the upper edge of the amphitheater at the foot of the mountain, where we unpacked. Then distributing the outfit among us, we made the rest of the ascent on foot. In a little less than a thousand feet we had gained the spur of the mountain that commanded the desired views. While resting a bit before getting to work, we ate lunch. Storm clouds began to gather around us early in the afternoon so we were able to get only three large plates before we were enveloped in a dense cloud of mist with rain and hail. The Doctor and Gardner stood it until about three o'clock and then went down the mountain in a hurry.

We remained an hour longer, hoping for a break in the clouds so that one or two more negatives might be made; but it was useless, and we also beat a retreat in double quick time with the mist so thick we could hardly see ten paces ahead. We got back on the return trail a little after five, and by pushing our animals pretty hard, we were out of the heavy timber and into comparatively open country before darkness set in. It was nine o'clock, however, before we found camp and then only through the instinct of the mules. We were wet to the skin and our boots were full of water. Reviving the camp fire, we partly dried ourselves. We then found something to eat and, hunting our blanket rolls from out of the darkness somewhere, we were soon wrapped in them sound asleep.

Our next task was to get back to the headwaters of the Arkansas and replace the broken negatives made from La Plata. Taking the same Indian trail, we crossed Taylor River and camped at the foot of the pass over the divide. The cooks were ordered

LOOKING NORTH OVER THE SAWATCH RANGE. August 17, 1873. Copy of modern print from wet plate negative.

The view is from the summit of La Plata, 14,333 [14,336] feet high. Colorado has forty-seven peaks above 14,000 feet. The official count now stands at fifty-four "fourteeners," with thirteen subsidiary peaks listed at over 14,000 feet (Borneman 1994, 250). This number will always be debated as many of the massive mountains contain multiple summits and secondary ridges.

"In approaching the mountain we are enabled to ride within 1,500 feet of the summit, the rest of the ascent being easily accomplished on foot, the huge blocks of gneiss, of which the mountain is composed, being so disposed as to afford excellent footing, like a great stairway. . . ." In the photograph "are seen the amphitheaters, or heads of canons, flowing either way, those on the right into the Pacific and those on the left into the Atlantic. In them originated the great glaciers" (Jackson [1875] 1978, 58–59). Courtesy U.S. Geological Survey.

RED ROCK FALLS, ELK MTS. August 14, 1873.
Copy of modern print from wet plate negative.

The exposure time for a wet plate photograph was often
more than a few seconds. All of the images that involve
moving water that Jackson photographed during his
years with the Hayden Survey show the movement to
be a silky blur. Courtesy U.S. Geological Survey.

to have us up by three in the morning, as Gardner wanted to reach Twin Lakes the
same day. John was on time as usual, but a dense fog overhanging the entire valley
made it hard to find our animals. Coulter and I got ours among the first and we struck
out ahead with the photo-pack.

The fog hung about us until we reached the top of the pass. Here it lifted and gave
us a magnificent view, looking back over the valley of Taylor River, where the fog
clouds covered everything like a great white blanket. Between passing showers I
made a few negatives of the cloud effects. The rest of the train having passed us while
at the work, we took up their trail and were soon at the old camp ground at the foot
of La Plata Mountain, with the serious business before us of remaking the negatives
destroyed on Rock Creek. This duplication, however, was accomplished next day
with better results than before, and then we made haste to join Gardner in the quest
of the Holy Cross.

Chapter Eleven

Photographing the Mountain of the Holy Cross

August 1873–September 1873

Gardner, as chief topographer of the Survey, was engaged in making primary triangulations from the highest mountains as the groundwork for more detailed map making to follow. When we rejoined his party after retaking the pictures from La Plata, he was about to make one of these stations on the Mountain of the Holy Cross, and we went along at the same time to photograph this mysterious mountain.

The name was a familiar one to Colorado people. Many had heard that over on the western side of the range somewhere there was a mountain with a great snow cross on one side, but we knew of no one who had ever seen the cross. The mountain itself is of such a commanding height that our topographers had located it from the surrounding, distant peaks. The cross itself can be seen under favorable conditions from far-away Grays Peak, but on nearer approach this feature of the mountain mysteriously disappears; from all usual points of observation it is not visible. It is cut off by a high ridge called Notch Mountain, which confronts the eastern face of the mountain carrying the cross. In fact, a near view can be had only from this ridge or from some higher point in the distance overlooking it.

After crossing Tennessee Pass, we followed an Indian trail that made easy traveling except for a detour around Eagle River Canyon. Passing this, we came to a valley leading directly up to the base of the Holy Cross Mountain itself. This valley seemed to offer an easy approach, but we found it impracticable. The fallen timber, rocks, and bogs made such difficulties that we finally turned back and camped on the banks of the Eagle for the night.

After a lively discussion around the mess table the next morning as to the best way to approach the mountain, we decided to have Gardner pilot the way. Following his

~

"No man we talked to had ever seen the Mountain of the Holy Cross. But everyone knew that somewhere in the far reaches of the western highlands such a wonder might exist. Hadn't a certain hunter once caught a glimpse of it—only to have it vanish as he approached? Didn't a wrinkled Indian here and there narrow his eyes and slowly nod his head when questioned? Wasn't this man's grandfather, and that man's uncle, and old so-and-so's brother the first white man ever to lay eyes on the Holy Cross—many, many, many years ago? It was a beautiful legend, and they nursed it carefully" (Jackson [1940] 1994, 216).

~

VALLEY OF THE SHEEP BACK ROCKS [ROCHES MOUTONÉES] AND THE MOUNTAIN OF THE HOLY CROSS. August 25, 1873.
Copy of modern print from wet plate negative.

The cross faces into the amphitheater between the two peaks and can be seen in its entirety only from Notch Mountain to the left. Upon retreating from the mountain, Jackson and Tom Cooper, packer, remained behind the main party to photograph the polished glacial rocks and tangled timber that the party had labored to avoid on their approach. Courtesy U.S. Geological Survey.

lead, we went down stream a short distance, then turned to the left and made a stiff climb from the valley to the top of the ridge lying west of the creek. Almost immediately we got into a bad windfall of small timber. Through this we chopped our way to an open space in the plateau, where we picked up an old game trail, which we followed until it was lost in another thick tangle of fallen timber. We eventually got so involved in one windfall after another that we decided it was a hopeless task to continue. It was nearly night and we had made less than five miles in a long day of hard work. We camped in a little grassy ravine, where there was hardly more than enough room to unpack the mules.

Experience had proved that our party, consisting of sixteen persons, with more than that number of animals, was altogether too large an outfit for the purpose at hand. The next morning it was decided to send back to a camp on the Eagle all who were not to participate directly in the ascent of the mountain. Coulter and one of the packers remained with me, while Gardner, Dr. Hayden, and Holmes with three or four others made up the triangulation party. Taking with us four pack mules, we started out again. Two or three axmen went ahead and chopped a way out of the worst timber immediately in front, enabling us finally to come out on a high point overlooking the entire valley with a fine view of the mountain itself from that side.

It was decided here to abandon the ridge and again attempt to make the approach up the valley. I remained behind to photograph the mountain from this point, and then joined the others in the descent, a drop of nearly fifteen hundred feet, but fortunately most of the way over soft soil. We found traveling conditions in the valley fully as bad, if not worse, than where we had made the first attempt. As it was practically impossible to get our animals through, we decided to go into camp and finish the job afoot the next day.[1]

The little way we had taken the animals into the valley was rough work for them. It was just one bog hole after another between the smooth glaciated rocks, the intervening spaces filled with a network of fallen trees. While we were making camp, it began raining, which did not improve the situation. To gain time, Gardner, with some of his assistants, carried his instruments to the foot of the mountain and left them there.

Next morning everyone was up long before sunrise, and after a quick breakfast the photographers shouldered their packs and began the difficult climb up the high, rocky ridge from which we hoped to get a good view of the snowy cross. Tom took the cameras, Coulter the plate boxes, and I had the tent and chemicals, a matter of forty pounds for each one. Meanwhile Gardner's party also got off, proceeding straight up the creek to the foot of the mountain. It was a clear and wonderfully bracing morning.

In starting out, we made the mistake, as we found out later, of first following up the creek instead of striking up on the ridge at once. The logs and rocks were all white with frost and the foliage was heavy with the rain of the night before. In passing through the thickets of willows and alders, we were showered with water, which soon soaked us completely. After fording the creek two or three times, we had had enough of it and made for higher ground.

I usually kept some distance in advance of my assistants in order to prospect about for the best points of view before they came up. In this instance, after we had agreed upon our general direction, I struck out ahead, climbing directly up for about a thousand feet until near the crest of the ridge. Then I continued along it until I came out above timber line at the foot of Notch Mountain, fifteen hundred feet higher yet, the attainment of which was to reveal the cross.

For some time I waited here for the others to come up, but as there was no sign of them, I continued on over the great masses of broken rock, eager to reach the point that would determine the success or failure of our efforts. I now began to hear faintly across the intervening gorge voices from Gardner's party, although I could not see them. They were ascending the mountain itself. Clouds began to gather, and as they drifted about among the peaks the top of the Holy Cross Mountain was hidden, except for occasional rifts and breaks. Pressing on steadily, I finally gained the summit of the ridge, and working along its crest, at last stood face to face with the Holy Cross in all of its sublime impressiveness.

After some moments of silent contemplation of the marvelous mountain on which nature had drawn with mighty lines of snow the symbol of the Christian world, I sat down to wait for my companions. First, in response to the call of hunger, I disposed of the sandwich I had with me, and then made myself as comfortable as possible by wrapping the folds of my dark tent around my shoulders as some protection from the cold wind, mist, and intermittent spats of rain. All this time the

THE MOUNT OF THE HOLY CROSS. August 24, 1873 (Jackson 1873, 40). Copy of modern print from wet plate negative.

The mountain, 13,978 [14,005] feet in elevation, as viewed at sunrise from Notch Mountain. The vertical arm of the cross is 1,500 feet in length. "This photograph . . . is the first picture ever made of the Mt. of the Holy cross" (Elwood P. Bonney Collection of William Henry Jackson Material 1996. MSS 1643, ff. 364. Jackson wrote the notation on the back of another copy of the same photograph). William Jackson was never able to photograph the "cross" as vividly as he did during that initial exploration in 1873. This was due in part to a deterioration of the right arm caused by subsequent rock slides. Nor was he ever there again for the early morning light that highlights the cross. "The fine effect obtained in those old first negatives of the mountain and the cross was due mainly to their being taken soon after sunrise. . . . It is only by the early morning light that the strong lines of the mountain and cross are clearly brought out. Few photographers cared to spend the night on Notch Mountain to secure this effect" (Jackson to Fryxell, Jackson April 30, 1933. Fritiof M. Fryxell Papers. 1853–1973. MSS 1638, Box 29, correspondence file). Courtesy U.S. Geological Survey.

clouds were surging around, breaking occasionally to afford brief glimpses of the surrounding peaks, then closing up so solidly that I seemed isolated in space, the only object in view being the rock on which I was sitting.

It was about two hours before the boys emerged from the edge of timber line. As I was now well rested, I descended the ridge to meet and assist them to the top. On the way up we saw floating on the mists below us a rainbow that was almost a complete circle. The colors were clearly defined, and in the brief intervals when the sun broke through above it, the rainbow lay apparently in the midst of the clouds a thousand feet below, its circle broken only by the shadow of the rock we were standing upon.

We remained on the summit until nearly sunset. Then despairing of doing any photographing at that time, we carefully stowed our apparatus away under the rocks and descended to the edge of timber. Here we passed a seemingly endless night, supperless, without coats, catching such little snatches of sleep as we could between our foraging for wood to keep the fire going.

About the time we started our fire, a light flashed out of the darkness on the other mountainside. It carried the information that the topographers were faring no better or worse than we were. The distance was not so great but that our voices carried over, and all night at intervals their "Hellos!" would float across to be echoed by us. Thus we kept up a feeling of companionship as we watched the little red star of their fire glowing all through the long night. Sometimes it waned to almost complete extinction and then, replenished with fuel, flared again with cheering light.

Sunday morning came without a cloud in the sky. As soon as it was fairly daylight, we exchanged final greetings with our comrades across the gorge and then, before the sun had warmed us with its genial rays, we were once more on our way up the fifteen hundred feet to the crest from which we could view again the Holy Cross. The feeling of lassitude and weariness due to the fasting and the hard work of the day before made this second climb painfully fatiguing.

On reaching the summit we faced the problem of finding water to wash the plates after development. The day before all the snow banks had rivulets running from them, but this morning everything was frozen solid. Not a drop of water could be found until the increasing warmth of the sun started the snow melting again.[2] Setting up my dark tent among the rocks, I worked rapidly. I coated, sensitized, exposed,

SOME OF THE GROUP THAT MADE THE TRIP TO THE MOUNTAIN OF THE HOLY CROSS. August 25, 1873. Copy print.

At the left is Dr. Hayden and [James] Stevenson [general manager; W. S. Holman, Jr., meteorologist and assistant; S. C. Jones, general assistant; and an unidentified packer above Jones]; at the right James Gardner [topographer; Prof. Wm. Dwight Whitney, guest of the Survey from Yale]; with William H. Holmes [geologist] in the background. "Made a fair start in the A.M. Dr. [Hayden] and I went ahead to prospect for views of the roches moutonnes & when the packs came up Tom [Cooper, chief packer] & I remained behind a couple of hours to photograph. . . . No. 3 of our mules, that went ahead with the others, rolled down the hill & cut herself so badly on the rocks as to render herself entirely useless. After dinner cut up a couple of 11/14 plates and made 5/8 groups of the party . . ." (Jackson 1873, 41). Courtesy National Park Service/Rocky Mountain National Park.

~

"My marriage to Emilie Porter took place on October 8, 1873, before I returned to Washington. Since I was a relatively recent widower, Emilie, her parents, and I had agreed it would be most fitting to omit the traditional trappings. And so we were married with the utmost simplicity, in Cincinnati, at the home of Emilie's brother, Samuel" (Jackson [1940] 1994, 219).

~

and developed eight 11×14 and 5×8 plates. They were rinsed well after development, but I deferred fixing until my return to camp.

It was a perfect day for the making of the first photographs of the Mountain of the Holy Cross. The early morning is the best time for this particular subject. I do not think it can be successfully photographed later in the day. Having but one point of view from which to make the negatives, I was through before noon. Quick time was made in assembling and repacking the apparatus, and we got down the mountain in much less time than it took to go up. I struck out ahead and reached camp by two o'clock. Coulter and Tom, taking things more leisurely, arrived two hours later.

Gardner and Holmes, of the other party, came in at six. Dr. Hayden with two or three others had returned from the mountain the evening before. We had a pleasant time that night around the camp fire, reviewing the events of the two preceding days. The Doctor was immensely pleased with our success; and all were greatly interested in the negatives, as none had seen the Cross itself, except our photographic party of three.

By previous arrangement our parties now separated. My work was done, but Gardner and the geologists had other peaks to climb. No one was more eager than I to be homeward bound, for in October I was to be wedded to the Maryland girl whom I first met when photographing among the Omaha Indians out in Nebraska. It was her father who helped me get the pictures of the Pawnees.

By rapid marches we returned over Tennessee Pass and crossed Mosquito Pass to South Park, whence we struck out for Denver by way of Kenosha Pass and Turkey Creek Canyon. Then after carefully packing and shipping our negatives, we were soon aboard a Pullman bound for Washington.

WINTER QUARTERS. February 22, 1863. Colored pencil drawing.

Although Jackson's Civil War enlistment was relatively uneventful, he was assigned a duty he found to be an interesting challenge—that of sketching camp life and creating maps. "Commenced snowing some time during the night and by morning was some 4 or 5 inches deep. This evening it is about 8 or 10. Made sketch of [our] quarters under its wintry aspect" (Jackson 1862–1863, February 22, 1863). Courtesy National Park Service/Scotts Bluff National Monument.

YOKING UP. Circa 1920–1930.
Hand-tinted colorized glass lantern-slide.

Jackson's initiation into life as a
bullwacker was memorable. "Most of
[us] had never seen an ox yoked, much
less driven one. The corral was crowded
to the limit, many of the oxen were
unbroken, others had forgotten all about
it in running the range and some of the
more refractory ones had to be lariated
and drawn to a wagon wheel to be
yoked. The wagon boss helped as much
as possible and occasionally an old-timer
lent a hand. But about all that could be
done in individual cases was to have the
ox pointed out to the prospective
bullwhacker, and let him go about it as
best he could" (Jackson 1931, 193).
Courtesy National Park Service/Scotts
Bluff National Monument.

CALIFORNIA CROSSING. Circa 1950. Lithographic print from hand-tinted photograph.

Because the transcontinental railroad had not bridged the Western United States, the Oregon Trail was still teeming with activity as Jackson headed west, fording the South Platte near Julesburg, Colorado, in 1866. The river, more than half a mile wide, was filled from bank to bank with teams. Courtesy National Park Service/Scotts Bluff National Monument.

MITCHELL PASS, NEBRASKA. Circa 1950. Lithographic print from hand-tinted photograph.

Jackson wields his bullwhip as his train passes around Scotts Bluff. The artist did other paintings of this scene where the larger "prairie schooner" wagons of earlier times replaced the double "back-action" wagons used in the train he was traveling with. This print was one of a series done for Harold Warp in the 1950s. Courtesy Harold Warp Pioneer Village.

OUR WAGON TRAIN PASSING CHIMNEY ROCK.
December 2, 1866. Watercolor wash.

They were . . . on the North Platte east of Scott's Bluff. In the distance appear several curious rock formations. On August 1 "our noon camp was opposite 'Chimney Rock.' . . . Made carefully detailed drawings, and then as it appeared to be hardly more than a mile away, a few of us, right after 'grub pile' started out to investigate it at closer quarters. Needless to say we were very much deceived as to distance; had a stiff two hours walk and did not succeed in getting a much better view than was to be had in camp" (Jackson 1923, 15–16). This watercolor and the one below were two of a series done while living near Salt Lake City, subsequent to Jackson's trek across the plains. Courtesy National Park Service/Scotts Bluff National Monument.

INTERSECTION OF ECHO AND WEBER CANYONS.
December 30, 1866. Watercolor.

William Jackson's trek west was drawing to a temporary close. Abandoning his gold-laden dreams of Virginia City, he joined another wagon train heading for Salt Lake City. "At the mouth of the cañon it was quite wide and the road very good. Turned to the left up the Weber River and corralled for the night some two miles from the mouth of Echo. Farmhouses begin to line the valley & it looks something like civilization. Went up to farmers & bought a gallon of milk for 50 cents. Had a genuine treat on fresh milk" (Jackson [1866–1867a] n.d., October 10, 1866). Courtesy National Park Service/Scotts Bluff National Monument.

OUR LAST ATTEMPT. Circa 1930–1940. Oil painting.

Upon reaching California in 1867, Jackson accepted a job driving horses. There were difficult and dangerous adventures. The vaqueros tried "to force the horses to swim across the Green River. Mounting old Bally bareback, I plunged in while everyone on shore crowded the horses in right after me" (Jackson 1866–1867, July 9, 1867). It took William Jackson five tries on two different horses to cross the river. On the fifth try he was able to successfully navigate the swift currents to the opposite shore. Unfortunately, the unruly stock never followed. It was late in the day, and Sam McGannigan finally agreed to pay the fare to ferry the horses across. After an exhausting and frustrating day, the men spent a nearly sleepless night battling one more natural element—mosquitoes. Courtesy American Heritage Center.

VIEWS OF OMAHA. 1869.
Albumin stereoview.

After procuring a photography business, Jackson settled in Omaha. This view is "Looking east on Farnham from 3rd Street: Omaha, Nebraska."
"Omaha was a fine location for business. The town was old, as age is reckoned beyond the Mississippi—the first house built in 1853—and it had at the same time the enormous vitality of a boom town. . . . By the time Jackson Brothers got underway Omaha was the unrivaled metropolis west of Chicago and north of St. Louis" (Jackson [1940] 1994, 172–73). Courtesy Union Pacific Museum.

EXPEDITION OF 1870. Circa 1920–1930. Hand-tinted colorized glass lantern-slide.

This scene occurred on August 24, 1869, at Red Buttes at the junction of the North Platte and Sweetwater Rivers. Standing left to right are members of the United States Geological Survey of the Territories: "Potato" John Raymond, cook; "Val" . . . cook; S. R. Gifford, landscape painter and guest; H. W. Elliot, artist; James Stevenson, assistant; H. D. Schmidt, naturalist; C. P. Carrington, zoologist; L. A. Bartlett, general assistant; and W. H. Jackson, photographer. Sitting, left to right: C. S. Turnbull, secretary; J. H. Beaman, meteorologist; F. V. Hayden, geologist in charge; Cyrus Thomas, agriculturist; "Raphael" . . . hunter; and A. L. Ford, mineralogist (United States Geological Survey Photo Library [1869–1878, and 1883] n.d., #282). Courtesy National Park Service/Scotts Bluff National Monument.

Virginia Dalf Station. October 1870. Lithographic print from hand-tinted photograph.

Jackson created this painting in 1932. His son Clarence later fashioned the hand-tinted print for Harold Warp. Jackson's 1870 photograph *The Robber's Roost* was the inspiration for his painting. It depicts "a stage station on the line of the old overland route, which attained an unenviable notoriety during 1860 and 1863, while kept by Jack Slade, a noted desperado of that time" (Jackson [1875] 1978, 19). Courtesy Harold Warp Pioneer Village.

THE 1871 EXPEDITION EN ROUTE IN
YELLOWSTONE PARK. Circa 1920–1930.
Hand-tinted colorized glass lantern-slide.

Some of Jackson's best-known
photographs were taken in the
Yellowstone region. The Survey
entourage is "... upon the trail between
the Yellowstone [River] and the East
Fork, showing the manner in which all
parties traverse these wilds" (Jackson
[1875] 1978, 31). Lieutenant [Gustavus]
Doane is leading, with Dr. Hayden and
[James] Stevenson following. Next comes
[Antoine] Schönborn [Anton],
topographer, and [F. L.] Goodfellow with
his odometer cart for measuring trails.
This view was taken in camp at Mirror
Lake west of the Lamar River on the
Mirror Plateau. Courtesy National Park
Service/Scotts Bluff National Monument.

THE ANNA. Circa 1920–1930.
Hand-tinted colorized glass lantern-slide.

Jackson claimed it was "the first boat ever launched upon the [Yellowstone] lake. Its frame-work was brought up from Fort Ellis and then put together, and covered with tar-soaked canvas. A tent-fly made the sail. In it two adventurous members of the survey visited every arm and nook of the lake, and made all the soundings. It is so named to compliment Ms. Anna Dawes, a daughter of the distinguished statesman whose generous sympathy and aid have done so much toward securing these results" (Jackson [1875] 1978, 29). "I was able to 'borrow' [the skiff] on several occasions, and I thus had the means for reaching many vantage points otherwise inaccessible to me. It was a tiny, frail craft, and how it survived the loads I put in it has always been something of a mystery to me" (Jackson [1940] 1994, 201). Mr. Elwood Bonney, a close personal friend and associate of Jackson later disputed this claim, stating, "WHJ told me he did not use [the boat]" (Elwood P. Bonney Collection of William Henry Jackson Material. 1996). The notation is found in Bonney's personal copy of *Miscellaneous Publications No. 5* (Jackson [1875] 1978). Pictured from the left are James Stevenson, Survey general manager, and Chester Dawes, general assistant (Merrill 1999, 142). Chester Dawes was Anna Dawes's brother. In all probability prehistoric Native Americans were the first people to navigate the lake, not Hayden Survey personnel. The original photograph was created on July 28, 1871 (Merrill 1999, 171). Courtesy National Park Service/Scotts Bluff National Monument.

HAYDEN SURVEY. (1871) 1935. Oil painting.

Jackson painted four murals for the Department of the Interior. One of each of the Great Surveys of the American West was produced: the Hayden Survey, the Powell Survey, the King Survey, and the Wheeler Survey. In the center foreground is Dr. Hayden followed by N. P. Langford, who became Yellowstone's first superintendent, and Thomas Moran, artist. In the background is William H. Jackson preparing to photograph the Old Faithful Geyser. Jackson claims to have taken only a small party over to the Firehole Basin where Old Faithful is located. "We had but one day and confined our visit to the Upper Basin only. My photographic work was limited to details of formations about the geyser cones and but one of them—the Grotto, was caught in eruption" (Jackson [1871] n.d., 13). Some of the people in the painting did not visit the Upper Basin during the 1871 season. Langford journeyed with the Survey in 1872, not 1871 as depicted. "I intend some of the horsemen to be portraits—Hayden and Langford on their favorite horses—symbolic of first discoveries. The Hayden party entered the geyser basins from the east so I have them coming out on the Giantess plateau for a first view of Old faithful in action" (Jackson to Fryxell, September 8, 1935. Fritiof M. Fryxell Papers. 1853–1973. MSS 1638, Box 29, correspondence file). This mural depicts the Survey's contribution of presenting the wonders of Yellowstone to the world, rather than a historical representation of an actual event. Courtesy U.S. Department of the Interior Museum.

PAWNEE INDIAN NAMING CEREMONY.
Circa 1950. Lithographic print from
hand-tinted photograph.

A Pawnee village of mud lodges on the
Loup Fork, Nebraska. Its location was
"about 100 miles west of Omaha. It was
divided into two parts, the Skeedees
occupying one part by themselves and
the other three bands jointly in the
other. The entire village accommodated
about 2,500 people. Each lodge was
capable of holding several families; they
were formed by erecting several posts in
a circle, forked at the top, into which
cross-beams were laid, and against these
long poles were inclined from the
outside toward the centre [*sic*]; all was
then covered with brush, and finally
with earth, leaving a hole at the apex for
the escape of smoke, and a long tunnel-
like entrance at its base. This village is
now (1876) entirely destroyed, and the
Indians removed to the Indian
Territory" (Jackson [1877] 1978, 68).
The original photograph was taken at
the end of the 1872 season with the
United States Geological Survey.
Courtesy Harold Warp Pioneer Village.

PHOTOGRAPHING IN HIGH PLACES. 1936.
Watercolor painting.

The pioneer photographer's workshop on the plateau west of the Three Tetons. In the first edition of this book, Jackson adapted his original 1872 photograph (see page 83) by painting horses and a camera on the distant ledge, a physical impossibility given the ledge was only a few feet wide. Jackson's intention to demonstrate the cumbersome process of wet plate photography was further explored in this later watercolor. More photographic equipment was added in the foreground, and Alec Sibley, the pack animal assistant, was added beyond the photographers. Courtesy National Park Service/Grand Teton National Park.

(left) *ADVENTURE OF MR. STEVENSON.* Circa 1872–73. Graphite and watercolor.

While attempting to scale the Grand Teton in 1872, "Captain Stevenson . . . had made several ineffectual efforts to reach [an] overhanging ledge of the rock, and losing his foothold, his entire weight coming upon his hands while he hung with his face to the wall. It was impossible without a leap to reach a standing place, and by loosening his hold without one he would drop several hundred feet down the mountain. Fortunately, there was a coating of ice and snow, which reached midway from his feet to his arms, and into this, by repeated kicks with the toe of his boot, he worked an indentation that afforded a poise for one foot. This enabled him to spring on one side to a narrow bench of rock, where he was safe" (Langford 1873, 151). Courtesy National Park Service/Yellowstone National Park.

SELF-PORTRAIT. 1873. Oil painting.

Finding an idyllic vista in the Colorado Rockies which satisfied the photographer's critical eye and Hayden's demanding needs often took time, patience, stamina, and luck. Jackson depicts himself high in the mountains. Courtesy Brigham Young University.

HOLY CROSS. 1936. Oil painting.

The photographer and his assistants gaze at the Mount of the Holy Cross in 1873 with storm clouds superimposed around its summit. After laboriously ascending Notch Mountain, Jackson's emotional first glimpses of the mountain peeking between the clouds are captured on this canvas. Courtesy National Park Service/Scotts Bluff National Monument.

PHOTOGRAPHING THE MOUNT OF THE HOLY CROSS. 1936. Oil painting.

This composition depicts one of the crowning achievements of Mr. Jackson's illustrious photographic career. It shows the men on the ridge of Notch Mountain photographing the Holy Cross. Jackson discusses his artwork: "I have just sent off the two Holy Cross paintings. Am fairly well pleased, myself, with the cloud view [previous page] but not so well with the other [seen here]. Foreground doesn't suit me and have even considered doing the entire picture all over again. Seen not too critically, however, it may serve its story telling purpose" (Jackson to Fryxell, October 28, 1936. Fritiof M. Fryxell Papers. 1853–1973. MSS 1638, Box 29, correspondence file). Courtesy National Park Service/Scotts Bluff National Monument.

THE SUMMIT OF BERTHOUD PASS,
COLORADO. 1874.
Hand-tinted colorized glass lantern-slide.
Circa 1920–1930.

The camera is looking north towards
Middle Park, with Harry Yount, big
game hunter for the Survey, the first
ranger of the Yellowstone National
Park. "Height of pass, 11,313 [11,315]
feet. View made . . . from a point 800 feet
above the lowest point of pass [on July
27, 1874]. James' Peak, with an elevation
of 13,283 [13,294] feet, is near the center,
while away in the distance on the left is
the group around Aaraphoe Peak"
(Jackson [1875] 1978, 66). Courtesy
National Park Service/Rocky Mountain
National Park.

FISHERMAN'S CABIN ON GRAND LAKE

FISHERMAN'S CABIN, ON GRAND LAKE. Circa 1920–1930. Hand-tinted colorized glass lantern-slide.

According to Jackson this was the home of a hermit fisherman. While approaching the lake in the mountainous Colorado wilderness in 1874, "a severe hail storm came up accompanied with intense lightning and deafening thunder. The hail pelted so hard that it annoyed our mules very much and they disliked exceedingly to face it. . . .We reached the lake in a drenching downpour. Slung off the packs in double quick order and took refuge in a fisherman's hut until the worst of it was over" (Jackson 1874a, July 30). Jackson's photographic team spent three days camping near this cabin, doing photographic work when weather permitted. The log cabin was photographed on the morning of August 2 as they were preparing to break camp. Courtesy National Park Service/Rocky Mountain National Park.

DISCOVERY OF TWO STORY CLIFF HOUSE, MANCOS CANYON. 1936. Oil painting.

"Our first discovery of a cliff house ruin that met our expectations was made late in the evening of the first day out from Merritt's [ranch]—We had finished our meal of bacon, freshly baked bread and coffee & were standing around the sage brush fire—enjoying its genial warmth—in the contented and good natured mood that follows a day of hard work and a good supper & were in a humor to be merry. Looking up at the walls of the cañon that towered above our camp at least 800 feet, we commenced bantering Steve who was a large heavy man about the possibility of having to assist in carrying the photo boxes to the top of the cliffs to photograph some ruins up there—no one imagining at the time that there were any at that particular place. He asked Moss to point out the particular ruin we had in view. The Captain pointed to the highest point of the cliff at random. 'Yes,' said Steve 'I see it.' and behold upon close observation in the waning light there really was something that looked like a house with spots indicating doors and windows sandwiched between the strata of the sandstones very near the top. Forgetting the fatigue of the days work all hands started out at once to investigate" (Jackson [1874] n.d., September 9). Two Story Ruin can be seen nestled in a crevice high on the massive sandstone cliff in the upper left quarter of the painting. Courtesy National Park Service/Mesa Verde National Park.

RACING. Circa 1920–1930. Hand-tinted colorized glass lantern-slide.

In Montezuma Canyon, Utah. Insisting upon having us go to their camp, and animated by mischief, these Indians got behind us and with quirt and lariat lashed our frantic animals into a breakneck race with them down the canyon. Jackson's photographic party had several unpleasant encounters with Utes. Courtesy National Park Service/Scotts Bluff National Monument.

5 PORCHES, 1 DOOR.
March or May 1877. Watercolor painting.

While traveling with the Reverand
Sheldon Jackson through northern New
Mexico in 1877, William Jackson visited
Santa Fe. This painting shows a
territorial-style adobe building.
Courtesy National Park Service/Scotts
Bluff National Monument.

INDIAN WOMAN. Circa 1877. Watercolor painting.

The loss of Jackson's 1877 photographs was compounded by the fact that he kept no journal of his travels. The hurried stay in New Mexico allowed no time for careful note taking. As there is no detailed sequence of events for Jackson's travels in 1877, little is known about this colorful Native American woman in the sketch. Courtesy National Park Service/Scotts Bluff National Monument.

The Rock Citadel at the summit of Fremont Peak, Wyoming. Circa 1920–1930. Hand-tinted colorized glass lantern-slide.

Seated on the rock summit are the topographers and geologists of the survey. On August 8, 1878 "I found the whole party of six or seven, topographers and others, gathered on the little citadel of rock that forms the apex of the peak. By the way, this is undoubtedly the same rock that Fremont mentions, where he would allow only one man at a time to go upon it for fear of dislodging it and being precipitated down the mountain" (Jackson [1878a] n.d., 7).

Jackson was experimenting with dry plate photography. This photograph has a large blemish in the center of the rock outcropping, which was retouched and used in the first edition of *The Pioneer Photographer.* "I developed the plates exposed on the peak, getting fair results all around, except for drying marks caused by unequal heating over a hot shovel" (Ibid., 9). Courtesy National Park Service/Scotts Bluff National Monument.

Chapter Twelve
Photographic Adventures among the Ute Indians

July 1874–August 1874

M y photographic operations in Colorado, the first year of the Hayden Survey in that territory, were confined to the northern half of the Rocky Mountain region included within imaginary lines drawn west and north from Colorado Springs. Most of this territory was little known before the days of '59, and some portions were almost entirely unknown except to the hardy prospector and the pioneer.

In 1874 the field of operations for the Survey was extended over the mountainous region, reaching from Wyoming to New Mexico's border line. The same organization of small parties and division of territory was made. The photographic party, as before, was expected to keep more or less in touch with all the others, but was to give more attention to the sections having the greatest scenic attractions. My final instructions were to go first to Middle Park by way of Berthoud Pass, thence south to San Luis Park, and from there up the Rio Grande into the heart of the San Juan region.

With office work, completing reports for publication, and preparing sets and albums of photographs for distribution where they would do the most good, we were kept in Washington till rather late in the season. A long session of the Congress further delayed our departure since we had to wait for our appropriation. It was the middle of July before we left Washington for the Denver rendezvous, two months later than the preceding year.

My photographic party was entirely new. It comprised Ernest Ingersoll, naturalist and correspondent for the *New York Tribune*,[1] with the same relation to the party as [John] Coulter formerly had; two boys of about eighteen, [Frank] Smart and C. H. Anthony, who were expected to make themselves generally useful; Bob [Mitchell] and Steve [Stevens], expert packers; and Charlie, late waiter at Charpiot's

A LINE-UP OF THE PHOTOGRAPHIC DIVISION OF THE SURVEY. 1874. Copy of modern print from wet plate negative.

The Survey party is ready for the photographer with the pack animals in the background. The team is ". . . on the way to Los Pinos and the Mesa Verde. Left to right: [Frank] Smart [general assistant], [C. H.] Anthony [Photographic Division assistant], [Robert] Mitchell [assistant packer], [Bill] Whan [packer], Ernest Ingersoll [naturalist and correspondent], and Charley, cook. Dolly, one of Jackson's favorite mules, stands between Charley and Ingersoll" (William Henry Jackson Photograph Collection [1869–1878, and 1883] n.d., #512). There was little time for photographic fieldwork in 1874. As congressional funding was politically delayed until late in the summer season, "and since the plan was primarily to select fields of operation for the next full season, 5 × 8 plates and stereos would serve admirably" (Jackson [1940] 1994, 223). Both 5″× 8″ photos and stereoscopic views could be produced with the same smaller camera using different lenses. Courtesy U.S. Geological Survey.

~

The Survey's season lasted from July 15 to October 12. "Quite apart from any lasting value that classifying and cataloguing might have, there was the immediate need for the Survey as a whole to organize its findings and to prepare them for publication. Whether or not there was an active public demand for such a report, it was imperative that the Survey justify, and keep on justifying year after year, its practical usefulness before Congress. And regularly every year all of us passed through a season of fits and trembles until the chosen representatives of the people should vote the money we needed to take the field again. . . . The Panic of 1873 threw a staggering burden upon the congress which convened shortly before Christmas. . . . One of the inevitable results was that the Geological Survey should be pushed into the background. The appropriation came through so late that we never got out of Washington until July" (Jackson [1940] 1994, 221–22).

~

restaurant in Denver, who served as cook. Outfitting was about the same as before, only this year we used aparejos for all the pack mules, except the one who carried the photographic kit. For this we used the sawbuck saddle, as it was more convenient for a light pack and quick work. For greater expedition in my own work, I took out only one size of camera, a 5 × 8, which served for single as well as stereoscopic pictures. For a dark room I went back to the folding box form of '70 and '71.

Everything being ready at last, we struck out on July twenty-first directly west into the foothills along the north side of Clear Creek. We had a fine-looking outfit, new aparejos, white canvas mantas over every pack, and animals in fine condition owing to the lateness of the season. The first few days of breaking-in, however, were hard ones. As we went up and down the steep mountain roads, our packs were continually slipping and made plenty of work and worry for a time.

At the foot of Berthoud Pass we fell in with one of the other divisions of the Survey when we had to lay over a day on account of heavy rain. The morning after was clear with a warm sun, one of those days when it is a joy to be out on the road. As we ascended the pass, fine views of the prominent peaks along the divide began to open up and we went into camp near timber line to do some photographing.

The summit of the pass is 11,350 [11,315] feet above sea level; but with the photographic kit on little crop-eared Mexico, we sought still higher points for commanding views up and down the range and made a half dozen negatives, the first of the season. As it was too late to go on down the pass that evening, we remained in camp. Near us a party of Hoosier tourists was also lying by for the night. They were not of the "auto tourist" variety of today, but a group of four men and two women, with three horses and two packs, and they evidently took turn-about riding, and walking. I mention our experience in crossing this pass, not that it differs a whit from many others, but merely to show the difference from present conditions—a broad, paved highway over which motor cars are humming at the rate of forty to fifty miles an hour.[2]

Once over the pass, our descent was quite rapid into a deep gorge that soon opened out into boggy flats. Here our troubles began. Heavy spring rains and melting snows had saturated the mucky soil with water. Within a dozen miles there were at least twenty places where the pack mules sank so deep in the mire that they had to be unpacked and their loads carried out to firmer ground before they could be pulled out themselves. But once out of the woods into the open, our train was speeded up, and we overtook our comrades of the other party in camp on Frazer River. We had a jolly time around the fire that night before going our separate ways on the morrow.

Our experiences, photographic and otherwise, at Grand Lake, through Middle Park, and up the Blue River into South Park again, where all the high peaks were white with newly fallen snow, then down into San Luis Valley by way of Poncha Pass, were much like those of the year before. We began to strike a new type of scenery to photograph, however, as we got into southwestern Colorado, and also we had adventures of a different sort, especially in the land of the Colorado Utes.

From our camp on the southern side of Poncha Pass it was a long ride to the little Mexican town of Saguache.³ The sun beat down upon us with unaccustomed heat, which was only slightly tempered by occasional showers. Off to the left the splendid panorama of the Sangre de Cristo Mountains was beautiful through a summer haze, but we could not photograph it. Passing down the valley, we met a round-up of more than five thousand cattle on their way over the pass, and we had some trouble in taking our little train through the vast herd.

Leaving the San Luis Valley, we turned westward up the Saguache River, where the bottom lands for several miles were occupied by small Mexican and American ranches. As we progressed, the road made many detours over the basaltic mesas and hills that encroached upon the river. In one place among the hills we ran into a traveling band of Indian families, trooping along with their pack ponies running at random all over the hills each side of the trail. The ponies were loaded with the paraphernalia of their camp life—big bundles of skins and rattling buckets and pans tied to every available place on the packs. Generally there was a papoose or two on top and the tepee poles dragging behind.

When we met this noisy horde in a narrow ravine, there was an immediate stampede of our outfit. Our pack mules bolted up the sides of the hills to a most precarious footing. My riding mule, Dolly, had always shown great antipathy to any and all Indians, and in the present instance was well-nigh uncontrollable, being strongly inclined to follow the pack mules. The Indians drove by unconcernedly, however, paying little heed to us, and the rumpus was soon over with no greater damage than the loosening of some of the packs. Soon after this adventure we passed a small group

FALLS AT THE FOOT OF ROUND MOUNTAIN.
August 1, 1874. Gelatin bromide print.

"The Grand River [Colorado River] is here but a brawling brook, falling down the mountain in continued series of cascades and falls, one of which, of about 50 feet tall, is shown in this view" (Jackson [1875] 1978, 66). Courtesy National Park Service/Rocky Mountain National Park.

VIEW IN THE MIDDLE PARK. August 6, 1874.
Copy of modern print from wet plate negative.

"Took photo pack & saddle animals with the intention of crossing the Blue [River] & going down into the cañon of the Grand [Colorado], but were unable to ford the stream below camp, its treacherous banks, sluggish current and soft bottom, making it dangerous if not unpassible [*sic*]. . . . Spent the day on a prominent spur which over looks the junction of the Blue & muddy [water of the] Grand & secured a fine set of negatives" (Jackson 1874a, August 6). William Jackson's photographic outfit is showcased in the foreground. Courtesy U.S. Geological Survey.

of tepees with some two hundred horses grazing near by in the meadows, the combination making a picturesque scene. Our day's march ended in rain and hail, which flooded the country with a deluge of water.

Ingersoll and I rode out ahead of the outfit next morning, as we were eager to reach the Los Pinos Indian Agency, one of the objective points of the trip, and to get the mail matter supposed to be there. Leaving the Saguache, we passed up a canyon into groves of aspens and spruces and finally out on the open elevation of Cochetopa Pass.[4] Descending the western slope to Cochetopa Creek, we passed another encampment of some seventy tepees of Ute Indians, with hundreds of ponies scattered over the meadow lands up and down the valley for more than a mile. The Agency buildings, four or five miles away, were now in sight, so we stopped at the last crossing of the creek and spruced up a bit.

The Los Pinos Agency then consisted of a dozen or so log houses with a larger frame building of more modern appearance, the agent's residence.[5] The agent himself we found in the carpenter shop,[6] and after introductions we explained that the main object of our visit was to obtain photographs of the Indians. He was glad to meet us and promised to assist in every way possible, but it seemed to us that he was more interested in the opportunity to get portraits of himself and his family and pictures of the Agency buildings than in helping us photograph the Indians.

After this preliminary arrangement we rode out to find a camping place for our party, locating it about half a mile back of the Agency. As the train was now in sight down the valley, I sent Ingersoll to intercept it and guide it to this new camp while I remained to read my letters.

Next morning Ingersoll and I had an interview, arranged by the agent, with Ouray, chief of all the Utes.[7] This big chieftain occupied a small adobe house in one corner of the Agency square. We found him alone, reclining on a rude couch covered with Navajo blankets. The single room was furnished very simply with a few chairs and stools and couches, or lounges, of rough boards thickly covered with blankets. Some cheap prints and several articles of beaded buckskin apparel decorated the walls. The rather lengthy interview ended with satisfactory arrangements for photographing the chief and his wife. He agreed also to use his influence in inducing others to have their photographs taken.

I became interested in his stock of Navajo blankets, which he said he had brought from Arizona, the proceeds of a season of horse racing with the Navajos. One of the larger blankets I bought for twenty dollars and a smaller one for a saddle blanket for two dollars. The best of his collection he held at forty dollars and fifty dollars each.

No one was ready for pictures in the forenoon. After dinner in camp, we returned and began photographing the agent's family, extemporizing an outdoor studio on the porch of the residence. Ouray in full beaded array and his wife, a most comely young woman, likewise in Indian dress, were included in the sittings. A rainstorm then put an end to any further work for that day.

It was arranged that we were to photograph the Indians in their camp next day. Noontime came before I got down there prepared for work. The agent and his family had preceded us in their carriage. Soon after we arrived Ingersoll and I had a preliminary pow-wow, in one of the tepees, with a group of the head chiefs. The pipe was passed and matters were discussed at some length. It soon developed that some of the medicine men probably had prejudiced the others against being photographed. The chiefs united in declaring that it was "no bueno." Shavano, Guerro, and some others said they would have nothing to do with it.[8]

Despite their objections, however, we unpacked our outfit in front of Peah's tepee.[9] This chief had been very friendly towards us, and we now counted upon his influence to see us through, having further enlisted his support by the purchase of two of his best blankets. Getting to work in earnest, after these delays, we succeeded in rounding up several groups in front of their tepees, the men donning their big feather war bonnets and beaded buckskin dress for the occasion. Just as everything was going along all right, the inevitable afternoon storm stopped further operations. We took refuge in Peah's tepee and had a long talk with him in a medley of English, Spanish, and Ute, with sign language to supplement our conversational efforts. Peah's household consisted of his squaw and three papooses, with an old man who declared himself to be "heap lazy."

The rain ceased in about an hour's time, but the clouds hung low and it was so dark that we packed up and went back to camp. As I was preparing to mount, my mule, nervous and excited in the presence of Indians, dashed off before I could get

PIAH [PEAH] AND OTHER UTE CHIEFS. August 20, 1874. Albumin half-stereo print.

The "medicine men had a prejudice . . . against our work. . . . Notwithstanding however we unpacked our [photographic] outfit in front of Peah's tent—counting upon his friendship and good nature to keep us through, which was helped materially by Ingersoll and Anthony buying a couple of his good blankets. Got to work in good earnest and succeeded in rounding up several groups in front of their tents, when the inevitable afternoon shower came up and stopped further operations" (Jackson [1874] n.d., August 20). Courtesy Smithsonian Institution National Anthropological Archives.

CHIEF PEAH'S PAPOOSE. Disputed date.
Type of negative unknown.

"By a little maneuvering in which we were assisted by
the [Indian] agent's wife I got a capital negative of Chief
Peah's papoose" (Jackson [1874] n.d. August 21). The
origin and date of this photograph are suspect. In the
first edition of *The Pioneer Photographer* it is discussed
as an 1874 image but the Colorado Historical Society
lists it as a post-survey New Mexcio photograph.
Courtesy Colorado Historical Society.

into the saddle. We had half an hour's chase to catch her and made camp just in time to protect ourselves from another heavy rainfall.

The presence of so many Indians about the Agency at this time was due to one of the periodic distributions of annuity goods, when beef, flour, sugar, and many other articles were issued to them. We anticipated great photographic results from the crowds that would be in attendance. I set up my dark box in a corner of the stock corral early in the morning and prepared for a busy day.

As the Indians were slow coming in and would probably not be in full force until nearly noon, we began our exposures on some tepees near by with groupings of ponies about them. By some conniving, in which we were assisted by the agent's wife, we got a capital negative of Peah's papoose. I tried to get his squaw, but when the chief observed what we were doing, he ordered her away most peremptorily. Peah appeared to have suddenly changed his attitude towards us and now seemed intent on obstructing our work as much as possible.

Failing to get some of the individual groupings that I wanted, I planted my camera on the Agency porch for the purpose of taking in the general gathering on the issuing ground. At once Peah and five or six other Indians rode up in front of me, protesting vehemently, meanwhile pulling away the tripod legs, jerking the focusing cloth from over my head, and occasionally throwing a blanket over the camera and myself. They protested that "Indian no sabe picture"—"make 'em all heap sick—all die—pony die—papoose die." They would listen to no explanation whatever. Peah's idea seemed to be that no harm would result from making a picture of one man, or two or three together, but I must not attempt to include their squaws, papooses, or ponies.

Defeated in this quarter, for they were persistent and apparently had appointed a guard to follow and watch me closely, we went over to the cook house with our camera, intending to get a general view from the doorway. Just as I was about to expose a plate, an Indian rode up and tried to spur his horse through the doorway. Failing in that, he wheeled the animal across the entrance and, throwing his blanket over his arm, completely blocked the view. It was no use arguing with him, for he was determined and was backed up by a number of others, mounted like himself, who waited upon his orders. As so much antagonism was shown, and no assistance came from either the agent or Ouray, we gave up any further attempts.

Even after I had packed up, Peah made an imperative demand that I give up the plates already made, at the same time trying to take the plate box away from me; but this was going too far and we made him understand it. Regardless of this situation, however, no more picture making was possible as the usual afternoon storm was threatening and the sky was overcast with dark clouds.

The rest of the afternoon was devoted to watching the distribution, and a lively, bustling scene it was. Squaws, nearly all with papooses on cradle frames, sitting on the ground in a semicircle, received their sugar, tea, and other small supplies in rotation. The beef was issued by apportioning one steer to each group of six lodges. Instead of dressed beef in quarters, it was received on the hoof. The Indians were lined up in groups representing their lodges. As the cattle were released from the corral, one by one, each little group selected their steer and gave chase, as if on a buffalo hunt, and with rifle and pistol brought down their game.

The scene was picturesque and exciting. Indians were racing all over the valley in groups of eight or ten, chasing their particular steer and popping away with firearms. Some of the cattle were too tame and old to make much of a run and were quickly dispatched. Others, wilder and more gamy, gave a lively chase for their lives and were pursued a mile or more before they were finally brought down. The skinning and cutting up began at once, and the meat was divided among the members of the group, nearly everything from horns to hoofs being utilized. Altogether it was a thrilling scene, which a moving picture camera could have caught, but such possibilities were not even dreamed of in those early days.

Later in the evening, just as we had finished supper, one of the chiefs known as Billy came over to our camp and had a long talk with us. He said he came to see how many there were in our party and to learn how long we intended to remain. He wanted to know where we were going and what we were doing there anyway. The chief further gave us to understand that this was their country, that they did not recognize boundaries as marked on maps, but claimed all the western slope of the Colorado Rockies as their reservation. He complained bitterly of the encroachments of the white man's toll roads, of the miners, and of the hunters, who were driving away their game. His talk showed us clearly that we were operating in a country of hostile-minded people, so we were ready to pack up and seek more friendly fields.

~

The Utes put a stop to Jackson's photographic endeavors. The next afternoon Chief Billy returned. "I decided it might be well to answer Chief Billy in the way he could best understand. Motioning to Bob and Steve, who were crack shots with both rifle and revolver, I got them to put on a little exhibition of target shooting, in which I also joined. After a dozen rounds Billy departed. Neither he or Peah, who had been audacious enough to demand our exposed plates, tried any further interference with us" (Jackson [1940] 1994, 228).

~

THE RIO GRANDE. September 27, 1874.
Copy of modern print from wet plate negative.

This "view" is "about one mile below Wagon Wheel
Gap, a wild picturesque gorge, where the river has
forced its way through a volcanic gorge, two or three
thousand feet in height" (Jackson [1875] 1978, 68). The
men went past the upper reaches of the Rio Grande
twice. This photograph was taken on the return journey.
Courtesy U.S. Geological Survey.

Chapter Thirteen

Among the Peaks of the San Juan

August 1874–October 1874

From the Los Pinos Agency we struck across country for about eighty miles, as the trail goes, until we came to the headwaters of the Rio Grande opposite Cunningham Pass, the eastern approach to Bakers Park.[1] Most of the time we were at altitudes of from 9,000 to 11,000 feet among strikingly bold and interesting basaltic mesas. Only a few stops were made for photographic work, as we were anxious to get on among the higher peaks before it would be too late in the season. Beautiful little Lake Santa Maria hidden under the mesas near the Rio Grande,[2] and a view looking over Antelope Park were scenes that could not be passed by indifferently.

Our last camp on the Rio Grande was at Jennison's, a sort of road house and grocery store. The "ranch" was one of the primitive log cabins common to the frontiers. Its only occupant at the time of our arrival was a comely young woman. We happened to be all out of bacon and coffee, and in reply to our request for these supplies, she said that her husband, who was away somewhere fishing, would probably accommodate us, but confessed that about all they had to sell was whiskey and tobacco.

Sending the train ahead early next morning, I remained with Ingersoll and Anthony to do some photographing in the immediate vicinity. With the photographic outfit packed on little Mex, we went up among the cliffs to make negatives of the more interesting features of the curiously weathered rocks, and to work along the river for canyon views. When we got back about noon, we found dinner ready with a fine mess of trout, which our hostess had prepared at our request.

Hurrying away to overtake our train before nightfall, we followed an old trail until we reached an elevation of over 12,000 feet. Snow-clad peaks towered 2,000 feet higher, while the canyons or gulches sank into the earth for greater depths. Our descent to the valley below was a precipitous zigzagging by short tacks over the rocks, thinly covered by the black muck that is usually found in dense pine forests. Recent rains had made the soil slippery and treacherous. The wonders of the mountains, the canyons, and the cascades, which seemed to be dropping down from the sky, so engrossed our attention, however, that we paid little heed to what was happening under foot. The steepest part of the trail extended about two miles in a direct line, and this brought us into the depths of Cunningham Gulch. Howardsville, our destination, was six miles farther.

The trail continued to be rough and rocky. The mountains towered higher and higher, and slender cascades were tumbling down over the rocks for thousands of feet. Just as the sun was setting, we came into the open space at the junction of the Cunningham and the Rio Las Animas [Animas River], where the little mining settlement is situated. The first people we met chanced to be Wilson's party, the San Juan division of the Survey.

It was a jovial reunion for all. The first and most important consideration was our grub. We had expected to find our supplies at this place, but nothing had come and none were to be had in town. Wilson had information, however, that they were at San Juan City in Antelope Park.³ So Steve and one of Wilson's men were dispatched with two pack mules to bring in the much-needed provisions. The round trip would be about one hundred miles and we allowed them four days to make it.

Wilson was to make a station on Sultan Mountain, one of the high summits overlooking Bakers Park.⁴ As a fine mountain panorama could probably be had from that picturesque viewpoint, I decided to go with him. Charlie, our cook, volunteered to go along as my assistant.

Our route lay through Howardsville, which consisted of about half a dozen log houses grouped without much order close up under the bluff.⁵ Crossing the river, we followed along the right side, over what they were pleased to call a wagon road, until we passed through year-old Silverton and bivouacked for the night at the foot of a spur running down from Sultan.

Everyone was up early next morning, but the prospect was not encouraging. Clouds hanging low over the mountains threatened rain. Nevertheless, we got ready, and with riding animals well cinched and with Mex carrying the photographic outfit, we began the climb up the spur. A blazed trail, little used, through the thick timber led

Jackson separates into chapters his archaeological explorations and Pueblo Indian adventures from the work done in photographing the Colorado Rockies. Thus, the order of events in 1874 is somewhat confusing. It was at Jennison's roadhouse that he met E. H. Cooper who kindled Jackson's desire to visit the Four Corners region. The party spent a few more days photographing in the San Juan Mountains and then proceeded to John Moss's camp on the La Plata River (chapter fifteen), which was the starting point for this anthropological side trip to numerous prehistoric ruins and the Hopi Indian villages. Following this hurried excursion, Jackson returned to the Colorado Rockies for some late-season photography.

BAKERS PARK AND SULTAN MTN. August 29, 1874.
Albumin print on Hayden Survey mount.

"A view looking down the mouth of Arrastra Gulch.
The Animas [River] is here closely confined between
high walls of dark volcanic rocks, that are weathered
into many fantastic forms" (Jackson [1875] 1978, 69).
Courtesy Colorado Historical Society.

directly to where we wanted to go. The ground, wet and soft, and the steep trail, made it far from easy climbing. Most of the way we walked, leading our animals. At timber line we tied up, and fitting the different pack loads to our own shoulders, began clambering up over the rocks.

Clouds were scudding around us everywhere, completely covering the top of the mountain. After getting up about a thousand feet, we got into such a storm that we had no doubt as to the kind of weather we were likely to have for the rest of the day; so we retreated down the mountain, not stopping until we reached the previous night's camp at the foot. The wind and rain made everything most disagreeable. We spent the next hours, under an improvised tent, drying stockings and clothing. Our blankets got so wet that we did not have a very comfortable time during the night.

Morning opened with a promise of clearing weather. Mex, however, turned up missing; so we put our photographic outfit in knapsacks, hung them over the horns of our saddles, and started up the mountain again. It had cleared finely by the time we reached timber line. Here we tied up at the last bunch of trees and distributed our packs on our own shoulders as before. The climb was not difficult, just a long, steady pull upwards for three thousand feet. It was hard on Charlie, who was not accustomed to this sort of thing; but he stuck to it manfully, and though nearly played out, reached the top only a little way behind us.

The panorama of mountain peaks extending around us on every side was splendid. Sultan, being central in the San Juan group and partly isolated, gave us an advantageous viewpoint, although some of the more notable peaks were too distant for the best photographic effects. From the summit in about three hours I made fourteen negatives, sweeping nearly the whole horizon and including all the prominent peaks.

The day was fair but so cold and windy that Wilson worked with gloves, and despite a warm coat I was shivering most of the time. We got through and down to the foot of the mountain by four o'clock, tired and hungry. Little Mexico had not been found, so after getting something to eat, we packed the apparatus on the cook's horse and started for camp with Charlie walking. Our missing mule turned up just beyond Cement Creek, and we made a quick change of loads. The rest of the way we covered in faster time, but it was dark before we got back to Howardsville.

After this came the ten-day side trip to the Mesa Verde Cliff Ruins, described in Chapter Fifteen. Wilson and his party also had been across the range to the San Miguel River and returned to Bakers Park the same day we did. They were enthusiastic about the scenery over there and said I must get views of it by all means, before returning to Denver.

The season was late (September 20) for high mountain work, with heavy snowstorms likely to happen any day, and there was a 12,410-foot pass over the divide. I decided, however, to make the trip and started off next afternoon, taking Steve and Smart with two packs. Passing through Silverton, we turned to the right up Mineral Creek and camped in an aspen grove at the foot of a peak that Wilson advised me to ascend for the fine view to be had from it. The next morning we were up early for the mountain climb. A steep but fairly practicable route soon took us above timber line into the midst of a group of splendid peaks. But the wind was blowing a gale, and it was entirely too cold to think of working from the summits, so I confined myself to views at lower altitudes.

We passed another cold night among the aspens. A heavy coat of white frost covered everything as we started out in the early morning to cross the high divide. We passed first through a belt of spruce so thick that our packs got some hard jolts. Then, after an interval of open ground for a short distance, we got into another stretch of scrubby timber, where we had bad traveling. At length we emerged into the open above timber line. Rising rapidly over rocky slides between the towering flanks of mountain peaks, we reached the summit, where a magnificent view over the San Miguel Valley was spread beneath us. Near by a delightful little lake nestled among the barren rocks;[6] then came alternate belts of forest and grassy meadows leading to beautiful Trout Lake in the distance. The lofty peaks of the background were banded in lines of red, yellow, and gray volcanic rocks in pleasing contrast with the somber gray-green of the upper line of forest, which lower down was relieved by the brilliant yellows of the aspens.

We hurried on, eager to get to work. This required but little exertion, except to restrain a tendency to tumble heels over head down the steep trail. Skirting Trout Lake over grassy ridges, we passed beyond and camped by a rivulet far up the mountain on the opposite side, in order to command a general view overlooking the lake with its

THE PHOTOGRAPHIC DARK TENT ON THE SUMMIT OF SULTAN MOUNTAIN. August 31, 1874.
Copy of modern print from wet plate negative.

"The view from the summit was grand although a little too distant for my purposes. Spent about three hours and made 14 negatives, sweeping nearly all the entire panorama & taking in all the prominent peaks. Made some group pictures of the boys at work" (Jackson 1874a, August 31). Courtesy U.S. Geological Survey.

Sierra San Miguel. Date unknown. Type of print unknown.

The Photographic Division's camp commanded a view of
Trout Lake (first known as San Miguel Lake), with its
background of brilliantly colored peaks and of the pass they
came over from Baker's Park. This photograph was given the
date 1874 in the first edition of this book but both the Denver
Public Library and the Colorado Historical Society list this as
being taken between 1881 and 1890. The clouds show up
clearly which was generally not the case with the earlier
Hayden Survey photos. "The wet plate . . . was unduly
sensitive to blue and violet rays with the result that our skies
were either blank white, or in the case of a thin negative too
smudggy [sic]. . . . Once in a while . . . passably good cloud
effects were obtained on the wet plate due to favorable light
conditions, but more particularly to conditions in the collodion
and silver bath" (Jackson to Taft, November 30, 1933. William
Henry Jackson Collection. 1875-1942). Courtesy Denver
Public Library.

background of gorgeously colored peaks. There was barely time to make a few negatives, but they were not satisfactory, as increasing cloudiness made a dull, flat lighting.

As the sun went down, it began to rain, gradually turning to sleet. We had made
up our beds for the night beforehand, taking pains to get them as comfortable as possible, as we had no tent. A group of large spruce trees afforded some protection. The
animals were securely picketed on meadow lands some distance below camp. The
night was one of rain, sleet, and snow. Our fire, although well supplied with logs,
soon went out and no one cared to get out and replenish it. I was warm and comfortable, however, a heavy tarpaulin over my blankets making ample protection.

There were other things which were even more disturbing and which kept us
awake most of the night. First, a mountain lion came out on the rocks above our camp
and filled the air with shrill, blood-curdling cries. Next some wolves or coyotes could
be heard below us on the meadows where our animals were picketed, and we had
visions of cut ropes and of finding ourselves left without mounts.

The long night wore away, however, with no greater trouble than our fears.
When we stuck our heads out from under our blankets at daylight, it was a wintry
world we looked upon. Everything, ourselves included, was covered with a thick
mantle of snow—valleys, uplands, and mountain peaks. It was a damp, heavy snow,
and all available fuel was wet and soggy, making the starting of a fire a slow and
tedious task. Finally a few ounces of collodion from my chemical box helped us to
get a cheery blaze going.

After breakfast we got to work, first drying some of the camp equipage. My dark
box, which had been left overnight set up all ready for work, also had to be dried
out. Then we had to wait for the heavy clouds to rise from over the mountains. During the forenoon a few breaks occurred, clearing the range so that a general view
could be had. I made a few exposures, but it soon began storming again, putting a stop
to any further photographic work.

We decided that we had better pack up and get out as quickly as possible. It was
not a pleasant prospect to be snowed in on the wrong side of the range with our meager stock of supplies. As we started off, the sleet was falling fast. By the time we
reached the shore of the lake, it had turned to snow, which came so thick that we who
were behind could hardly see the leaders of our little party. This kept up until we

reached the foot of the steepest part of the ascent, when the clouds cleared away for a little while, revealing a scene of startling beauty and grandeur. Oh, that I had had a kodak, by means of which such passing effects could have been instantly secured!

Toiling upwards, we found the snow getting deeper and deeper until on the summit it was nearly knee-deep. The trail was so obscured that it was almost impossible to trace it, and we had to walk, leading our animals. In one way, however, the heavy snow proved advantageous. On the way over we had had to pick our steps carefully in the narrow trail that wound around and among the larger rock masses, but now these same rocks were so completely blanketed that we could walk over most of them with comparative ease, except for trudging through the deep snow.

We reached our former camp in the aspen grove just at dusk. A glorious fire was soon drying our clothing and blankets, and we passed a comfortable night.

Returning to our Bakers Park camp, we began preparations at once for the homeward journey. Everyone was eager to get away, particularly the two boys and the cook, who had been left behind while we were off on our side trips. We had the animals all newly shod, and sold all surplus provisions in order to make packs as light as possible for the hurried homeward trip.

Going back over Cunningham Pass was harder than coming in. The morning we left I sent the train on ahead with instructions to follow the new wagon road, while Ingersoll and I were to take the trail and do some photographing on the way. When we came to the point where the road left the trail, we saw that the packers were not making much progress. On some parts of the road the grade was steeper than on the trail, and the more heavily laden mules could not make it, or they slipped their packs in the effort and had to be frequently repacked. We therefore gave up our plan, in order to help the packers, for the two boys and the cook were of little assistance. One of us went ahead, leading each mule by halter strap, while two others, following behind, with shoulders under the pack boosted it up over the hardest places. It was stiff work for man and animals, but we finally got to the snow-covered summit a little before sunset, and then dropped down to a camping place at the foot of the hill before it was quite dark.

Passing rapidly down the Rio Grande, we came to Del Norte late one afternoon and camped at the bridge about three miles below.[7] In the neighborhood were several

~

Jackson and Ingersoll had gone ahead to take care of some business in the town of Del Norte. The rest of the train passed them. "[We] remained behind for an hour or so and then on our way down [to camp] came across Charlie our cook lying dead drunk in the road & the two boys trying to get him along. Could do nothing with him so we took his horse along with us and left him lying there to get over his stupor as best he could." The next morning "Charlie came wandering in, a pretty sorry looking individual and no doubt was feeling bad. He would have been only too glad for a little rest, but we had a long days ride before us, a full 40 miles across the hot sage brush plain of the San Luis Park & no water until we reached the slopes of the Sangre de Cristo [Mountains] on the other side. We had no ambulance and so he jogged along all day until late in the evening on his jaded bell horse & had ample time for repentance" (Jackson [1874] n.d., September 28 and 29).

~

The Survey entertains a guest at dinner. 1874. Albumin half- stereo print.

Jackson's pencil notations on the photo state "WHJ," showing his position in the upper right, and "Hayden," who is directly below him. Courtesy National Park Service/Scotts Bluff National Monument.

Mexican adobe shacks with cultivated fields about them. The crops had been harvested and the grain was lying on the threshing floors. It was nearly dark when the boys made camp, and the stock was turned out to graze on vacant fields near by. During the night they wandered away some distance and broke through the fence surrounding one of these threshing places, where the grain had been left on the ground in little heaps after the usual primitive Mexican fashion. This was a fine picnic for our hungry mules. They undoubtedly had a great time, not only in eating their fill of the garnered grain, but also in rolling around in what was left and scattering it over the floor again.

Steve was sent out early in the morning to bring in the stock. After being away nearly an hour, he returned to report that some Mexicans had corralled our whole bunch of animals and were holding them for the damage done to their grain. The owners were reenforced by local officials and a number of neighbors. A long parley ensued, ending finally by the payment of fifteen dollars to square the matter. The amount was exorbitant, but there was nothing else to do, as among so many Mexicans we were at too great a disadvantage.

When crossing San Luis Valley, Ingersoll and I struck out ahead of the train and reached San Luis Lake after sunset. Here we stopped at a lone cabin of a cattle ranch. Our host proved to be Lafayette Head, Lieutenant Governor of Colorado.[8] He owned a large horse and cattle ranch in the valley and this log cabin was one of the outlying stations for his herders. He happened to be there at this time looking after his interests.

The best feature of the place was a roaring blaze in the big fireplace. Supper, as well as breakfast, was of beef ribs, roasted on the coals before the fire, and black coffee—both taken straight without condiment or seasoning. With the aid of our saddle blankets, we made a fairly comfortable night of it.

At Canon City[9] I found a letter from Dr. Hayden, urging me to join his party at Colorado Springs as soon as possible. Leaving Ingersoll to pilot the party, I hurried on by train. The Doctor wanted me to join his party for a few days and make a series of studies of the working of the field parties, personal groups, and other details. Three days later, when the packs came up, we joined the Hayden party in Monument Park, where we made nearly a hundred negatives, not only of the special groupings

JOHN, THE COOK BAKING SLAPJACKS. October 6, 1874.
Copy of modern print from wet plate negative.

The "slapjack" was added later to the negative, as the long exposure time would not have allowed for its being frozen in midair. There are other examples of Jackson using his artistic skills to alter or add detail to his negatives throughout the Hayden Survey period. Courtesy U.S. Geological Survey.

STUDY OF PICTURESQUE PINE AND CASTELLATED ROCKS.
October 6–8, 1874. Albumin print on Hayden Survey mount.

William H. Holmes, artist and geologist with the Survey from 1872 to 1878, is pictured. The "castellated rocks . . . [are] delicately tinted, creamy-white sandstone, weathering into horizontal lines, presenting, from a distance especially, quite a castellated appearance" (Jackson [1875] 1978, 68). The photographer was north of Colorado Springs near Monument, Colorado. This was a return visit as Jackson photographed here in 1873 (page 101). Courtesy American Heritage Center.

THE TRAVOIS AT FISHER'S RANCH. October 12, 1874.
Albumin print.

On the last day of the season for the Survey, Jackson, "Mr. and Mrs. Shanks and Mr. and Mrs. Stevenson went out to Fishers Ranch where a device [a travois] was rigged up to represent the apparatus by which Mrs. Shanks was hauled out of Sick Camp in the Elk Mountains. Dark rainy and stormy, but succeeded in getting two poor negatives" (Jackson 1874a, October 12). Jackson's "reconstructed diary account differs from this diary entry, stating it was "young Shanks stricken with mountain fever" who was hauled out on the travois (Jackson [1874] n.d., October 12). The poor quality of this print is due to rainy weather that dulled the light and added a significant amount of exposure time to the wet plate. This was the final use of the camera for the season. Courtesy Museum of New Mexico.

required, but also of the monument rocks all along the foothills from Colorado Springs south of the divide, to Perry Park on the north side.

There I took leave of all the boys and, with a pack mule carrying my working outfit, "lit out" for Denver, thirty-eight miles distant. It required precious little time to unpack, turn in the outfit, and call it the end of a season's work.

Chapter Fourteen

Adventures with a Larger Camera

June 1875–October 1875

The main purpose of my 1875 expedition was to follow up my work among the cliff ruins in '74 by another trip to the Southwest, as will be related in Chapter Sixteen. I could not, however, pass through the mountainous San Juan region again without paying particular attention to its outstanding scenic features. On my first trip I had used only a 5 × 8 camera, but I had been so deeply impressed with the snow-clad peaks, rugged canyons, and lovely lakes and valleys that I thought so small a picture wholly inadequate to their proper representation. My ambition ran to something larger even than the 11 × 14 plates of '73 and I finally decided upon a 20 × 24 outfit as the extreme limit as to size, which I could safely venture.

When one realizes what this meant—not only the packing of so large a camera (not the compact, folding ones of today) with the necessary plates and chemicals over hazardous mountain trails, but also the difficulties in manipulation of wet plates magnified many times—it is a wonder to me even now that I had the temerity to undertake it.

Nowadays bromide papers furnish ready means of enlargement to almost any extent from small negatives. In the seventies, however, such papers were not in general use, and large photographs were made from equally large negatives. I have mentioned elsewhere that there were no ready-made dry plates at this time and also no prepared printing papers; the photographer purchased plain paper and sensitized it himself as required.

My first try-out of the large camera was not made until we were well up on the Rio Grande on our way to Bakers Park. Making a detour over to the Lake Fork of the Gunnison, we pitched camp on the shore line of the beautiful Lake San Cristoval [Cristobal]. Here we set up the dark tent, and after some unexpected mishaps I finally got a satisfactory negative.

~

The order of events for the 1875 season is somewhat difficult to reconstruct due to the way the first edition of this book is organized. The men started south from Denver in 1875, going back to the Silverton area and the San Juan Mountains to photograph with the "big camera." Leaving supplies and this larger camera behind, they retraced their 1874 footsteps into the La Plata region in southeast Colorado. The focus became anthropological and archaeological as the party headed west down the San Juan River, south up the Chinle Wash, and west to the Hopi pueblos. Returning to the San Juan Mountains, Jackson did further work with the large camera. He did not arrive back in Denver until October 13, after more than four months in the field.

~

The bulky camera was used only for one season. It caused numerous problems. It required a larger dark tent, more chemicals, and very large glass plates. The whole outfit was extremely difficult to transport. The results were not worth the effort. "Explanatory note: —For the 1875 season's photographic work I was outfitted for stereoscopic, 5 × 8, and 20 × 24 sizes of plates. The 20 × 24 was the largest camera ever taken into the field by pack mule transportation . . ." (Jackson [1875] n.d., June 24).

~

THE BIG CAMERA IN PERIL. 1929. Copy of image from
The Pioneer Photographer.

Jackson was on the way to photograph Uncompahgre
Mountain. The sketch shows Old Mag in distress with
the bulky "big camera."

The next subject was to be a close-up view of Uncompahgre Mountain, one of
the highest on the northern flanks of the San Juan group. Taking Bill Whan to assist
with the two pack mules, we began climbing the foothills about two miles below
Lake City. It was a stiff climb and Old Mag had a hard time of it with her bulky, top-
heavy pack. At one place, in attempting to get by a tree that obstructed the trail, she
lost her balance, and falling backwards off the trail, was saved from destruction by
lodging against other trees. On the steep hillside it seemed impossible at first to get
her up without incurring the danger of rolling farther down the mountain; but while
I checked any tendency that way by a firm hold on the halter strap, Bill finally got the
lash ropes loosened, the camera carried to where it could be repacked, and Maggie
on her feet again, with no greater damage than the delay. It was demure Old Mag
that always came in for the hardest knocks because of her assignment to photographic work.

We made a camp at timber line about noon, and after a hasty lunch staked out our
animals securely, as we thought, and then went off with our guns to prospect for
viewpoints and incidentally to bag some game. I finally found a location for a near
view of the peak to which we could take the pack mule. This was at an elevation of
about 11,000 feet, so that its whole height of 14,286 [14,309] feet did not seem so
very much higher.

Returning late in the afternoon to our timber-line camp, I found that Bill had
brought in a fine mountain sheep; but as our animals in the meantime had pulled up
stakes and vamoosed, he had gone in pursuit. I followed their trail half way down
the mountain and then, concluding that both Bill and the stock had gone all the way
to the lake camp, I went back to my lonely bivouac to await their return. After getting supper, I built a big fire, hung the sheep well out of the reach of prowling animals, and rolled up in my blanket for a good sleep.

Bill was back with our mules and horses before I was through with breakfast.
The morning, however, was cloudy, and by the time we had reached our view location a troublesome wind was blowing across the high plateaus. The dark tent was
set up, plate prepared, and an exposure made, but without success, for the wind
shook the camera so that I got only a blurred image, due mainly to the long exposure required, as instantaneous work with wet plates was impossible.

With a storm impending, we cached the apparatus under the rocks and retreated to our timber-line camp. A long dreary afternoon of drizzling rain and fog dragged along while we waited for a change in the weather. This was followed by a bright, clear morning that promised good work—and a celebration as well, for it was the Fourth of July.

Anxious to take advantage of early morning conditions, I went on ahead to set up dark tent and camera while Bill followed later with the animals. There was time for but one exposure; the wind was rising, and before we had finished packing up, clouds were drifting over the peak with intermittent flurries of snow. With our main object accomplished in securing a good negative, we made quick time in getting down to our lakeside camp.

No more large negatives were made until after our return from the far southwest limits of our trip among the old ruins. From Bakers Park, Sultan Mountain was photographed, although we had to wait several days, with tent and camera set up, for rains to cease. Then Mag was called upon again to make the hard climb over the

INTERIOR OF THE DARK TENT.
Circa 1929. Ink wash sketch.

Preparing a 20 × 24 plate for exposure in the camera. "For [darkroom work] I had a tent, built on the same lines as the one I used in 1873, but on a proportionally larger scale, and for the silver sensitizing bath, a wooden tray" (Jackson 1926, 21). This bulky tent was necessary in order to accommodate the larger-sized glass plates and chemical bath trays used in 1875. Courtesy Brigham Young University.

HEAD OF ASTRA [ARRASTRA] GULCH. July 11, 1875. Copy of modern print from wet plate negative.

Although this ravine looks pristine in this view, areas of it had been heavily mined. When visiting there the previous year Jackson describes the mining activity: "The wrecks of the old arrastras [small circular ore crushers, usually operated with mules or horses] that were put in some twelve or fourteen years ago . . . have given the gulch its name. It was also worked in that time for placers, but with no success. It is now more favorably known through its silver mines, which are among the richest of this region" (Jackson [1875] 1978, 69). Courtesy U.S. Geological Survey.

CAMP OF THE MINERS. July 12, 1875.
Copy of modern print from wet plate negative.

The miners were "of the North Star and Mountaineer lodes, on King Solomon Mountain, above Cunningham Gulch" (Jackson [1875] 1978, 77). Courtesy U.S. Geological Survey.

TRAIL IN THE SAN JUAN MTS. July 13, 1875 (Jackson 1875b). Albumin print on Hayden Survey mount.

We "started up the trail for the summit of King Solomon Mountain [from the camp of the miners seen above]. Within half a mile of the camp we came to a place where the trail had been blasted out of the perpendicular face of a spur of the mountain deep enough for the burros with bags of ore, but hardly commodious enough for our larger animals. We finally got around however by taking off the packs & saddles and compelling the animals to crouch down and crowding them through" (Jackson [1875] n.d., July 13). Courtesy American Heritage Center.

13,000-foot pass[1] to the San Miguel for larger negatives of Trout Lake, as the smaller photographs of our former trip failed to do justice to this region.

We spent a day locating a high waterfall, said to be in the canyon below the lake. We came upon one, which, though rather picturesque, did not measure up to the descriptions that had been given. Just as I had finished making a large negative of it, one of the packers reported that he had found another fall, larger and much finer than the one just photographed. Going down the canyon, I found it so much better that I decided I must have a view of it.

The day was waning and we must hurry. While I was cleaning off and preparing a plate, all the others joined in getting the camera down into the gorge and up to the falls. I followed later with the plate holder strapped on my back. I had to go nearly half a mile and then make a precipitous descent of some four hundred feet down into the gorge in which the fall is located, and then follow up stream over the rocks to a favorable point of view. The exposure was made all right; but as a result of the effort to get down and back in the shortest possible time, when I opened my plate holder in the dark tent I found that the plate had slipped from the corners and, rubbing against the side of the holder, was completely ruined. I developed it, however, and found the exposure had been all right. This was about the longest time I had ever had a plate in transit from sensitizing to development. The back of the plate had been thickly covered with wet paper and the holder wrapped in wet towels. My satisfaction in noting how well the plate kept was some compensation for the failure of the picture itself.

It was too late to make another exposure so we returned to camp. Signs of gathering storms warned us that our work here was about done for. It was already late in September and we escaped another snowstorm "by the skin of our teeth," as snow began falling heavily as we crossed the divide on our way back to Bakers Park.[2]

On the long outward journey from Denver we had used a wagon as far as Bakers Park for carrying the greater part of our outfit, as two mules could pull more than seven or eight could pack, and make better time. Getting out of the park with this wagon was quite another matter, as we were to leave by another pass than the one by which we entered. For three or four miles before reaching the summit at the head of the Animas River, we passed over rock slides by a narrow trail, impossible for a

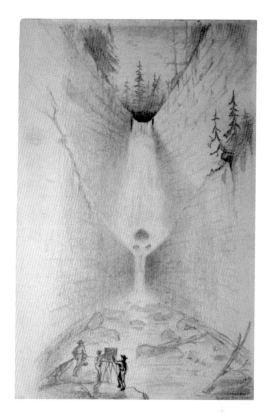

FALLS AT RIO SAN MIGUEL. n.d. Pencil drawing.

A page in William Jackson's *Diary* (1875b, page following the September 20 entry) has a sketch done on site depicting Mystic Falls. That diary sketch was the basis for this later drawing. Note the photographers with the 20″ × 24″ camera. Jackson regretted losing this photograph. He went back in the 1880s and duplicated his earlier effort as his first negative had been destroyed before it could be developed in 1875. Courtesy National Park Service/Scotts Bluff National Monument.

⁓

Because money and food were short, Jackson sent some of his men home early. "With Jack [packer] I take three pack animals, my two photo outfits & as much grub as we can get. . . . It will take us fr. 10 days to two weeks . . . . Gave the other party $5, and keep 4 for myself" (Jackson 1875b, October 4). The packer, Jack, had joined the party late in the season after Bill Whan and Bob Mitchell had a falling out.

⁓

wagon, so that we were obliged to take it apart and pack it across on the mules. Thereafter we had fairly good roads, over Cochetopa Pass into San Luis Valley, and then to the upper Arkansas. Here I divided my party, three of them, with the wagon, going direct to Denver, while I retained two pack mules and one of the packers as an assistant, for further work with the big camera outfit.

Crossing over to the head of Blue River by way of Hoosier Pass and then over Argentine Pass, we photographed Grays Peak, Georgetown, and other mountain views. It was rather a hard trip for the two of us, where I was assistant packer as well as photographer; but it was replete with incidents that might add to the pictures already drawn of the difficulties that beset the pioneer photographer at every turn.

Crossing the mountains from Georgetown to Idaho Springs, where we first met the railroad, we transferred our pack loads to the cars, and then driving the two mules ahead of us, raced them into Denver, fifty-two miles distant, in time to clean up for an early dinner.

Chapter Fifteen

Discovery of the Cliff Ruins

September 1874

The Mesa Verde, a green table-land, named from its forests of cedar and piñon pine, is an elevated plateau of about one hundred and twenty square miles in the southwest corner of Colorado. The Mancos River runs through one portion of it. Along this river and in its side canyons are many cliff dwellings and other remains of an ancient people.

That throughout the Southwest there were extensive ruins of "cities that died" long before the arrival of the first Spanish explorer was a well-known fact. This Mesa Verde group, the most remarkable of all, however, was entirely unknown except to nomadic Indians and a few prospectors until, with my roving photographic division of the United States Geological Survey, I passed through it in September, 1874.[1] Ernest Ingersoll one of my companions on this trip, wrote the first account of these ruins, as seen from Mancos Canyon, for the *New York Tribune* of November 3, 1874.[2] This article and the reports made by the Survey, including contributions by W. H. Holmes in 1875, were all that was known of them until fourteen years later, when the Cliff Palace and similar ruins were discovered in the more remote canyons. These were so remarkable from every point of view as to attract world-wide attention. Ultimately, for their better care and protection, they were all included in the Mesa Verde National Park.

Space will not permit detailed descriptions of these old ruins. There is plenty of good literature on the subject, much of which can be had from the National Park Service at Washington for the asking. All that we shall be concerned with here is the adventure of their discovery and the pleasure of photographing them.

On our way to Bakers Park in '74, I met a former acquaintance, who gave an entirely new direction to my investigations for the remainder of that season. We had

Aerial Habitation. 1876. Lithographic print.

Jackson was the first American explorer to document many of the prehistoric Pueblo ruins, based on his 1874 explorations. Courtesy National Park Service/Scotts Bluff National Monument.

⁓

The exploration of prehistoric cultural remains was short and hurried. For two weeks the Survey split up to accomplish different goals. Jackson's Photographic Division "did not get away until noon, the whole forenoon being spent in shoeing the stock we take with us, sorting out the plentiful supply of grub we had just received, and storing everything not needed in a little wickyup [*sic*] under a tree. [A. D.] Wilson [topographer] did the same also as he is off on a side trip likewise & expects to return about the same time we do. Left the two boys [Frank Smart and C. H. Anthony] with the cook [Charley] in charge of camp & the 8 animals we do not use —taking with us three light packs only" (Jackson [1874] n.d., September 2). Fast travel and long drives were possible because the party carried very little gear. "We had three pack mules. Mexico carrying the photo outfit. A little sot of a mule but a good climber and could jog along at a lively clip without shaking up the baths and plates too much. 'Muggins' and 'Kitty' carried the grub outfit & blankets and as both were reduced to bare necessities only, their packs were light also & could be pushed along as fast as we cared to [travel]" (Ibid., September 9–15, 1874). On September 17, fifteen days after Jackson's anthropological explorations in the Four Corners region began, he arrived back in camp two hours behind Wilson's surveying party.

⁓

gone into camp early in the afternoon at the Jennison ranch, as already mentioned, for the purpose of doing some photographing in the neighborhood. While the boys were taking off the packs, a train of six or seven burros and three men came up and camped near by. As they passed us, we were greatly amused at the comical appearance of one of the men sitting astride a little burro, with another man following with a stick, trying to keep the pair up with the rest. Shortly after this burro train went into camp near by, this same man came over to our camp, and I immediately recognized in him an old friend, E. H. Cooper of Omaha.

After supper, grouped around a generous camp fire, we talked long into the night. Cooper explained that he belonged to a party of miners working a placer claim on the La Plata River and that he and his companions had been to Del Norte for supplies. As he seemed to be acquainted with this region, we were of course much interested in his descriptions. He told us of the Mesa Verde, only a short distance from their camp, where he said there were cliff dwellings and other ruins more wonderful than any yet discovered. Understanding in a general way the nature of our work, he advised us to go over to the La Plata and said that he would show us something to photograph that would be well worth while. This proposition was so attractive that before we turned in that night we had decided to make the trip, although we had not intended in going beyond Bakers Park.

Cooper had not seen any of the cliff dwellings himself, but got his information from John Moss, head of their mining operations. Moss, he explained, was the "hy-as-ty-ee and high-muck-a-muck" of the La Plata region who had been all over the Southwest from the San Juan [River] to California and knew the location of all the principal ruins.

A few days later I made up a party for this trip, consisting of Ingersoll and myself with the two packers, Steve [Hovey] and Bob [Mitchell], and three light packs. Taking the Bear Creek Trail to the right of Sultan Mountain, we overtook and passed Cooper and his outfit the next day. They had had a hard time of it on the trail to the left of Sultan. Both trails were said to be so bad that, whichever one was taken, the traveler would regret not taking the other.[3]

At Castle Springs[4] we met a group of men who had just left Animas Valley, having been warned away by Indians. In their haste they had left their belongings, besides their houses and growing crops. Passing rapidly through a beautiful country, we came to another group of men, settlers from below, who also had been ordered out by the Indians for being on their reservation. We camped that night on Hermosa Creek in Animas Valley. Some deserted ranches near by invited a foraging expedition, with the result that we filled our saddlebags with green corn, potatoes, turnips, and enough other vegetables to make a bountiful supper. The few ranchers we met said they were going to remain and see what would happen; they did not intend being frightened away from their possessions by the redskins.

Soon after leaving the Animas on our way to the La Plata, we were overtaken by Moss himself, jog-trotting along on a little roan pony with the evident purpose of catching up with us. He said Cooper had told him of our expedition, and then explained briefly what we might expect to find. He also promised his cooperation and possibly his company in our investigations. Moss, at this time, was apparently between thirty-five and forty years old, of medium height and slender, with long dark hair flowing over his shoulders. He was reserved in manner and speech on first acquaintance, but we found him later to be a jolly good fellow in camp life.

Regarding the Indian situation, he said there was a good deal of dissatisfaction among the Southern Utes over a recent treaty by which the boundaries of their reservation had been changed. By the terms of the treaty they not only had been excluded from the San Juan mining regions, but had suffered the loss of their best hunting grounds. A further grievance was that the promised awards in compensation had not been made. As a consequence, they were ordering off all white men from their part of the reservation. They had a particular animosity for surveyors. No actual hostilities had yet occurred, but among the whites there was much unrest and apprehension, for there was no telling what the irresponsible young bucks might do.

Moss explained his own security in this threatening situation by saying that when he had brought in his party of miners a year earlier, he made his own treaty with the head chiefs of this region. By this treaty he had acquired mining rights over twenty-five square miles along the La Plata, through the payment of a liberal annuity in sheep, horses, and some other things. This purchase had placed him and his companions on friendly terms with all the Indians of the region.

JOHN MOSS—OUR GUIDE TO THE CLIFF RUINS. September 6, 1874. Copy of modern print from wet plate negative.

"The Captain is the hyastyie of this region, a great man among both whites and Indians, & I think the pioneer mover in all that is going on in this region. He speaks all the Indian languages of the region, Mexican, etc. is an old Californian of 25 yrs experience & brot [sic] with him to start this camp, 17 men from Lower California. He made a sort of treaty or purchase with the Indians by which he acquired 25 sq. m. [miles] of territory about the La Plata Mountains, paying them 60 horses partly, I think" (Jackson 1874a, September 5). Courtesy U.S. Geological Survey.

MERRITT'S RANCH. September 15, 1874.
Copy of modern print from wet plate negative.

The log and stone ranch house was in Mancos Valley, Colorado; the only house in the San Juan basin west of the Animas River. We "got into Merritts just after dark. The light showing thru the chinks of the ranch made a cheerful picture. Threw off the packs at the door and got supper in partnership. Merrit[t], who keeps the ranch, is one of the same crowd of Californians as the La Plata [miners]. He has several acres under cultivation & just now is bewailing a frost which came & nipped his corn" (Jackson 1874a, September 8). The photograph was taken on the return trip. Courtesy U.S. Geological Survey.

Moss's camp consisted merely of a few small tents and some brush wikiups. The mining operations were confined to a ditch line for carrying water to a gravel bench below, which was supposed to yield enough free gold to make it pay. Ingersoll and I were given claims on this bar, but it didn't mean anything to us in the way of dividends.

These operations were financed by California capitalists, with Moss as their representative. Just at this time they were all worked up over an election about to be held for county or township officers of the newly acquired territory. Moss, who had in the meantime arranged to go with us, was one of the candidates and had to remain until all votes were in. To expedite matters, all our party voted with the miners, there being no residence requirements, and as soon as this formality was over we started the packers off on the first stage of our journey. The rest of us waited until Moss closed the polls. Then we made a rapid ride over to Merritt's ranch on the Mancos,[5] where we put up for the night. Merritt was one of Moss's outfit who had taken up a ranch site on the river, built a log cabin, and was experimenting in raising vegetables.

Our little company left the hospitable Merritt ranch the next morning, eagerly expectant as to possible discoveries. To this was added a spice of adventure because of the uncertain temper of some of the irresponsible Indians we were likely to meet. As we rode away on the trail down the broad, open valley of the upper Mancos on a crisp and bracing September morning, we had with us "Cap" Moss as guide. His knowledge of the country and its wandering tribes was of great service. Ingersoll and I, with the two packers, represented the Survey. Cooper, the sixth member, was included on account of former acquaintanceship and because he had brought us to the La Plata camp. He was rather indolent and content to follow along behind with the packers. Loquacious and full of wonderful stories, mainly concerning himself, he furnished most of the amusement and banter around the camp fire after the day's work was over.

The discovery of the first cliff dwelling that came anywhere near our expectations was made unexpectedly. The day's ride into the deepest part of the Mancos Canyon had revealed nothing more than surface indications. These consisted of mounds and broken pottery, and a few small cave ruins here and there along the trail, just enough to sustain interest in making further discoveries. After supper that evening as we were warming our backs against a generous sagebrush fire, we fell to speculating about the cliff dwellings that had not been seen thus far, but which were to be found, Moss said, near the top of the canyon walls, at this point about eight hundred feet high. There was some joking with Steve and Bob about carrying the photographic boxes up to these almost inaccessible heights. Moss asserted that there were cliff houses right above camp and that it was going to be a hard climb to get up there in the morning.

Steve, interested, wanted to be shown just where they were, and Moss by a sweep of his arm indicated the highest part of the canyon. Steve scanned the heights for a few minutes and declared he had found one of them anyway, right up there near the top. This was a great surprise to Moss, who had been joking all along. Sure enough, closer inspection into the dusky shadows of the western walls of the canyon revealed the square lines and small dots indicating a house with windows, sandwiched between layers of sandstone far up the canyon walls.

Everyone was on the jump at once and started out to investigate. The first five or six hundred feet of the climb was steep but not difficult. It brought us to the foot of a vertical wall of rock about two hundred feet high, in the face of which, some fifty feet above its base, was a shallow eave occupied by a neatly built, two-story cliff dwelling.

Ingersoll and I were the only ones who persisted in the climb right up to the ruin. The others, realizing they would have it to do all over again in the morning, made a brief survey from below and returned to camp. It was getting dark, but we were determined to see all there was of it before quitting. I was eager to find out how it was to be photographed, and Ingersoll wanted first-hand impressions for his articles.

How to get up to the little house puzzled us for a while. We found an old dead tree, however, which we propped up against the rock, and climbing this, reached some ancient handholds and footholds cut into the rock, which made it comparatively easy to scramble up the rest of the way. Thus we finally stood face to face with the Two-Story House—our first discovery. It was a glorious view, from this height, over the surrounding canyon walls, while far below us in the deepening shadows our camp fire glimmered like a bright little star.

Next morning, by tacking back and forth across the steep slopes, we got Mexico with the photographic pack to the foot of the wall under the cliff house. Sending one

CLIFF RUIN, MANCOS CAÑON, COLORADO. September 10, 1874. Albumin print on Hayden Survey mount.

Our first discovery—the Two-Story Cliff House in Mancos Canyon, with John Moss and Ernest Ingersoll. "A two-story house of hewn stone, built in a narrow crevice of the sandstone mesa 800 feet above the valley at its feet. It is in a fair state of preservation, the overhanging rock protecting it from the weather. The ground-floor shows a front room about 6 by 9 feet square, and back of it two smaller ones. The stories were a little less than 6 feet in height; the flooring which formally separated them has decayed or been removed. Inside, the walls of the front rooms of each floor have been plastered with a fine adobe cement, painted with red and banded with white, giving them quite a finished appearance. In front a sort of esplanade has been cleaned out from the rock, some 20 feet long and 10 broad, the only level spot about the place" (Jackson [1875] 1978, 71). Courtesy Museum of New Mexico.

of the men up ahead with a rope, the rest of us found it an easy matter to follow with the apparatus. I was soon busy with my plates. It was an interesting experience, making these photographs of the habitations of a people that had long since passed away.

We were naturally eager to make discoveries of other cliff dwellings. As everyone lent a hand in camp work and packing, we were generally off on the trail quite early, frequently before sunrise. By fast traveling we made long drives, despite many diversions for investigations and photographing; but we did not go up the side canyons, where more important ruins were found later.

On the fourth day of our trip, at Pegasus Springs[6] at the head of the McElmo [Creek], we got a late start, where it was particularly desired to make an early one. This was due to the wanderings of our animals. Usually they were tired enough to remain near camp, if water and feed were sufficient. Sometimes a few of them were hobbled or picketed, but wherever we felt they could be trusted, we preferred to let them run loose, for it was but a scanty picking they got at the best.

So this morning, with the prospect of a long, hot ride down the canyon, we had breakfast disposed of before sun-up. While the rest of us gathered up the camp outfit,

MANCOS CANYON NEAR ITS OUTLET TO THE SAN JUAN VALLEY. September 11, 1874. Albumin print.

Near the top of the bluffs at right, cliff dwellings were found. "In the high bluff [upper right], are some of the most curious and unique habitations yet seen. While jogging along under this bluff, fully 1,000 feet in height, and admiring its bold outlines and brilliant coloring, one of our party, sharper-eyed than the rest, descried, away up near the top, perfect little houses, sandwiched in among the crevices of the horizontal strata of rock of which the bluff was composed. While busy photographing, two of the party started up to scale the height, and inspect this lofty abode. By penetrating a side-cañon some little ways, a gradual slope was found, that carried them to the summit of the bluff. Now, the trouble was to get down to the house, and this was accomplished only by crawling along a ledge about 20 inches in width, and not tall enough for more than a creeping position. In momentary peril of life, for the least mistake would precipitate him down the whole of this dizzy height, our adventurous seeker after knowledge crept along the ledge until the broader platform was reached, upon which the most perfect of the houses alluded to, stands. The ledge ended with the house, which is built out flush with its outer edge. . . . The masonry is as firm and solid as when first constructed, the inside being finished with exceptional care. . . . The position of these houses . . . is near the summit, just above the most precipitous portion of the bluff, generally at a height from 600 to 800 feet above the level of the cañon" (Jackson in Hayden 1876, 375). Courtesy Museum of New Mexico.

Steve went out to bring in the stock, which was supposed to be somewhere along the narrow strip of moisture and scanty grass below the springs. The packing up was soon done, but no mules or horses were in sight. Finally, after an hour of impatient waiting, we saw Steve coming up the canyon in the far distance, accompanied by an Indian, but with no animals. Moss and I ran down to meet them. Steve reported his failure to find any trace of the herd. The Indian, who said he was the father of the Capitan of the Weminuchis,[7] told Moss that our man did not know how to follow a trail and that our animals had left this valley and had gone up a northern branch leading towards the mountains.

Moss's familiarity with Ute language enabled him to get all the information that the Indian was disposed to give in regard to the stock. He learned also there was a small party of Indians camped below. We surmised they might have had something to do with the disappearance, in hope of later picking up strays from the bunch. However, we accepted his protestations of good faith and sent him up to our camp with Steve, while Moss and I struck out at once to pick up the trail. A mile below we found where it branched off to the right. High up on top of the mesa overlooking

CAVE DWELLINGS NEAR THE FORTIFIED ROCK ON THE MCELMO. September 13, 1874. Albumin print on Hayden Survey mount.

"A ruined town on the Hovenweep, a tributary of the San Juan lying just within Colorado, occupying a prominent rocky bluff overlooking the unusually dry bed of the creek. It consisted of a solid mass of small houses not more than about six by eight feet in diameter, arranged in a semicircle, the convex side flush with the edge of the rocky bluff, and inaccessible, while the concave side, which was depressed like an amphitheater, was occupied by much lower and less important buildings, now almost unrecognizable" (Jackson [1875] 1978, 72). Courtesy Colorado Historical Society.

this part of the canyon, we heard, but could not see, Indians calling or signaling in the long-drawn-out, far-reaching voice peculiar to them—whether to guide us or to direct others of their own party, we could not determine.

Following the trail on a jog trot, or running, as our endurance or the nature of the country permitted, we met two young bucks with their horses well loaded down with skins. They said they were on their way to the Navajo country to trade and intended stopping at our spring—the only water in that vicinity. They assured us that if we did not find our animals they would help in the search after they had had a little rest. We trotted on, keeping up a rather stiff pace, passing the dry Five Mile Spring and then coming to a big bend in the canyon. Moss made a cut-off across, while I followed the trail around, and when we met at the foot of the last hill leading up to the Mancos-Dolores divide,[8] we found the animals all together under a tree, whisking their tails in contented indolence.

We had traveled five or six miles in our roundabout course, but by taking a bee-line cut-off over the hills, we returned in half the distance. Mounting bareback, with trail ropes for bridles, we rushed our little band over the hills at a lively clip, getting back to the camp about ten o'clock—to find it full of Indians, all on horseback. The Capitan himself was among them—a venerable, gray-headed man. The others, with the exception of the one we met first, were young bucks on their way to the Navajo reservation.

They were good-naturedly respectful and did but little begging. The old Capitan wanted to know what we were doing down here, and when the nature of our work was explained to him, they all laughed boisterously, not comprehending how anyone could be interested in these mounds and piles of old stones.

After all these delays and diversions we set off for the Hovenweep Wash, now known as Yellow Jacket [Canyon] and included in the Hovenweep National Monument.[9] This was the western limit of our expedition. The ride was a long one and the sun, beating down into the dry and barren wash of the McElmo, made it most uncomfortably warm and sultry. Owing to the lateness in getting started, we did not attempt any photographic work, deferring that until the return trip; but we noted everything of interest as we went along.

One stop only was made and that was for water, late in the afternoon, at a place where the trail left the McElmo to make a cut-off across the mesas to the Hovenweep. We expected to find running water here, but the bed of the wash was as dry as an old bone. Moss said water could be found by digging. We had a shovel in one of the packs and the boys took turns digging. Water was struck at a depth of about three feet, but the sand caved in so fast that we could not get more than a cupful at a time. After taking a drink all around ourselves, we filled our hats with water and gave each one of the animals a taste, at least. While the digging was going on, they had stood around whinnying in eager expectancy and were quite appreciative, apparently, of our efforts to afford them some relief.

On the return trip from the Hovenweep we were three days getting back to the La Plata. It was a busy time for all of us, making photographs and doing some digging around the ruins. In going from Pegasus Springs to the Mancos, Ingersoll got interested in looking for fossils and fell behind until the rest of the party was out of sight. He failed to follow our trail and got on another one. After spending most of the night in Lost Canyon, he finally took the back track till he picked up our trail again[10] and rejoined us at Merritt's ranch a little after sunrise the next day.

After making a few negatives of the ranch, we "lit out" at a rapid pace for the La Plata, reaching there just before dark. The miners had moved down from the upper camp and were making a new one for the winter—the ditch having been brought down to that point. Before parting with Moss and his companions, we talked over plans for meeting them again next year for further explorations among the ancient cliff dwellings.[11] We reached our home camp in Bakers Park the next day, taking the trail to the east of Sultan Mountain, which we found not so bad as reported.

On our way through this picturesque region we passed several beautiful lakes. The views down into the canyon of the Animas were particularly fine, while beyond it the quartzite peaks towered over all majestically. The outstanding feature of this trip, however, was the success of our search for ancient cliff dwellings and the photographs we had obtained, revealing to the world these "cities that died."

OLD TOWER NEAR THE MCELMO. September 11–13, 1874. Albumin print on Hayden Survey mount.

"Watch-tower on the Mancos [the incorrect name given in Jackson's catalogue of photographs]. This is a circular tower, 10 feet in diameter, built upon a rock some 12 feet in height, with perfectly smooth perpendicular faces, rendering the superstructure inaccessible except by ladder. Occupying a bench half-way up the side of a cañon, it commands an old deeply-worn trail winding up past it to the plateau above" (Jackson [1875] 1978, 72). John Moss, guide, can be seen directly below and to the left of the tower. Courtesy Andrew Smith Gallery.

THE PHOTOGRAPHIC DIVISION OF THE GEOLOGICAL SURVEY. 1875. Type of print unknown.

Standing, left to right: Harry Lee, guide; W. H. Jackson; and Bill Whan, packer. Sitting: Bob Mitchell, packer; E. A. Barber, naturalist; and William Shaw, cook. "Barber, in a quite informal way, represented the *New York Times.* But on the rolls of the survey his name was followed by 'naturalist.' For some reason that never became entirely clear to me all newspaper men, as well as any other persons who had no specific qualifications, were carried as naturalists. They never seemed to mind, and I suppose it gave the Department of the Interior some vague satisfaction . . ." (Jackson [1940] 1994, 237). Courtesy National Park Service/Grand Teton National Park.

Chapter Sixteen

In the Land of the Cliff Dwellers

July 1875–August 1875

In summing up the operations of the United States Geological Survey for 1875, Dr. Hayden referred at some length to the work of the Photographic Division in its brief side-trip exploration of the Mesa Verde the previous year and the general interest in the subject created thereby.

"The first trip proving so successful," his report reads, "Mr. Jackson was dispatched again this season with instructions to ascertain, as far as possible, the extent and distribution of these ruins north of the present Moqui [Hopi] pueblos. Associated with him in the enterprise was Mr. E. A. Barber, naturalist and special correspondent of *The New York Times.* A guide, two packers, and a cook constituted the whole party. With six weeks' supplies, the party started from Parrott City, on the head of the Rio La Plata,[1] August twenty-seventh, the general course being down the Rio San Juan to the de Chelle,[2] up that to near Fort Defiance,[3] and then over to the seven Moqui 'cities.' Returning, they crossed the San Juan at the mouth of the de Chelle and traveled northward to midway between the Sierras Abajo [Abajo Mountains] and La Sal Mountains, and then returned to the starting point across the heads of the canyons which run southward to the San Juan."

When we arrived at the La Plata, we found the miners had moved down from their camp of last year to Parrott City, where there were three partly finished small frame houses, in one of which Moss was busily engaged in preparations to leave for San Francisco. On learning our plans, he regretted very much that he could not go with us, but recommended Harry Lee as a guide. Lee had been with him on several trips over the region of our proposed route.

An immediate concern, however, was about supplies for the continuation of our trip. We expected to find them here, but they had not arrived. Moss said he had some

bull teams on the road with supplies for his camp, and a few days before he had sent men with burros to meet them and bring back a portion of the goods in advance of the slower moving oxen. Nothing had been heard of our supply teams. Cap Moss was very friendly and offered to share with us whatever he had until our train came in. He had a large flock of sheep and told us to come for mutton whenever we liked.

Our anxiety was shared by Holmes, who arrived at the La Plata camp with his party about the same time we did. He was making a geological survey of this region and at the same time paying particular attention to its archaeology, a field in which he later became preeminent.

Meanwhile I had a good bit of photographing to do, following up the La Plata into the mountains to the source, where it first trickles out of snow banks and runs down in many pretty cascades. Some of the miners who had been working on the ditch were up there shoveling gravel into sluice boxes along the gulch, and others were locating gold-bearing quartz lodes.[4]

Many Indians were hanging about camp nearly all the time. It was fortunate for us that they were there, Moss said, for it gave him the opportunity to explain to them the object of our presence in the country. He told them particularly that we had nothing whatever to do with the surveying of the new lines of the reservation. Among the Indians was a picturesque lot of young bucks, who said they were going over to the Animas to meet Ignacio, Chief of the Southern Utes,[5] and other Indians, who were escorting a party of line surveyors to a conference over the running of the line. None of these Indians were disposed to recognize the recent purchase, claiming that much of their best land had been sold by Ouray and they had received nothing themselves in return. If the government was to take it, they said, the purchase price must be paid before a stake was driven.

Moss fed every delegation that came to his camp, serving them bread, meat, and coffee. Consequently, they one and all swore by John Moss as the big chief of the San Juan. With the delegation that came in from the McElmo was old "How-de-do," to whom I had promised presents the preceding year. He was eagerly waiting to get them, but didn't want any of the other Indians to know what he was to get.

Just before going on one of our side trips I sent two men with six pack mules to meet the supply train and bring in some of the food for which we were waiting. On our return we found they had brought in twelve hundred pounds of flour, bacon, sugar, and other supplies; the next day the wagons followed. The men with the wagon train reported that they had left Tierra Amarilla[6] on July second and had been nearly four weeks on the road and had had a hard time of it. Bad roads, high water, and frequent breakdowns were responsible for the delay.

With a six weeks' supply of grub, our two parties now started off together, while I remained behind to wait for the arrival of the overdue mail carrier, as I expected a number of things, which I intended for presents to Indians and for trading with them. He didn't show up until the afternoon of the second day of waiting, and then came limping in on an old horse, with a sheepskin for a saddle and the mail bag slung over his shoulder. He said he lost his horse for a whole day in Animas Valley and had left a large part of the mail, among which were all the articles I had promised the Indians.

I made an agreement with Harry Lee that he should go with us as guide and interpreter for twenty-five dollars a week and twenty-five dollars for the use of his horse. He remained with me until the mail carrier arrived, and then together we made a fast ride to the Mancos ranch. The next day we overtook our parties at Pegasus

Spring on the McElmo. Old "How-de-do" was camped near by with all his relatives in a group of small wikiups, and the whole lot of them came up at once to see what we had for them. Although I didn't have all the things I intended giving them, I satisfied the old man with some powder, lead, and caps, and then had the cook fill them up with bread and coffee.

In the canyons and on the table-lands about us were ruins of many kinds. With all of our exploration of this region, however, we failed to discover the group of remarkable towers that are now included in the Hovenweep National Monument, so completely do they blend into the natural features of their setting.

Both parties now moved on together. We followed first the deep, winding wash, or arroyo, made by the Hovenweep and the McElmo, finally coming out into the broad, open valley of the San Juan. The groves of cottonwoods here, of a brilliant emerald green, made a pleasing contrast with the gray sagebrush plains and red and yellow bluffs.

After passing the Montezuma Wash, our groups parted company, Holmes going off to the right, while we continued down the San Juan. Our trail for the greater part of the way followed the river, with high bluffs bordering close upon it. In these bluffs were many ruins of the rock-shelter kind, some near the water's edge and others on precarious shelves or in caves a hundred feet or more above, with no apparent means of reaching them.

A half day's ride below the Montezuma we discovered on the other side of the river two or three miles away a great circular cave, occupying nearly the whole height of the bluff in which it was situated. After many attempts to find a practicable ford, we crossed the river and found the cave to be about two hundred feet in height, with an approximately circular opening running back to a hundred feet in depth and with a perfect dome overhead. Midway around the cave a shelf of harder rock supported a row of small connecting rooms extending around more than half the entire circle. The great dome over all echoed and reëchoed with marvelous distinctness every word we said.

Below the Casa del Echo, as we named this ruin, the river plunged into an impassable canyon, forcing the trail upon the plateau. Most of the way we traveled over the upturned edges of red and white stratified sandstones, following in the tracks of sheep and goats that a band of Indians had taken across this mesa the day before.

CLIFF DWELLINGS. August 2, 1875. Pencil drawing. "Moved down the Hovenweep & McElmo [Washes] 28 miles to the San J [San Juan River]. Intensely hot & disagreeable. Nothing but sand, sagebrush & sun. Found more ruins at the junction of the McElmo [Wash] on big rocks under the cliffs. . . . As we approached the San Juan I never saw a more beautiful green than that of the Cottonwoods along the banks of the river. A refreshing sight contrasted with the barrenness of the days trip" (Jackson [1875] n.d., August 2). Courtesy National Park Service/Scotts Bluff National Monument.

CASA DEL ECHO. August 4, 1875.
Albumin print on stereoscope card.

"The whole appearance of the place and its
surroundings indicates that the family or little
community who inhabited it were in good
circumstances and the lords of the surrounding country.
Looking out from one of their houses, with a great
dome of solid rock overhead, that echoed and re-echoed
every word uttered with marvelous distinctness, and
below them a steep descent of 100 feet to the broad
fertile valley of the Rio San Juan, covered with waving
fields of maize and scattered groves of majestic
cottonwoods, these people, whom even the imagination
can hardly clothe with reality, must have felt a sense of
security that even the incursions of their barbarian fees
[foes] could hardly have disturbed" (Jackson in Hayden
1878, 419–20). Today it is variously known as Seventeen
Room Ruin or Fourteen Window Ruin. Nestled in its
protective sandstone cave three miles east of Bluff, Utah,
it overlooks present-day Navajo cornfields. Courtesy
Colorado Historical Society.

Dropping down to the San Juan again, we came to where the Chin-li [Chinle] Wash
came in, and crossing over, we made camp near its confluence with the river. The San
Juan disappeared in a deep canyon a short distance below.

Our camp was not a pleasant one—nothing but sand and sagebrush, with a landscape of bare red rocks. It was all right, however, for photography; and the first thing
in the morning we were off with the pack to see how far we could get down in the
canyon. There was no trouble until we had passed through the sandstones into a
limestone region,[7] where there was no beach line whatever, barring further progress.
Getting back to camp about noon, after making several negatives, we had little to do
for the rest of the day except to try to mitigate the intense and depressing heat. The
thermometer registered 100 in the coolest place we could find; 125 in the sun, where
we were most of the time; and 140 when it was placed in the sand. The most refreshing place of all was out in the river, with the temperature of the water at 88.

From this hot camp we made our long detour southward to the pueblos of the
Moquis, now more generally known as the Hopis. Something more than two hundred miles was covered in the trip there and back. As we wished to make it in quick
time, by traveling light, we cached in the sand everything except a few essentials.

Leaving the San Juan, we swung to the right around the canyon of the Chin-li. On the plateau the trail divided, the right-hand branch leading toward the Colorado Canyon. I wanted to follow that trail as far, at least, as Monumental [Monument] Valley, the towering rock forms of which seemed tantalizingly near at hand, but we were headed for an equally interesting place. The packers, who had gone on ahead, had taken this trail and were well on their way to the rocks before they could be overtaken and turned back.

From the plateau we had a fine view of the bluffs along the Chin-li wash. The groves of brilliant green cottonwoods promised plenty of water, but we had no need to go so far, as on the way down we happened on a small spring, cool and clear, in a most unlikely place. It gave us a refreshing drink all around. A search later up and down the wash failed to locate water, except a few warm, muddy pools; so I sent the train back to make camp at the spring. Harry and I meanwhile explored the canyon for ruins, and at last were rewarded by finding the largest and most important one I had seen so far.[8]

This was in a long, shallow cave about fifty feet above the base of a bluff, two or three hundred feet high, with the deep arroyo of the wash sweeping close under it. The ruin was really a compactly built town running along the face of the bluff in a continuous series of rooms for a distance of nearly two hundred yards, a tower-like room in the center being three stories high. Digging into the accumulated débris of some of the rooms, we found a number of fine corrugated-ware jars and some glazed pottery of artistic design and finish. Many stone implements and finely chipped arrow and spear points were also discovered.

Fifteen miles farther south, over a plateau of white sandstone and drifting heaps of fine sand, we passed the so-called diamond fields of Arizona.[9] These had acquired great notoriety three years previously, when they were "salted" with a few precious stones for a stock-selling scheme. We lingered on the bare rocky plain, which had promised much and given little, only long enough to gather a handful of garnets. The sun beat down upon it with such intensity that I doubt whether we should have stayed longer had there really been diamonds there.

Soon after this we dropped down into the Canyon Bonito Chiquito,[10] a gash across the rocky plateau, into which we had some trouble finding a way. But what a

CAVE TOWN OF THE RIO DE CHELLY, ARIZONA.
August 7, 1875. Albumin print.

A group of dwellings in a long, shallow cave on the Chin-li wash near the San Juan River running along the face of the bluff. "They are nearly 600 feet in length.... A central three-story tower is a prominent feature among them" (Jackson [1875] n.d., August 7). "Weather was so extremely hot that I had trouble in making my [photographic] plates working from below [the ruin]. Finally moved my tent into the cave of the ruins where it was cooler" (Jackson 1875b, August 7). Courtesy George Eastman House. This site is known today as Poncho House.

⌣

The men were heading south from Pancho House approaching the Hopi pueblos when the following incident occurred: "Bally the frisky mule. Bob [Mitchell, packer] traded to Copper [guest] for his horse. Gave us a little diversion this morning while packing up by scattering his load all over the country in the sage brush. Because of a sore back we gave him a small load and with it was a small keg of whisky—antidote for snake bites & bad water. As the final hitch was being made, securing this keg on the top of the pack, something alarmed the mule & he bucked & bolted, scattering his load right and left. The keg however remained attached by a handle to one of the sling ropes and during the escapade over the sand dunes and sage brush was thumped and banged about very much as a tin bucket tied to the tail of a rampageous dog. The cork came out and at every jump there was a liberal spurt of the precious fluid over the dry sand and dusty sage, throwing out an aroma that was [an] aggravation because of the failure of the boys to round up the animal until the keg was empty" (Jackson [1875] n.d., August 8).

⌣

contrast! Abundant green grass, with a long line of the tall, reedy growth common to damp lands, made a change grateful to man and beast. Climbing out of this canyon, we soon came again to the Chin-li, bordered with groves of fine old cottonwoods. The arroyo, in which were pools of clear water, was so deep as to be almost inaccessible; but a band of wandering Navajos, with a large flock of sheep and goats, had passed this way a few days previously, and by following their trail we found a rather easy way down into it.

There were many interesting cliff ruins in this locality, and the exploration and photographing of them kept us busy during our brief stay.

For the next two or three days we were traveling over a flat sage-covered valley, bordered by low but abrupt sandstone bluffs. Among and in these we discovered occasional ruins. A striking feature of this section was the detached red sandstones rising out of the plain in monumental forms to four hundred feet in height. One of them had a large window-like hole through it, which could be seen twenty miles away.[11]

We were now in the land of the Navajos. Many of these Indians were in the neighborhood, and one afternoon they all crowded our camp eager to do some trading. We bought a lot of green corn and melons from them, paying in silver, but what they wanted more than anything else was leather. They looked with covetous eyes upon our equipment of saddles, cantinas, and aparejos. Since we had heard much of their thieving propensities, we took extra precautions to have everything made of leather as near to us as possible when we made our beds for the night.

After careful consideration I decided to divide our party here and continue the trip with only Barber and Harry and two packs, sending the rest back to Canyon Bonito to await our return. The prospect for water and grass was altogether too precarious to warrant taking the whole train any farther. At Bonito there was both, and the animals could recuperate in our absence. While we were getting ready for the separation, the Indians brought in quantities of green corn for sale, and we bought as much as we could carry.

With the boys off on the back track, we set out ourselves, at a lively jog trot, for "Moquitch." We soon came into an extensive farming region, and for several miles passed through a succession of cornfields in the harvest season. Numerous small hogans (the Navajo name for their earth lodges) were scattered about, and many of the Indians came out to the trail to meet us, always with the salutation *"buena hay"* or *"adonde va!"* Leaving the cornfields, we struck off southwesterly, skirting on our right the line of high cliffs of the Great White Mesa.[12] Until noon we traveled rapidly; then we stopped for an hour under a group of peculiar red rocks, near which was a small pool of water. Our thirsty animals would not touch a drop of it, however, probably because of the sheep odor.

Just before sundown we came to a spring in a ravine, around which were camped several families of Navajos with a multitude of dogs. As we rode up, we were surrounded by a yelping pack of curs, which raised such a rumpus that it was difficult to get a word with the Indians. The dogs were eventually quieted, and we made our camp in peace. Several of the Indians who had their summer hogans in the neighborhood were in our camp all the morning, importuning us to trade. They said there was to be a big corn dance next day and they wanted us to remain for it, but we could not accept their invitation, as our time was too limited.

In the morning we struck out in an almost bee line over the broad, open valley, passing point after point of the great mesas. About noon, while still fifteen to twenty miles distant, we could make out, with the glasses, the mesa upon which stood Tewa, the first of the Moqui towns.[13] It was the last of the mesa promontories; otherwise we might have passed it without noticing the line of rock-built houses upon its summit, so like are they to their surroundings. Riding on rapidly, we were soon among Moqui cornfields, where we met a herder, who directed us to a place where we could get water. Because of the many trails, we had difficulty finding the tank or reservoir. It was a shallow well, walled with stone.

Passing on through a small peach orchard, we met a man who pointed out the right trail for ascending the mesa with our animals. The trail was cut out along the face of the bluff, being walled up in places. Part of it was like being on a steep stairway. We made the four-hundred-foot climb with ease and came out finally at the very door of the Capitan's house.

What followed I will let Barber tell in his letter to *The New York Times,* of October 1, 1875.

"As we dismounted from our animals at the entrance of the town, two men advanced to meet us—one, the foremost, a bright, fine-looking young fellow . . . who took off his hat, shook hands, and in broken English, interspersed with Spanish, bade us welcome. . . . After we had shaken hands with several more of the prominent men,

PUEBLO MAIDEN. 1875. Pencil drawing.

Num-Pa-Yu, a Hopi maiden of the Pueblo of Tewa, later the most famous pottery maker of all the pueblos. Jackson was struck with this young woman's beauty, intelligence, and charm. He photographed her, sketched her from the photograph, and talked about her in his writings. He states, "Made my neg. of Num-Pay-U, or 'the Serpent-that-has-no-teeth,' the good looking sister of [Captain] Toni," the pueblo chief (Jackson 1875b, August 14). Courtesy National Park Service/Scotts Bluff National Monument.

our mules were taken from us and lavishly fed with corn, and our host invited us to enter his house. Following up a ladder to the roof of the second story, and thence to a third by a series of stone steps, we passed through a low aperture into a room on this floor. Here we were bidden to be seated on a raised platform at one side of the room, on which had previously been placed robes made or woven from rabbit skins. Behind us a maiden was grinding corn in the primitive manner of the Moquis. Scarcely had we become seated when a beautiful girl approached and placed before us a large mat heaped with pee-kee, or bread. . . .

"The pretty Moqui princess who had waited upon us sat down in another part of the room and resumed her occupation of shelling corn from the cob into a dish. From where we were seated we could gaze upon her unobserved, and many an admiring glance was sent in that direction. She was of short stature and plump, but not unbecomingly so. Her eyes were almond shape, coal black, and possessed a voluptuous expression, which made them extremely fascinating. Her hair was arranged in that characteristic Oriental manner, peculiar to her tribe, which denoted her a maid. It was parted in the center, from the front all the way down behind, and put up at the sides in two large puffs, which, although odd to us, nevertheless seemed to enhance her beauty. Her complexion was much lighter than that of her family, and every movement of her head or exquisitely molded hands and arms or bare little feet was one of faultless grace.

"All the surroundings of the place, our reception, and the presence of this damsel, so unexpected and novel to us, overwhelmed us for a while with mute surprise, and we could only eat and look about us, almost believing we were acting in a dream. We had entered abruptly and awkwardly enough, with our hats un-removed and our garments ragged, travel-stained, and dusty; but on the approach of the modest and beautiful Num-pa-yu—[Nampeyo] signifying in the Moqui tongue a snake that will not bite—every head was uncovered in a moment, and each of us felt clumsy, dirty, and ashamed of our torn garments and unshaven faces."

Num-pa-yu later became the most famous of all pueblo pottery makers, her designs gaining wide celebrity. She is still living (1927), but now has greater concern for the welfare of her grandchildren than for the decoration of jars.[14]

SHE-PAUL-A-WEE [SIPAULOVI]. August 14, 1875.
Albumin print on Hayden Survey mount.

The plaza of Sipaulovi, one of the seven Hopi
pueblos of Arizona. In the center are Jackson's mounts
and two pack mules. "A view within the court of one of
the villages upon a mesa about six miles west of Te-qua
[Tewa Village]. The houses are accessible only from
within, the outside walls presenting a perfect blank"
(Jackson [1875] 1978, 80). Courtesy American Heritage
Center.

Our introductory visit over, we were directed to a place on the west side of the mesa where we could camp. Two boys were sent along to show us the way. Our photographic apparatus was left in the Capitan's house for future use. Since there was no grass in the neighborhood, we laid in an additional supply of corn for the animals.

Breakfast was late next morning, owing to the scarcity of fuel, but with that disposed of and the animals securely picketed, we went up into Tewa and began photographic operations by making a picture of Capitan Tom and his attractive sister on the terrace of their house. Then we carried our boxes to the other end of the mesa and made several views around Walpi.[15] Crowds of naked youngsters followed us around and, perched upon the rocks, watched with eager interest all we were doing.

In the afternoon we started off for the other pueblos. Oraybi which was too far away for the time at our disposal, was the only one omitted.[16] Views were obtained at Shungapavi, Mishongnovi, and Shepaulavi,[17] and at each pueblo the Capitans entertained us with the usual layout of wafer bread and stewed peaches. Wherever we

PATIO OF A PUEBLO. 1875. Pencil drawing.

Jackson was treated to a farewell party. "Had a gay
lunch in the house of the Captain of Gualpi [Walpi]. All
of our party with Traux [Indian Agent], [Billy] Keams
[trader] & half a dozen of the Moquis were gathered in a
little porch or vestibule of the Captain's house and by
the light of the moon only partook of a liberal supply of
mayavi [wafer bread] and stewed pumpkin. Our fingers
were all the utensils provided and everyone dipped in
alike" (Jackson 1875b, August 14). The drawing is
fashioned after a preliminary sketch found in Jackson's
diary. Courtesy National Park Service/Scotts Bluff
National Monument.

went, we were surrounded by curious throngs, pressing upon us so closely that we
had but little room for getting our meals. For the two nights we were away from the
first mesa, we had to make camp on the bare rock, where there wasn't a spear of grass
for mules and horses. Corn on the cob without roughage was hard on them.

On our return we took our whole outfit up into Tewa and made our camp in its
little court or plaza, where again we had nothing but corn for the animals. During the
afternoon two other white men came in, W. B. Truax, the new agent on his first visit
to the pueblos, and Billy Keams the Agency trader.[18]

Buying modern pottery and baskets as well as fetishes and small idols from Tom
and his family, we spent all our cash and also bartered away nearly everything else
we had to trade. When we finally gathered up all our purchases, we wondered how
we were going to carry them. My photographic work was concluded by making
another negative of Num-pa-yu.

Later in the evening we had a farewell party in the house of the Capitan of Walpi.
Here the three of us, with Truax, Keams, and five or six of the Moquis, gathered in a
porch or vestibule, and by the light of the moon only, joined in a feast of wafer bread
and stewed pumpkin. Our fingers were the only utensils available, and everyone
dipped into the same bowl.

Next morning we started off on a jog trot for the return trip. We made the camp
on Bonito Chiquito by sunset of the third day and found everything all right. The
boys were glad to have us back.

Next day, while we lay over to let our animals recuperate, Barber and I went
down the canyon afoot over the bed rock about two miles to a two-story cave house.
Here we made careful measurements, with sketches, for a future model. Another
day took us back to the Cave Town on the Chin-li. Then sending the train on to the
San Juan, I went over to the big cliff ruin again and made several more negatives of
it. It grew oppressively hot before we were through, but I stayed with the work until
I had photographs enough to give all the data required for making a reproduction.

We arrived at our former camping place soon after the train. The caches we had
made in the sand were found undisturbed. A refreshing bath in the river, even though
the water was quite turbid from heavy rains farther east, prepared us for an invigor-
ating sleep.

U.S. Geological Survey.   Plate XLVII.

PLATE XLVII, HAYDEN'S TENTH ANNUAL REPORT. 1878. Lithographic print.

The men were returning to the San Juan River on August 20 (Jackson 1875b). "[In] the cañon of the Chelle [Chinle Wash] we found the house shown. . . . It was reached from the valley by a series of steps cut into the rock, but now so eroded away as to be impracticable. . . . About 20 rods above, at the foot of the bluff, there is a deep natural reservoir of water, formed by the accumulated rains upon the plateau above pouring water over the rocks and scoping out a basin 30 feet in diameter and fully as deep, that seems to retain a perpetual supply of water" (Jackson in Hayden 1878, 424). Courtesy Museum of New Mexico History Library.

Chapter Seventeen
Further Adventures with the Indians

August 1875–September 1875

The group traveled up Epsom Creek (now Comb Wash), located across the San Juan River from the Chelle (Chinle Wash). It runs south from the Blue Mountains. "Fifteen miles up Epsom Creek a side cañon comes in from the left, down which trickles a scanty stream of brackish water with the peculiarity of taste and action which has given the name to the whole valley" (Jackson in Hayden 1878, 425). "This Epsom water has a very disagreeable effect upon all of us, men & animals. Blinkey [the Mule] had two of his usual tumbles" after drinking it (Jackson 1875b, August 22).

Our next objective was the Blue Mountains—the local name for the Abajo and La Sal peaks in eastern Utah. It was a mysterious region, reputed to be the haunt of a band of outlawed, renegade Indians, recruited from the surrounding Utes, Navajos, and Apaches. We approached this region, therefore, with some apprehension, but had confidence in Harry Lee's familiarity with the country and in the probability that he would know some of the Indians we might meet.

A brief explanation of what had happened before our arrival, of which we were in entire ignorance, will account for the actions of some of the Indians we met, for they probably knew more than we did. In planning the itinerary of the different parties of the Survey, it had been arranged for us to meet Gardner's party, which included Gannett's division, somewhere around Sierra Abajo. He arrived there a week before we crossed the San Juan on our way north to meet him. As he and his party were approaching Cold Spring on the Old Spanish trail, they were attacked by about one hundred Indians. For nearly two days they were under fire behind rock barricades, but finally escaped with the loss of all their camp and instrumental equipment and four mules killed.[1]

Knowing nothing of this trouble, we proceeded on our way. The route we chose lay to the right of Sierra Abajo [Mountain].[2] We first put in a day of photographic exploring by going up one of the side canyons on the west until it became impassable, with walls a thousand feet or more in height. Many interesting ruins were found—small individual tenements in eaves built along high cliffs and perched on isolated rocks.

The third day out from the river we met a small party of Pah Utes [Piute Indians]. They first made their presence known by calling down to us in their peculiar,

CAVE ROCKS. August 27, 1875.
Copy of modern print from wet plate negative.

Red sandstone bluff with dome-shaped caves near Sierra La Sal, Utah; Scene of the raid on [James] Gardner by renegade Indians. The Utes were especially angry with government surveyors; others had recently reapportioned their treaty-given tribal lands to make development comfortable for miners and ranchers. While photographing this rock, Jackson had no clue as to what had happened to Gardner's topographic crew. This distinctive landmark, known today as Casa Colorado Rock, is described in Jackson's photograph catalogue as follows: "Between the Sierra Abajo and La Sal, in the great basin-like depression falling toward the Colorado, are a large number of red and white sandstone buttes, which display in a marked manner their tendency to weather into great circular caves, affording the favorite building-sites of the prehistoric man of this region. These particular rocks give no indication of ever having been occupied" (Jackson [1875] 1978, 79). Courtesy U.S. Geological Survey.

James Gardner [topographer] tried to warn Jackson about the dangers he could face in dealing with the Ute Indians. Jackson didn't receive the communiqué until his return to Parrott City.

Parrot [Parrott] City, Aug. 21st. 1875.

My Dear Jackson:

The combined parties of Mr. Gannett and myself numbering 18 men with seven rifles were attacked by the Indians in a canyon 15 miles north of the Sierra Abajo known here, I believe, as the Blue Mts. We were besieged in a waterless place [Casa Colorado Rock]. We fought two days and a night without water under constant fire and at last escaped up the bluffs by cutting everything off the packs. None of the men were hurt, 4 of the animals were wounded and two killed. We rode 200 miles in four days to make this point when we met Holmes just coming in. His mules were stolen two nights after you left him but were retaken a few moments after their capture. In view of the state of things I think it is wise for you to return here as soon as practible [sic] and run no further risk. Mr. Holmes has completed his western work and goes north for 20 days. Two of Gannett's party were left by him on the Dolores [River] to watch supplies. I march tomorrow with six fighting men to rescue them if they are still alive. I have hired Mr. Giles at six dollars per diem and the other men at $5 to find you. Hoping that my fears for your safety are groundless I am

Truly yours,

Jas. T. Gardner

(Gardner to Jackson, August 21, 1875. William Henry Jackson Manuscript Collection. 1862–1942. MSS 341, Box 2, ff. 45)

﹏

far-reaching cry, from far up the bluffs above. It was only after some parleying with Harry that they ventured to come down. They were curious as to where we were going.

The Indians had some buckskins they wanted to sell, but we had nothing with which to trade. Following us to the next water, they were rather insistent that we should camp there, but we preferred to go on farther. About supper time the same Indians came into camp, and after being well fed, hung around until long after dark. Our animals, which we allowed to run loose, were restless during the night and made several rushes. Once they stampeded right through camp, nearly running over us and scattering pots and kettles in every direction and making a great rumpus for a while. It was the result, probably, of the same Indians prowling around the neighborhood.

Skirting the eastern flanks of the Abajo Peak, we rose out of the region of cliff ruins into another region of rich, abundant grass, clear mountain streams, and groves of oak and aspens.[3] Game signs were frequent; three deer crossed the trail ahead of us as we were riding along with the train. We met but one other party of Indians, a Weminuchi family with many horses and goats on their way to the Navajo country.

Our last camp on the mountain was in a fine grove of scrub oaks, where there was luxuriant feed for our animals and plenty of clear, cool water. This was so grateful to both man and beast after the desert experiences of the past month that I decided to leave the larger part of our party there to recuperate while I went on a side trip with Harry and Bill for an investigation of the country lying between the Abajo and La Sal mountains.

With two light packs, we struck out across country to pick up the Old Spanish Trail to an upper crossing of the Colorado, which Harry said was in this neighborhood. Dropping into a draw, or shallow canyon, we came to a copious and remarkably cold spring (the one that Gardner had been trying to reach when his party was attacked). As we followed down the gradually broadening canyon, we came on the old trail near a peculiar rock formation, known as La Tinaja. We were now in a broad, valley-like expansion of the gorges leading into the Colorado Canyon, where there was very little grass and no water. A dry camp was made, but we had a heavy shower during the night.

Until noontime the next day we roamed about looking for ruins, but found no indications whatever. The only object that warranted setting up the photographic outfit was a group of red sandstone bluffs with great dome-shaped caves that would have been a fine place for cliff dwellings.[4]

Returning by a different route, which bore around to the east, we struck an old trail under white sandstone bluffs. This was followed until we came to a side canyon, which took us, after a steep and rough climb, to the level, plateau-like summit. Leaving the trail here, we made a bee line in the direction of our camp, but had to tie up for the night when about halfway there.

During our day's rambling we had puzzled much over numerous tracks of shod horses and mules, plainly not Indian, which we found at various points in the vicinity of our first night's camp. There was also a fresh trail going east through the sagebrush, on the plateau over which we had just passed. Gardner was to make a station on the Abajo Mountain, but these tracks, if of his party, would indicate that he had not been there.

Returning to our camp among the oaks, after resting the animals a bit, we packed up for our return to the rendezvous camp on the La Plata. A direct route by the way of Montezuma Canyon was taken. Fortunately we happened on a practicable way down into it. The bottom of the canyon, as usual with those in this region, was flat, with a deep wash winding from side to side. It was rather narrow where we first entered it, but gradually widened farther down. Near sunset we camped at the junction of another large canyon. The main canyon was now some two hundred to three hundred yards wide, with the bottom lands literally covered with old ruins.

As this was a dry camp, in the morning I first sent the men up and down the canyon to locate water; but finding none, we started off down the trail. The ruins were so numerous now that frequently one or more were in view as we rode along. Arrow points were so plentiful that there was an active rivalry as to which one of us found the greatest number. Broken pottery of all kinds and beads and other trinkets also were collected. After passing two rather important ruins, we found running water a short distance below and went into camp while we investigated them.

Next morning our camp was moved down the canyon a little way for better grass, while I went back to complete my photographing. Near the previous night's

Perfectly Inaccessible, Hayden's Tenth Annual Report. 1878. Lithographic print.

"Camping here [15 miles up present-day Comb Wash in a side canyon], we extended our observations up this lateral cañon some 8 or 10 miles in quest of ruins, and found them numerous . . . although not of the importance of . . . the San Juan and De Chelle [Chinle Wash] . . . . A short distance above the entrance of the cañon a square tower has been built upon a commanding point of the mesa, and in a position perfectly inaccessible . . . . The stones of which it is composed are very nearly uniform in size, more so than in any of the buildings we have seen west of the Hovenweep" (Jackson in Hayden 1878, 425). Courtesy Museum of New Mexico, History Library.

RUINS IN MONTEZUMA CAÑON. August 30, 1875.
Albumin print on Hayden Survey mount.

"At the foot of one of the promontory towns a low
bench, tongue shaped, and only about 10 feet above the
valley, runs out from the mesa 200 feet in length and half
as broad, through the center of which runs a wall its
entire length; a portion of it is composed of the large
upright rocks shown in the sketch, the largest standing 7
feet above the surface and evidently extending some
distance below, in order to be retained so firmly in their
places. There are only seven of these standing, placed
about 5 feet apart, the rest of the wall line being
composed of a low ridge of loose rock extending up to a
mass of old ruins at the foot of the bluff" (Jackson in
Hayden 1878a, 429–30). Courtesy Colorado Historical
Society.

camp there were Indian cornfields, planted in white sand and not thriving very well.
Our stock got into the fields during the night, doing no great damage; but it was just
as well that the owners were not around.

In the afternoon, with Harry and Bill and the photo-pack mule, I started on a
side trip down the canyon to look for more ruins. About five miles from camp we
came to a right-angle bend to the eastward; and a few miles farther on, to a large Indian camp of brush wikiups. Between these two points we had a lively and exciting
experience. Soon after passing the big bend, we noticed up in the rocks to the left the
head and shoulders of an Indian boy. He beat a precipitate retreat down the canyon
on his pony as soon as he saw he had been discovered. A little later a single horseman met us, and after the usual "how-how!" turned back and rode along with us.

While Harry was trying to get some information from the Indian, we saw a cloud
of dust down the trail, and out of it came some fifteen to twenty Indians on ponies,

rushing full tilt toward us. Shouting their shrill "hi, hi" and swinging their guns over their heads, they did not stop until they had run right into us and, turning about, surrounded us completely. We had no idea what all this demonstration meant, but there was nothing to do but sit tight and wait to see what happened.

Crowding around us, all of the Indians joined in a noisy chorus of greetings and shaking of hands. Harry thought he recognized one of the men—he claimed acquaintance anyway—and through him replied to some of their questions as to who we were, where we came from, and where we were going. There was some hesitation in saying we were a part of the government surveys, as we knew of their hostility toward surveyors in general. Being none too sure of the temper of these young bucks in these remote canyons, Harry told them that we were prospectors bound for Moss's La Plata camp. They appeared to be friendly, however, and finally insisted upon our going to their camp. In a spirit of pure mischief or deviltry they got behind us, and with quirt and lariat lashed our horses and mules into a breakneck race, never letting up until we dashed among their wikiups. It was a regular stampede all the way, and it was fortunate that the photographic outfit on Blinkey was securely packed, for if anything had gone wrong, that would have been the last of it.

Old Pogonobogwint, their chief, who was present, met us with a friendly greeting, and by his invitation we joined them in a lunch of boiled green corn. They were insistent that we stop there overnight, as they declared there was no water, other than the spring near their camp, within a day's journey. We were equally determined about going on, however, and after supplying ourselves with a dozen ears of green corn, we continued down the canyon. In order to get away from the Indians, we were willing to take our chances for water.

All this time we had not told the Indians of the rest of our party that we had left up the canyon. We had a rather hazy purpose in mind of getting back to it by some roundabout, unobserved way and then leaving the country by another route that would pass around the Indian camp.

Soon after leaving, we noticed that we were being followed by two Indians on horseback. Spurring up and watching our opportunity, as the deepening shadows of late evening obscured our movements and tracks somewhat, we lost our pursuers by making a quick turn up a small side canyon filled with brush. Up this we worked

~

The photographs and text in *The Pioneer Photographer* lead to the notion that most of the discovered ruins were of the cliff-house variety. However, the diary entries for both 1874 and 1875 mention numerous surface ruins built on the canyon floors or mesa tops. Because many of these are older or more exposed than the structures nestled within protecting canyon walls, most of them had been reduced to piles of rubble that Jackson termed mounds. Generally, they were not worthwhile photographic subjects. The expedition was not equipped for extensive excavation, but they did take surface measurements and collected as many artifacts as their limited carrying capacity would allow.

~

our way to the top of the mesa, where we unsaddled for a dry camp just as the stars were beginning to shine brightly in a dark blue sky. We had eaten so much corn that we did not prepare supper, and after securely picketing our four animals, we rolled up in our saddle blankets for a sound sleep.

Until late the next afternoon we wandered around among canyons and over mesas. We found many ruins, but discovered no way to rejoin our party other than by going back over the old trail past the Indian camp. Making a virtue of necessity, for our animals had had no water for twenty-four hours, we rode to the spring, where they drank deeply. Nearly all the men of the Indian camp were away, but those who were there gave us another noisy reception and also more boiled corn. I do not know what Harry told them, but they seemed friendly enough. When we finally got back to our camp, the boys said that no Indians had been around there.

There seemed to be no other way of avoiding the Indians than by going up the canyon and finding a trail leading over the mesa to the south. We were so opposed to further contact with them that we took desperate chances to keep out of their way. There was no trail, but we began tacking back and forth up the sides of the canyon. Halfway up the pack mules began to weaken, some of them stumbling and falling over the loose rocks. We did not give up, however, until Old Mag, carrying a load of bedding in which was packed some of our pottery collections, fell backwards on a steep incline. The mule rolled heels over head, making a clear leap of about forty feet over a perpendicular ledge, and landed on her back in the top of a thick scrub cedar. I was below, at the rear of the train, when this happened, and thought it was surely the last of Old Mag as I saw her hurtling through the air, followed by a clatter of loose rock; but to my utter amazement she rolled out of the tree and landed right side up in the trail below, none the worse, apparently, for her experience.

Our difficulties seemed to be growing greater rather than less in trying to get over the mesa, so I ordered a right about and returned to our former camp. Next morning we decided to strike out straight for the La Plata rendezvous, Indians or no Indians.

Passing their camp, we were held up for the damage done to their cornfield by our mules, which had been discovered in the meantime. We had nothing to give them,

A LUCKY FALL. n.d. Ink wash, graphite, and tempera.

In an attempt to climb out of Montezuma Canyon, Old Mag, leg weary, rolled over the cliff, landing back down in a stout scrub cedar, which threw her out on her feet in the trail, none the worse for her experience. In some instances Jackson's various diary accounts disagree with the text. There are several reasons for this. Approximately half a century elapsed between the time of his tenure with the Hayden Survey and the writing of this book. Much of the book was taken from diary notes that were transcribed by Howard Driggs into readable text. Many of the diary entries are extremely hard to read because of their condition and age and also because of Jackson's handwriting. In this instance he tells the incident of the mule falling off the cliff differently in his diary entry. In an attempt to avoid more encounters with Indians [I] "started the whole outfit up the canyon intending to find a trail to take to the top of the mesa. Went up, about to camp, and finding no indications [of a trail] made up my mind that we would try it without finding a way & got the train half way up when the mule came slipping & falling & making such bad work of it—(Old Jake [not Old Mag] rolling down over 100 feet [making] in one place a clear leap of 50 feet lighting in a cedar & so breaking his fall) that I gave the word 'right about' and went back toward [our old] camp" (Jackson 1875b, September 2). Courtesy Brigham Young University.

and when they got ugly about it I had the packers rush the train ahead, while Harry and I remained behind to stand them off until we could make a get-away.

It was a long, forced ride to the Hovenweep. From there we went direct to the La Plata. Harry and I rode in a day ahead of the others, and as we passed the Mancos ranch, got our first news of Gardner's skirmish with the Indians. At the La Plata camp we found nearly all of his party and also Holmes's party—the miners and the Survey boys all in one company. Cap Moss, with a party from California, had also just arrived.

There was a regular jubilee for a time. The story of Gardner's party was repeated over and over again—how a band of renegade Indians had corralled them up against the bluffs for two days without water, in the place where we had seen the mysterious horse tracks; how they had lost several mules during the shooting, but had

~

By the time he explored and photographed the Four Corners region, William Henry Jackson had become an indispensable part of Hayden's Survey. He had become a celebrity; his photographs were known internationally. Thousands of his photographs had been sold as stereoscope cards and as Hayden Survey-mounts. His photographs and sketches had been duplicated as lithographs in the Survey's annual reports—the mass publication of photographs in books and periodicals was still a few years away. Examples of lithographs Jackson created to illustrate his article in Hayden's *Tenth Annual Report* (Jackson in Hayden 1878) are seen on pages 159 abd 163.

~

finally effected a retreat at night up over the mesa and then had made a bee line in double-quick time to this camp. Luckily none of the party was injured. The loss, as said before, was confined to the four mules killed and their entire camp equipment, which they were compelled to abandon. This was fine loot for the Indians.

Great anxiety had been felt for the safety of my party, as they knew we were to pass through the same country. Gardner had sent out two men from Parrott City to intercept us south of the Abajo Mountain and warn us of the danger. They had trailed us from the San Juan up to the Abajo, where they lost our trail, and being out of provisions, had returned just a day ahead of us. Preparations were under way to send out another party to find us, "or our remains," when we rode into the camp, none the worse for our experiences.

Our next move was on to Bakers Park for photographic work among the San Juan peaks.

Chapter Eighteen

In the Land of the Pueblos

January 1866–July 1877

The Centennial of the Declaration of Independence came in 1876. Instead of going west with the Survey, I was employed, with others, for nearly the entire season in the preparation of its exhibit for the Exposition at Philadelphia.[1] This offered an excellent opportunity to show the results of the various expeditions by publications, maps, and other objects. Photographs, of course, played an important part in the display. For this I was awarded the large bronze medal of the United States Centennial Commission.

Among the interesting features of our exhibit were models of some of the cliff dwellings discovered during the two years previously. From ground plans and measurements of the more important ruins, made with this object in view on my last expedition, I constructed models in clay. These were then cast in plaster and colored to represent the originals as nearly as possible. Later these models, as well as a number of duplicates, were distributed among the principal museums of the country.

While I was at the Exposition I paid special attention to the photographic exhibits from foreign lands. The panoramic cameras and the use of paper instead of glass for making negatives had special interest because of my field work. When I returned to Washington, I began experimenting with these new developments in photography.

With the aid of a model maker, I constructed a panoramic camera that would swing around the entire circle of three hundred and sixty degrees. This, of course, required the use of a roll and film and led to further experiments. I tried coating paper with what was then known as collodio-bromide, which was very much like the gelatino-bromide on the films and plates of the present time. This coating, when the photographic operations were completed could be stripped off as a film and transferred to glass plates.

A RESTORATION OF A PORTION OF AN ANCIENT CAVE TOWN ON THE RIO DE CHELLY, ARIZONA. n.d. Molded clay diorama cast in plaster.

Jackson did not do fieldwork in 1876. Instead, he worked for the United States Geological Survey creating models to be exhibited in Philadelphia at the Centennial Exhibition. His detailed notes, sketches, and photographs were used to create three-dimensional models of the historic and prehistoric dwellings of Native Americans. "With [William H.] Holmes [artist and geologist] and three or four assistants I spent the best part of six months shaping clay to exact scale models . . . . When the fair opened, this display attracted more attention than many of the photographs and all of the rocks and relics of Dr. Hayden's career. It drew almost as many visitors as Dr. Alexander Graham Bell's improbable telephone, and, had a Gallop Poll existed at the time, I am confident that nine persons out of ten would have voted my models a better chance of enduring" (Jackson [1940] 1994, 243). This model represents the ruin known as Pancho House (see page 153). Courtesy Harold Warp Pioneer Village.

◡

Spending a lot of time with the Hayden Survey topographers led Jackson to making photographic panoramas. He undertook the construction of a rotating panoramic camera. "Many times while photographing the encircling mountain ranges from some lofty peak I had wished for an instrument that would take the entire horizon with one continuous sweep instead of making separate plates and then joining them together to complete a panorama . . . . I picked up some useful ideas . . . while attending the Exposition at Philadelphia and after consulting every authority I could find. . . . In realizing these ideas the main difficulty concerned the preparation of a suitable sensitive film for the negative. I succeeded in doing this by coating paper with a substratum of rubber and on this a collodion emulsion, resembling in some respects the Eastman Transferrotype, except in my case [not using] . . . gelatine, the detachment of the film from the paper being effected by benzine.

"The final result of our efforts to make a revolving camera was a circular base, corresponding to the top piece of the tripod . . . .The works of an eight day clock, with strong springs, furnished the motive power that drove the camera around the circle at a regulated speed and at the same time unwound the film from one spool to another.

"With this apparatus I made several experimental exposures with the paper film, getting negatives of nearly 360 deg. radius that were everything desired as to definition but the difficulties in making, developing and stripping the films in addition to their being no immediate need for such work, induced me to lay it aside for the time being" (Jackson [1877] n.d., 2–4).

◡

The question may arise why I did not use this method, instead of the cumbersome wet plate, for my work on the expeditions. Simply because this new process was still an uncertain one; I could not afford the risk, so I stayed with the reliable old wet plate. Dry-plate methods, with deferred development, where the results were in doubt until it was too late to correct them, were used only by amateurs who could take these chances. The leaven, however, was working, and out of it was to come the perfected film and plate of today.

Instead of going out with the Survey in 1877, I undertook another trip to the Southwest for a further investigation of its ancient ruins. This plan of going out alone, dispensing with the usual outfit provided for the purpose, was a result of meeting Rev. Sheldon Jackson in Washington, who was actively engaged in attending to the affairs of the Presbyterian Board of Missions. He was about to make a tour among the pueblos west of the Rio Grande as far as the Moquis in Arizona. Our interests being almost identical as to the principal places to be visited, it was arranged that we go together. We were to get some sort of an outfit at Santa Fe and drive over the main part of the route.

It was to be a quick trip, for the Doctor's time was limited. If there was to be any photographing, my slow wet-plate equipment was entirely out of the question. Dry plates or films must be used or no photographing could be done.

While I was experimenting, an advertisement appeared in an English photographic journal describing a "Sensitive Negative Tissue supplied in bands for Roller Dark Slide." This promised a ready solution of the problem. I could have made such a tissue myself but had no facilities for making the required quantity. Correspondence with the English company resulted finally in my ordering enough of the 8 × 10 size for four hundred exposures. The tissue was not in a continuous strip, like a kodak film, but was made up of separate pieces pasted together in strips for twenty-four exposures. I had the roll holder made in New York from designs suggested by a description of what had been done with it abroad.

Delivery of the tissue in Washington was promised in season for a work-out trial before my departure, but it did not come in time, so I went on to Santa Fe without it. There I waited overtime, until finally the tissue arrived only the day before our final departure for the pueblo region. Trial exposures and development were made at once. The results were not equal to the old and well-tried methods, but I felt they would answer for the objects I had in view. At all events, the die was cast. There was neither time nor opportunity for anything else, so I started out with the hope, rather than a conviction, that all would turn out well.

There was no provision for daylight changing of films. This had to be done, by day, in a light-tight bag made for the purpose, or at night, in a room of some pueblo home. At one other place while on the road I had an opportunity to make a test development and found everything working as well as could be expected. So, with exposures made under normal conditions and each roll well sealed in its metal container, I was fairly confident that every section of the tissue was a possible negative.

It was not until I got back to Washington and began development that I could make sure of the results of the costly experiment. There I met with the bitter disappointment of getting only my test negatives for all my long journey and earnest efforts. No method I could think of in developing would bring out the faintest trace of an image on any one of the exposures made. There is no use in going into further detail; the undertaking was a failure, and that was the whole story. My theory was that if each piece of tissue could have been developed soon after exposure, it might have proved more successful.

Some twenty years later, while on a foreign tour, I had a similar experience. At this time I was using celluloid films, then in the pioneer stages. The first of these developed beautifully under all conditions. Others, presumably of the same kind, were received later, and on a test exposure and development seemed as good as the first. Then it so happened that because of rapid travel I accumulated some three hundred exposures at the end of a three-week period before any of them could be developed. The first ones exposed were flat failures; those taken more recently showed more or less of an image, according to length of time since exposure. If developed within a day or two, a perfect negative resulted. The celluloid used was quite different from the present film, which is practically "fool-proof."

But the trip into New Mexico and Arizona was not without interesting and worth-while returns, despite my failure to get a photographic record of it. Dr. Jackson and I arrived at Fort Garland, on the western border of San Luis Park,[2] late in the afternoon of March twenty-third. Before leaving Washington, we had been provided

~

Jackson ordered the new dry film from L. Warnerke of London. He did not use the film holders that Warnerke sold, but instead used holders he had made to order by two different companies in the United States. His notes indicate that he took every precaution with the film, following the manufacturer's directions as closely as possible. It is not clear whether it was the lag time in development or the film holders that allowed the film to deteriorate.

While at Fort Defiance, Jackson wrote to William H. Holmes, geologist and artist with the Survey from 1872 to 1878. He confidently discusses the new dry film he was using. "My paper film seems to be working all right, although I have developed one small lot only, but that came up so well, so easily and uniformly that I have banished all fears as to the final result. The only fault I found was that I had been over exposing. As the stripped film is quite thin I think it best not to remove any more negatives from the paper than the Specimen I have sent Frank [Franklin Rhoda, topographer from 1873 to 1876], until I have the opportunity to transfer to glass, or give additional coatings" (Jackson to Holmes, April 27, 1877. Fritiof M. Fryxell Papers. 1853–1973. MSS 1638, Box 29, correspondence file).

After returning to Washington and developing the deteriorated film, the reality of losing an entire season's photographic work was devastating. "My experience of 1877 was quite the most costly setback of my career. There was no going back, as I had done in Colorado in 1873, when my mule slipped his pack and broke so many of my glass plates. I considered the whole summer shot to pieces, and the fact that I had compiled a voluminous first report on the Chaco Canyon Ruins — now a National Monument — didn't comfort me much. My feelings were beyond the repair of Dr. Hayden's praise. They still are. I can never replace those lost pictures" (Jackson [1940] 1994, 246).

~

ADOBE DWELLINGS. March 26, 1877. Pencil drawing.

The North-side Village at the Taos Pueblo is depicted. "Laid over [in Taos] to hear preaching, but Monday made up for the loss of time by a hard day's work around the Pueblo" (Jackson to Holmes, April 27, 1877. Fritiof M. Fryxell Papers. 1853–1973. MSS 1638, Box 29, correspondence file). The letter is signed "Jack," a name often used by his colleagues on the Survey. The drawings done in 1877 are all that remain of his artistry as all of his photograph negatives deteriorated before they were developed. Courtesy National Park Service/Scotts Bluff National Monument.

with orders on the military posts of this Southwest Department for whatever transportation we required; so at this post we were furnished at once with an army ambulance and were off for Santa Fe that same afternoon.

Our first drive was to Costilla, just under the New Mexico line, and the next day we had another forty-mile ride to Rancho de Taos.[3] Our driver put his two lusty mules over the rough mountain roads at a pace that compelled us to hold tight to our seats. Sunday following, there was a lay-over for rest and for attending religious services conducted by Dr. Jackson. On Monday I had a busy day at the Pueblo de Taos with my camera, compass, tapeline, and notebook, securing details of ground plans and elevations for making the model I then had in view. Two more forty-mile drives brought us to Santa Fe.

We arrived at this city just before the departure of a party for the Navajo Agency at Fort Defiance,[4] to witness the distribution of annuity goods to the Indians. There were the pueblo agent, with two ladies; a local clergyman, likewise accompanied by two ladies; a paymaster, with his wife, going to Fort Wingate⁵ to pay off troops; and two other men. Dr. Jackson and I gladly accepted the kind invitation extended to travel with this congenial party on their trip.

For the continuation of our journey we got an order from General Hatch at Fort Marcy, on the outskirts of Santa Fe,⁶ for a buckboard and two good mules, with requisitions on all army posts for forage. Behind its single seat there was room for a roll of blankets, our luggage, with a small mess kit for emergencies, and my photographic outfit. Because of my experience, Dr. Jackson gave to me the care of the team and the selection of camping places.

The whole party got away on a Friday noon and drove down to Peña Blanca, on the Rio Grande. The next day we forded the river and had a hard time making it, being nearly swamped at one place, with the wetting of our luggage as the least of our trouble. We made fifty miles that day to Rio Puerco and had a lay-over there for Sunday services. A three days' drive around the San Mateo Mountains brought us to Fort Wingate for a one-night stop;⁷ and then we were off for Zuni on a four-day side trip. While Dr. Jackson was busy with matters of his particular concern, I was working my camera overtime in and around the pueblo of Zuni.

On our return to Fort Wingate we rejoined our Santa Fe party and went on to Fort Defiance. A wet snowstorm struck us just before our arrival. This, mixed with the soft adobe soil under the feet of thousands who were coming in to the Agency, made a fine mixture for "dobies" but a hard road to travel.⁸

Every Navajo in the country, young or old, seemed to be on hand to receive his share of the gifts of the government. The day after our arrival the distribution began by passing all the Indians into an enclosure with high adobe walls. Each was given a ticket on entering, and none could leave until all had been accounted for. This was to prevent any repeating, as it was difficult to distinguish one from another. By five o'clock more than nine thousand tickets had been issued, each one representing an individual Indian. All of this horde was crowded into the one corral, with the snow falling fast and the thick mud getting deeper as they milled about. Some two hundred chiefs and head men, drawn up in line on horseback, kept out of the mêlée by remaining outside and receiving tickets there.

PUEBLO WOMAN. n.d. Pencil sketch.

Any significant information about this sketch has been lost over time. Judging from the woman's dress, it was probably done in 1877 at one of the pueblos Jackson visited while touring the territory of New Mexico. It is conceivable, however, that it was created in 1875 when he visited the Hopi villages in Arizona.

When the enumeration was completed and the order to let the Indians out of the corral was given, there was an eruption of such a turbulent, muddy crowd of humanity as one seldom sees. They took it good-naturedly, however, and quickly scattered over the surrounding hillsides, where they soon extemporized little wiki-ups for shelter.

As night came on, hundreds of little camp fires were glimmering through the falling snow, some of them apparently far up in the sky, and the whole horizon was aglow with a soft illumination. At the same time countless moving figures were shifting about, in and out of their own little circle of light, while the air was filled with the cries of children, the admonitions of the squaws, the shoutings of the men, and the barking of every dog of the encampment. As a kind of finale for this interesting moving picture, the young bucks, in a hilarious mood, indulged in much reckless riding about the Agency, with an occasional fusillade of gunshots out among the encampments.

For our accommodation we had been assigned a log cabin with bunks, on which we spread our blankets. There was also a large fireplace, with an ample supply of pine and cedar logs near by. With a blazing fire illuminating the interior beyond any need for candles, we had a comfortable refuge when the day's work was done.

We had been advised to watch our property, as these Indians, of good repute otherwise, were notoriously light-fingered. With the door padlocked and the one small window securely barred, we thought everything safe, but some prowling Indian did get in and made away with my most prized possession, a new .45 Smith and Wesson revolver—nothing else. On my reporting the matter to the agent, he promptly assigned two Indian policemen to find the thief. Four days later, when we returned from a side trip to the Canyon de Chelle,[9] the men were back with the pistol. They reported that they had followed the man all the way to the San Juan River. I was so pleased to get it back that I forgot to inquire as to how they got on the trail of the right Indian.

On this trip to the Canyon de Chelle we joined the party that had come out from Santa Fe with us and two officers of the small force stationed at the Agency. Our first camp in the canyon was made at the foot of the Explorers Column.[10] Then came trips down to the great White House and other ruins in the neighborhood and up the Canyon del Muerto,[11] where I photographed everything in sight; that is, I went through the motions.

The day after getting back to the Agency and seeing the rest of our company off for home, we hitched our mules to the buckboard again and started for the Moqui pueblos, Billy Keams, my old friend of 1875, going along as interpreter. The first day out on the road was as fine as one could wish. The second day a heavy wind came up, and when we got out into the open country the flying sand, which neither we nor our mules could face, compelled us to turn aside into the timber and make a dry camp. The next day was about the same, but we managed to drive through it to the first mesa. The surrounding country was a sea of sand, and it seemed to be all in the air as we rode through it. There was little encouragement for successful photography under such conditions.

Contrary to expectations, another day dawned fair and clear. I made the most of it among the three pueblos of the first mesa, Tewa, Sechumevay[12] and Walpi. After this we got away for a tour of the other four pueblos, making with our buckboard nearly the same round that I had made two years previously, only this time reaching Oraybi and spending some time there.

On our return to Tewa we loaded up with pottery and other examples of Moqui handiwork and got as far as the Agency headquarters that evening. Our second day's return ride was through a snowstorm, but we made camp for the night in a bit of timber and were comfortable behind a brush shelter and a big piñon fire. We came near having to "hoof it" for the rest of the way, however. Usually we kept our mules tied up or staked out near by when in camp. This evening there happened to be good grass not far away, and I let them loose, with their picket ropes trailing, while supper was being prepared. We had been out on the road so long that we had little fear of their straying far from camp.

For some time we were so busily engaged with camp work that we paid little attention to what was going on around us, and then as we were about to sit down to our supper, I noticed that our two mules were out of sight. This was a serious matter. I jumped up, to discover that they were several hundred yards from camp, one trailing behind the other down the road and evidently bound for Wingate or some other place where they had been put up. The Doctor was no sprinter, so it was up to me to head them off and to be quick about it. Of course, as soon as they saw they were followed, the mules quickened their pace, and it began to look like a hopeless

FORT DEFIANCE, ARIZONA. Circa 1929. Ink drawing.

The rendering shows the fort in about 1880, maintained as a Navajo Indian Agency. Courtesy Brigham Young University.

trailing chase. The road, fortunately, soon ran into some piñon and cedar timber, where by making a wide detour and keeping out of sight, I succeeded in getting ahead of them in the road. Finally, picking up the trail rope of one, I mounted and made quick time back to camp, the other following, for two mules under such circumstances would never be separated.

While we were at the Canyon de Chelle, the two officers from Fort Defiance told me about Pueblo Bonito[13] in Chaco Canyon and the possibility of reaching it from the head of the De Chelle by way of Washington Pass.[14] I decided to go there, and on my return from Moqui tried to get a guide and companion at the Agency. No one except Indians could be found who knew anything about the country; and not one of them would undertake the journey at this time of the year, even at five dollars a day. At Fort Wingate the officers did all they could for me, but no guide was to be had. I was told, however, that there was a man in San Ysidro who would probably serve my purpose.

Dr. Jackson and I parted company at Fort Wingate; he to return directly east, while I was to take the buckboard back to Santa Fe after completing my tour among the pueblos and old ruins. Returning over our outward road as far as San Ysidro, I readily found the man recommended to me, Mr. Beaumont, living among the Mexicans very much as some white men live with Indians. He had never been over the country beyond the Puerco and knew of the Chaco ruins only by hearsay; but what served my purpose even better was his ability as an interpreter in both Spanish and Indian. Beaumont's first suggestion was to get as our guide Hosta, ex-governor of the near-by pueblo of Jemez, who accompanied the Colonel Washington expedition of 1849 against the Navajos. His portrait appears in Simpson's Journal of that expedition, where he is described as a fine looking and most intelligent Indian.[15]

We found old Hosta in the midst of his family, a small, thin man. His body was bent under the burden of more than four score years of toil. His eyes were dim with age, and straggling gray hair but thinly covered his head. He declared himself to be as good a man as any of us and ready to undertake to guide us over the country he knew so well. He stipulated only that one of his grandchildren, a lad of twelve or fourteen years, should go with him to help locate distant landmarks, as his eyesight was failing and he feared he might not recognize them.

The trader's store at Jemez furnished the only supplies to be had for our outfit-ting short of Santa Fe or Fort Wingate. Our needs were simple, however; a frying pan and a coffee pot with hard bread and bacon and a few extras, provided for the inner man. These, with a small blanket roll for each and my camera, were packed on one mule, our little party of four riding the same useful animals.

Our first day's ride was across country to the Cerro Cabezon,[16] where we crossed the Puerco by a bridge, as the water was running too deep for us to use the regular ford farther up. Turning northward, we came to the valley of the Torrejon and among Navajo cornfields, where they were beginning to break the soil. Beyond this point the valley narrows to a canyon, and the dry arroyo increased in depth until it became difficult to get either in or out of it. In this we finally made camp, as there was some grass for the mules and an accidental pool of water.

We soon left the Torrejon, and taking a northwesterly course, rose gradually over a comparatively open country to the continental divide. The transition from the waters of the Rio Grande to those of the Rio Colorado was so imperceptible that we could not tell within several miles when we had passed the actual divide. Low hills on either side of our course now gradually converged to a narrow passage between them, and the Chaco Canyon began to come into view. Passing some water holes, around which were several Navajo families with many sheep and horses, we came in sight of the first of the great ruins, the Pueblo Pintado,[17] while yet about five miles away. It resembled a ledge of dark brown sandstone, and it was only when quite near that we recognized its true character.

Chaco Canyon is best known through its most important ruin, the Pueblo Boni-to, which has now been made a National Monument. There are eleven ruins in the Chaco group,[18] with the Pueblo Pintado set rather apart from the others at the head of the canyon and twelve miles from its nearest neighbor. The other ten pueblos are distributed along the lower twelve miles of the canyon at various intervals, and the Pueblo Bonito, the largest of all is about midway in this lower group.

The first reference to these ruins that ever appeared in print was by Josiah Gregg, in the *Commerce of the Prairies,* in 1844.[19] In 1849 Lieutenant Simpson accompanied an expedition against the Navajos, during which he passed through Chaco Canyon for the purpose of examining the ruins. His report, illustrated with lithographs, was

Pueblo Bonito. 1878. Lithographic print.

This massive structure was a center of the Ancestral Puebloan (Anasazi) culture, built between 900 and 1125 AD. "Close under the perpendicular walls of the cañon are the ruins of Pueblo Bonito, the largest and most remarkable of all" the Anasazi structures in the Chaco region (Jackson in Hayden 1878, 440). It was the largest structure in North America until well into the nineteenth century. Jackson had little time and no skilled assistance with his archaeological fieldwork. Despite this, he "roughly sketched the external forms of the ruin" and took measurements that were used to create this detailed lithograph (Ibid., 440). Courtesy National Park Service/Scotts Bluff National Monument.

the first detailed and authentic account ever published of these wonderful ruins and the only source of information up to the time of my own report to the Geological Survey in 1878.

Several scientific expeditions have been organized for an extensive excavation program, particularly about the Pueblo Bonito, the most recent being the work promoted by the National Geographic Society, frequent notices of which have appeared in its magazine.

Our trip being a hurried one, my examinations necessarily were somewhat superficial, but during the four days devoted to the entire group, my efforts were as thorough as the limited time and means permitted. My useless camera was constantly employed. Then came the notebook with tapeline and compass for dimensions and orientation, and much going to and fro to determine ground plans under

ANCIENT STAIRWAY. 1878. Lithographic print.

Beyond the bluff above this carefully crafted sandstone staircase, known as "Jackson Staircase," Pueblo Alto awaited Jackson's discovery. Another artist created this lithograph, probably from Jackson's preliminary sketch. "While engaged in the examination of the [Pueblo Peñasca Blanca] ruin . . . I accidentally discovered with my field glasses some ruined walls upon the summit of the bluff. . . . Back of the Pueblo Chettro Kettle is an alcove with perpendicular walls about one-third mile in depth and 300 yards wide across its mouth. . . . Continuing around the alcove to its mouth opposite where I entered, I saw some steps and hand-holds cut into the rock . . . . Upon each side of these steps, in the steepest part of the ascent, are hand-holds so hewn out as to allow the hand to grasp them like rounds of a ladder; in the other places they are sunken cup-like cavities, just large enough to admit the fingers. Easily gaining the summit, I walked back over the bluffs, ascending by terraces some 200 or 300 feet above the bottom of the cañon, and then turning around the head of the alcove, my attention was drawn to the stairway, shown in the accompanying drawing, hewn in the smooth and almost vertical face of a bluff, parallel with, and but a short distance back of that which forms the alcove" (Jackson in Hayden 1878a, 446–47). Today it is known as the Jackson Staircase in honor of its discoverer. Courtesy Museum of New Mexico, History Library.

great piles of accumulated débris. At the same time I attempted a sketch map of our route through the canyon, using simply my compass for directions and bearing of prominent landmarks. I got distances by timing the pace of my mule, which could be estimated nearly as well as by an odometer—at least my map turned out to be approximately correct.

During the three days I was examining the lower group of old pueblos, we made our camp in the bed of the deep arroyo near Pueblo Bonito, where there were a few shallow pools of muddy water, so thick that it imparted to our coffee the appearance, if not the flavor, of cream. From this point we worked up and down the canyon, returning to it each night, as it had the only water to be found.

While working on one of the ruins situated upon a high bench at the lower end of the canyon, I accidentally discovered with my glasses what appeared to be another large ruin far back on top of the bluffs behind Pueblo Bonito. No such pueblo had been noted by Simpson, and this aroused my curiosity. Searching the apparently inaccessible bluffs, I finally found a line of steps and handholes hewn out from the rock, back of the Pueblo Chettro Kettle,[20] by which I easily gained the summit. Then walking back from the bluffs, ascending from terrace to terrace, I finally came to the ruin on an elevation that commanded the entire horizon, from the La Plata Mountains across the San Juan to the snow-covered peaks of the San Mateo in the south. From its dominating position, I named it Pueblo Alto. It is now regarded as one of the important ruins of the Chaco.

On the morning of our departure from this interesting region, while making a final inspection along the foot of the bluff back of Pueblo Bonito, I discovered a crevice, partly concealed by a large detached mass of rock, in which there was a rude stairway leading to the top of the bluff. Ascending this with comparatively little trouble, I came out directly over the Pueblo Bonito, and from this bird's-eye view was able to get a much better idea of its complex ground plan. But another discovery left regrets only in its train. In making my way across the bare, rock surface of the summit, I came on a series of potholes in a deep crevice, containing hundreds of gallons of cool, sweet water, something we had not seen since leaving Jemez. And the vexatious part of it was that I could take only one long, satisfying drink of it.

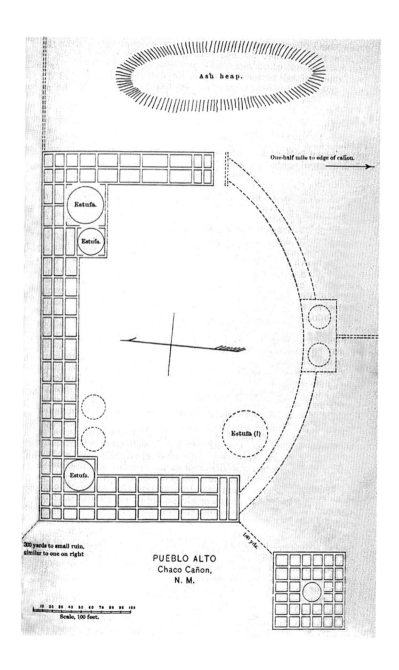

PUEBLO ALTO
Chaco Cañon,
N. M.

Scale, 100 feet.

Ash heap.

One-half mile to edge of cañon.

Estufa.

Estufa.

Estufa (?)

Estufa.

300 yards to small ruin,
similar to one on right

PUEBLO ALTO, CHACO CAÑON, N.M. 1878.
Ground plan print.

"This ruin is . . . nearly midway and above all the others—dominating them so far as its position is concerned. I endeavored to obtain some information from Hosta [the guide] as to its name among the Navajos or Pueblos. At first he professed entire ignorance of its existence, and said that none of his people or any of the Navajos knew anything of it. A day or two afterwards, however, while on the way home, he modified this statement by saying that there was a tradition among his people, of one pueblo among the others that was above them all, not only in position but in strength and influence, and was called El Capitan or El Jugador [the Captain or the Gambler]. He explains the latter name by saying that among his people the gambler was regarded as a type of a superior people. Whether this explanation was gotten up for the occasion, to explain something he knew nothing of, and yet did not wish to confess his ignorance, a manner in which most of these traditions are gotten up, it is impossible for me to determine; but as a compromise I have called this ruin Pueblo Alto." Employing simple tools, some ingenious methods, and his Civil War experience as a mapmaker, Jackson produced some relatively accurate ground plans of the major ruins at Chaco Canyon. Because no other Hayden Survey members were present, Jackson served as photographer, topographer, cartographer, and architectural draftsman while detailing the layout and construction details of Chaco's prehistoric human habitations. This ground plan was one of several appearing in Jackson's report (Jackson in Hayden 1878a, 447). Courtesy Museum of New Mexico, History Library.

LAGUNA. May 1877. Pencil drawing.

Jackson's rendering shows the Catholic Church altar at the Laguna Pueblo. Courtesy National Park Service/Scotts Bluff National Monument.

The return trip to Jemez and San Ysidro was made without particular incident, except for the long talks with Hosta about the various ruins of this region and his experiences while with the Colonel Washington Expedition. Our conversation was carried on through the interpretations of Beaumont. Hosta's grandson, Victoriana, was a bright boy, a worthy successor of his grandfather.

From San Ysidro I went to the pueblo of Laguna, sixty miles or more to the southwest, over a desert-like country.[21] There was merely a pretense of a road here and there and a poorly defined trail for most of the way. The whole region was almost entirely unoccupied except for occasional shacks near water holes, the homes of wandering sheep herders. The one-night camp I had to make on the way was out on the trail, away from even these poor habitations.

I had a trying time taking the buckboard over those trails. It was comparatively easy going across the upland country between water courses; the trouble came in crossing the many intervening arroyos and getting in and out of deep valleys, where the endurance of the buckboard was tested to a limit just short of a breakdown.

At Laguna I was entertained by the Marmon brothers, merchant traders for this region. They were helpful in many ways while I worked around the pueblo. They also accompanied me to the Acoma Pueblo, twelve or fifteen miles to the south, which on its lofty rock citadel is an unchanged survival from a time beyond recorded history. Two busy days were spent here in photographing, measuring, plotting, and sketching—gathering material for the model I was to make on my return to Washington.

Crossing the Rio Grande at Albuquerque, I passed through the numerous pueblos along the river from Sandia to San Domingo, making brief stops in each. Reaching Santa Fe about the last of May, I turned in my government outfit and was soon on my way to headquarters, to go through the heartbreaking experience of failing to develop even a single negative from several hundred films I had exposed. This hard trip, through the land of the pueblos, however, offered many compensations. It had brought some rich experiences and left many picturesque memories with me.

Chapter Nineteen

Along Old Wyoming Trails Again

July 1878–October 1878

The last expedition of the Hayden Geological Survey to the Rocky Mountain region was made in 1878. After that year it was discontinued, along with the Wheeler and other surveys. The present United States Geological Survey was then instituted for the better correlation of the work.

I went out with the expedition in 1878 with no premonition that it was to be my last service as a government photographer.[1] After two years' lay-off I was as eager as ever to get out into the mountains again at the head of a pack train. I was also happy to be going over Wyoming, where my first work with the Survey began.

Our outfit, as in 1870, was drawn from Fort D. A. Russell near Cheyenne. It was shipped over the Union Pacific to Point of Rocks.[2] From there we made our departure for the Wind River Mountains on July twenty-fourth, a late start for mountain work in the northern territories, as we were to learn to our discomfort. I had my separate party, as usual, but except for the time we were in the Yellowstone Park region, I traveled with the other divisions of the Survey on the long journeys to and from the railway.

As we traveled northward, there was no photographing until we got into the foothills beyond South Pass, except when we lay over for a day to witness a total eclipse of the sun on July twenty-ninth. We happened to be within the line of totality. I prepared to make photographs, but through some miscalculation of the time, the totality had passed before my plates were ready, so I got exposures on the last half only.

The first photographic work of importance was done around Wind River Peak from the headwaters of the Little Popo-Agie River.[3] Here, up near the timber line, I found some picturesque lake scenery, with the peak as a background. The early

Because this was the last year for the Survey, much of its work was never completed or published. There are no Hayden Survey catalogues containing photograph descriptions or numbers. "I did not keep a daily journal and have only a few random notes to assist me in recounting the many incidents and adventures connected therewith. It was an interesting experience in many ways, both as to the region traversed and the personal happenings, and I regret now that I did not make note of these, at the time, as faithfully as I did during our Colorado campaigns. I have'nt [sic] even a [complete] list of the views I made—one of the best kind of reminders—and as I have probably forgotten much more than I can possibly recall at the present time, [the 1878] notes will cover only such incidents as have survived the lapse of time in memories' storehouse" (Jackson [1878a] n.d., 2). More than forty days of notes were lost altogether.

"The Geological Survey was destined to be reorganized after the expedition of 1878; but in the spring we knew nothing about that, our concern was the usual one; how much money would congress give us; when could we start. . . . The turbulence of the early Grant years had been succeeded by the stodginess of the Hayes administration. In 1878 the amiable gentlemen of the House and the Senate just couldn't get going. It was late in July before we were in the field. . . . In respect to the season, our chosen theater of activity, Montana and Wyoming, was rather unfortunate. Before starting out I recalled the old saying about the three seasons of that country—'July, August, and winter'— and by September I should have occasion to think about it again" (Jackson [1940] 1994, 246–47).

WIND RIVER PEAK. August 2, 1878.
Copy of modern print from wet plate negative.

"Worked all day yesterday with 5/8 plates getting only two good exposures. Trouble with [wet plate negative] bath; very windy also" (Jackson [1878b] n.d., 1). The figure contemplating the grandiose scenery is A. D. Wilson, topographer. Courtesy U.S. Geological Survey.

morning was the best for picture making, as almost invariably the afternoons were windy, with low-lying clouds and sometimes rain.

Winding in and out among the glacial lakes and granite ridges of the western foothills of the range, we were gradually approaching Fremont Peak.[4] It had been in view for several days, and we finally reached a point as near its base as it was practicable to take the whole train. From here a smaller party was made up for the ascent, and with lighter packs we climbed on through the rocks and piñons to near timber line, camping there by the side of a rock-bound lake.

As the rest of the climb up Fremont Peak promised to be difficult, it was thought impractical to attempt packing up a wet-plate outfit, as I had done in Colorado. I had with me, however, a recently perfected collodio-bromide emulsion for making dry plates; and this was the time to try it out. Not that I had forgotten my trying experience of the year before in New Mexico; but in this instance I had more confidence in my material and was prepared for development soon after exposure.

Waiting until it was quite dark and working under one of our large tents, as my dark tent was too small for the purpose, I coated half a dozen plates. Proper drying was an essential part of the process, and this was accomplished by heating a shovel in the camp fire and bringing it into the tent.

Next morning, long before the sun appeared over the top of the mountains, we were climbing the historic peak. Before us, just beyond the lake, a granite ridge about five hundred feet high lay across our path, apparently the only one between us and the base of the peak. But this surmounted, we found another one of equal height; and so it kept on, one ridge after another, up five hundred feet and down the same, four or five times. Thus we were forced to make the most laborious part of the climb without gaining anything in altitude.

Reaching the base of Fremont Peak at last, we had before us a straightaway climb of some four thousand feet, rather steep and mostly over loose rock, with an occasional snow bank to cross. It was simply a scramble from one slide to another between intervening rocky ledges. With the summit gained, the whole party perched upon the little rock citadel that forms the apex of the peak. This must be the same rock that Fremont mentions;⁵ he would allow only one man at a time to go upon it for fear of its being dislodged and precipitating them down the mountain.

The view from the summit had the usual mountain grandeur. North, east, and south a wonderful array of sharply serrated peaks pierced the sky line, while directly below was a great snow field with glacial characteristics. The far distances were too hazy for clear definition. The Tetons and the Absarokas were only faintly visible, while the Big Horns were almost entirely out of the picture. Directly west was the great plain of the Green River Basin, suggestive of trappers' and fur traders' rendezvous. Nearer, at the foot of the peak, were granite ridges, among which were scattered many little emerald lakes—altogether a panoramic scene well worth the difficult climb.

While the topographers were locating the various peaks, I was busy with my camera, taking first the party on the rock and then a panoramic view into the mass of ragged mountain summits. For a wonder, there was neither wind nor clouds—nothing but the distant haziness to mar a perfect day.

THE TETONS FROM THE EAST. August 1878. Albumin print.

As William Jackson traveled through Jackson Hole for the first time "a smoky haziness . . . prevailed quite generally and it was only by taking advantage of early morning light that fairly satisfactory pictures were made" (Jackson [1878b] n.d., 9). This is often mistakenly credited as an 1872 image. Courtesy U.S. Geological Survey.

COLUMBIA SPG., RED MTN. BASIN. August–September 1878. Copy of modern print from wet plate negative.

The Hayden Survey named a small range of rust-colored volcanic peaks in southwestern Yellowstone the Red Mountains. The adjacent thermal area was termed the Red Mountain Basin. It has reverted to its original name today, the Heart Lake Basin. In fact, this name is a misnomer as the lake had originally been termed "Hart" Lake after Hart Hunney, a hunter who frequented the area, predating the Survey (Whittlesey 1988). Courtesy U.S. Geological Survey.

Returning to the camp far below, we packed up next day and moved on across the headwaters of Green River. Then by way of Hoback Canyon we entered into the broad expanse of Jacksons Hole, named for Dave Jackson, one of the partners with Jim Bridger in the Rocky Mountain Fur Company of earlier days.[6] The trail through Hoback was an attractive one so far as scenery goes, but it had some serious problems in the long, steep slides that crossed it frequently. These made precarious footing for riding and pack animals. One of the mules took a roll of about two hundred feet into the stream below, but fortunately with no serious harm to itself. None of us cared to ride over those slides.

Very little photographing was done in passing up through Jacksons Hole because of a smoky haziness that filled the air. From the Upper Gros Ventre Butte I did take some pictures of the Teton Range,[7] but with little hope of satisfactory results. I could not go by that splendid scene without making an attempt at least.

Following the Upper Snake River over obscure trails or no trails at all through the dense pine forests, we finally camped on the shore of Heart Lake under the shadow of Mt. Sheridan.[8] Our camp was in a little grove, back of which was a marshy meadow surrounded by the general forest growth. The isolation of this remote corner of Yellowstone Park was shown by the frequent appearance of the wild denizens of the mountains—elk, particularly, coming out into the open and gazing curiously at our little encampment, entirely oblivious of the danger lurking behind the strange intruders.

After four or five weeks spent in working along the headwaters of the Fire Hole, Madison, and Gallatin rivers, mostly old familiar scenes, we finally reached the Mammoth Hot Springs about the middle of September. Here we met General Miles, with his staff and a small escort. He was on an inspection trip.

The year before, the Nez Percé Indians, fleeing from General Howard and his troops, had passed through the Park. Some tourists happened to come in the way of these Indians, and two of them were killed and several wounded. There were rumors that more of these hostile red men were still lurking about the Park, and a small scouting party of cavalry patrolled the country during the tourist season.

None of our parties came in contact with these Indians, except Wilson's. While we were in the Lower Fire Hole Basin, we were much surprised one day to see Wilson and his four companions come into our camp afoot, packing their blankets and rifles. They reported that three days previously, while camped at Henrys Lake, their party had been fired on from ambush as they were lying around the camp fire after supper, and at the same time mounted Indians stampeded all their stock. None of the men were injured. Escaping into the woods, they eventually found their way to our party. I provided them with riding horses and a pack mule, with which they went back to recover as much as possible from the raided camp. Everything had been destroyed or carried off except the instruments, which they had succeeded in caching among the trees before making their escape.

It was September twentieth before we turned our steps homeward. Snow had already fallen, and the increasing cold warned us of the danger of lingering long in these high altitudes.[9] Following the old trails of former days, we passed over Mt. Washburn during a cold snowstorm,[10] and going on to the Yellowstone Falls, remained there for two or three days of photographic work. In addition to finding other new points of view, I made my first descent to the bottom of the canyon on the east side for a view of the Lower Falls.

Lower Basins, Mammoth Hot Springs. 1883. Lithographic print.

The photograph that was the basis for this lithograph was taken in August–September 1878. The last of the Hayden Survey reports, the *Twelfth Annual Report*, appeared in 1883. Numerous 1878 and 1883 Jackson photographs were used in the second volume as illustrations. Courtesy Wayne Johnson.

UPPER FIRE HOLE FROM OLD FAITHFUL. 1878 or 1883.
Albumin print.

The United States Geological Survey was reorganized after
the 1878 season, and Jackson's work for that year was not
organized or catalogued. His work at Yellowstone for the
U.S.G.S. continued in 1883 when he joined the Hague
Party. Those 1883 photographs are often confused with the
1878 photos because the work for both years was not well
documented either by the U. S. G. S. or in Jackson's
records. In all probability this photograph was taken in
1878 because this particular print is mounted in a way that
earlier prints were done for the Hayden Survey. It is
identified on the mount as a "W. H. Jackson Photo,
Washington, D.C." By 1883 Jackson was living in Denver
and no longer used such mounts. Courtesy National Park
Service/Scotts Bluff National Monument.

It was a problem for a while how to cross the river without going all the way to
the upper ford near the lake outlet. We finally attempted it in the rapids between the
Lower and Upper Falls. This was a precarious undertaking, for the river bed was
strewn with large boulders, with a rather stiff current running over them. Fortunately, owing to the lateness of the season, the water was not much more than leg
deep for our animals, and we made the crossing all right.

This lateness of the season, however, was a handicap in making the descent into
the canyon. A coating of ice on rocks and slopes from the drifting spray of the falls
made the undertaking hazardous. By using the packers' lash ropes and letting ourselves down over the steep places with the photographic outfit strapped to our backs,
we managed finally to get to the bottom of the colorful gorge. There was a little difficulty in finding a smooth and level place for the dark tent. With that set up, conditions were as fine as they could be for our getting a successful series of negatives of
the scene that has since thrilled thousands of visitors to this wonderland.

Leaving the falls, we crossed the river in the vicinity of Sulphur Hills[11] and struck
into our old trail around the eastern shores of the lake, where we were storm bound
for several days. We had some apprehension of running into hostile Indians, but luckily met none. At the head of the lake we passed the site of an abandoned Indian camp
that was hardly more than a day old, but the newly fallen snow obliterated all traces
of any trail showing which way they had gone. The snow increased in depth as we
got into the thick timber along the Upper Yellowstone River, concealing the trail
almost completely, so that we had to depend on the blazed tree trunks to find our way.

Along in the afternoon, when it was nearing the time to look for a camping place,
I was riding some distance ahead of the train with Dr. Hayden when we noticed bear
tracks crossing our course. They were so recent as to suggest the presence of a large
grizzly bear in the immediate neighborhood. The Doctor proposed that we follow
the tracks and see what the old fellow looked like. So turning aside, we trailed his
devious course around among the trees.

The signs grew fresher all the time until, at the end of about half a mile of this
kind of work, we caught sight of him in the distance, loping off through the timber.
He had scented our approach and was now trying to shake our company. We spurred
up and followed in his wake, just keeping him in sight until he came to a large fallen

tree across his path. He jumped over this but immediately turned around. Placing his paws on the tree, he faced us with an expression, which indicated plainly that he had been chased far enough and would like to know what it was all about anyway. By this time we had approached within less than fifty yards.

I dismounted quickly, my horse bolting at once for the train in the rear, but the Doctor stood by, although he had no firearms. Kneeling down, and throwing back the heavy cape of my army overcoat, I took careful aim with my breach loading Springfield. Old bruin meanwhile remained motionless, watching my movements with evident interest. I hesitated for a moment as to where to shoot. As his body was concealed behind the tree, there was only the head as my target. I concluded to aim for his eyes, reasoning that even if my bullet did glance off his thick skull, it might so blind him that I would have a better opportunity for another shot. At the crack of my rifle, he crumpled up in back of the log as if struck by a bolt of lightning.

Knowing well the bear's tenacity of life, I was careful to keep on my side of the fallen tree until by prodding his ribs with the rifle I was pretty sure he was not "playing possum." He proved to be a full-grown silvertip grizzly.

The train coming up, we went into camp near by. As soon as the preliminary camp duties were done, the packers completed my work by taking off the bear's skin. While this operation was under way, some surprise was expressed over the fact that there was no outward evidence of the bear's having been hit at all. It was only when the skull was bared that we discovered that the bullet had penetrated the brain through one of the nostrils without leaving a trace on the surface.

The green hide made a heavy pack for one of the mules. My intention was to take it to the Indian Agency at Camp Brown on Wind River,[12] which was on our way homeward, and there have it properly tanned and dressed as a trophy. It was ten days before we arrived there. While we were up in the mountains, the cold weather was all the preservative needed to keep the skin in good condition; but after getting down into Wind River Valley, we had three or four days of very warm weather. When I turned the skin over to the Indians, they declared that it was unfit for tanning. All I saved for a trophy was a set of the claws.

This hot spell was in decided contrast to the weather we had experienced along the Upper Yellowstone. One night we camped on Two-Ocean Pass, as near as we

WE MEET BRUIN "SILVER TIP." n.d. Pencil drawing.

The incident occurred on October 1 (Jackson [1878b] n.d., 2) while traveling with Dr. Hayden *near the headwaters of the Yellowstone River.* Jackson often sketched several different versions of the same event over time. This sketch is nearly identical to the one presented in the first edition of this book. He was impressed by this event; he did several almost identical sketches. Courtesy National Park Service/Scotts Bluff National Monument.

VIEW FROM TOGWOTEE PASS. October 4–5, 1878.
Copy of modern print from wet plate negative.

"... in Togwote [Togwotee] Pass I made several
characteristic pictures of the castellated trachytes [light-
colored, rough-textured volcanic rocks] that are a
prominent feature of the region" (Jackson [1878a] n.d.,
unnumbered page following page 18). Courtesy U.S.
Geological Survey.

could determine, for the Doctor wished to get definite proof of the existence of a large
spring on the summit of the pass, from which, according to Bridger, the waters
flowed both ways to the Atlantic and to the Pacific. Our bivouac was made in the
snow, where it was more convenient to sleep on our little tents than under them. But
whatever discomforts we had, they were not comparable to the plight of our poor
animals in trying to paw out a few blades of frozen grass from under the snow.

In the morning everything was frozen up as tight as a drumhead. But led by the
Doctor, half a dozen of us tramped all over a space of about forty acres, breaking
through the ice wherever a stream was indicated, to find which way the water flowed.
Finally it was determined to the Doctor's satisfaction that from this place water was
running both ways, one branch to the Yellowstone and another to Snake River. Water
from the same source reached both oceans.

When we got over into the headwaters of Buffalo Fork and away from the elevated Two-Ocean plateau, we were out of the snow for a while. It was a fine grassy
country, and there we saw great troops of elk forsaking these high feeding grounds

for lower altitudes in Jacksons Hole. But most attractive of all were distant views of the Three Tetons, with their majestic individual peaks clearly defined against the western horizon. These could not be passed by without setting up the big camera and thus carrying to others something of their beauty.

In crossing Togwotee Pass, we had some steep hill climbing, bad trails, and at the summit more snow. But the scenery made amends, and we frequently stopped to photograph the castellated volcanic rocks that are a prominent feature of that region. Dropping down into Wind River Valley, we finally rode in to the Washakie Indian Agency. Most of the Indians belonging to the Agency, Shoshones, were away on their fall hunting expeditions; but at the post were a lot of Bannack prisoners recently brought in by the troops. These were lined up individually and in groups for their pictures. At the Agency also we found Beaver Dick, who had been a guide for the Survey on several occasions, particularly around the Upper Snake River country. We got him to camp near by in his little tepee so that we could photograph him with his Shoshone squaw, three children, and a donkey.[13] Besides his own family, there were several relatives of the squaw, who also came in for their pictures.

Leaving Camp Brown, we had but one purpose, and that was to reach the railroad as soon as possible. The second day out we camped near the Three Crossings on the Sweetwater. It was snowing all the time we were passing through Muddy Gap,[14] a wet, heavy snow that gradually deepened to five or six inches, making disagreeable camping conditions, as wet sagebrush was the only fuel we could get for cooking and for warmth.

From the head of the Muddy to Rawlins on the Union Pacific was a broad open plain, which it took us two days to cross, most of the way through a snow-laden blizzard. From Rawlins we went on to Fort Steele,[15] where we turned in our outfit, and the next day we were on our way back to Washington, enjoying the luxury of a Pullman.

Thus ended my rich and pleasant days among the Rockies with Dr. Hayden and my other companions of the United States Geological Survey. The days of pioneer photography, too, were brought to an end with the close of the seventies. A new era of dry plates, compact cameras, enlargements, films, and kodaks had come. With these handier appliances, during the half century that has since elapsed, I have followed my

BEAVER DICK AND HIS FAMILY. 1872.
Type of print unknown.

Beaver Dick Leigh was one of our guides in the Wind River country. In the first edition of this book it was placed in this 1878 chapter. It was taken in 1872, the year Beaver Dick guided Jackson's Southern Division of the Hayden Survey through the Tetons and into Yellowstone. Left to right the group includes Beaver Dick Leigh, John, Anne Jane, Jenny holding William, and Dick Jr. on the donkey. Stricken with "Bea-inga-ta-sea," the white man's smallpox, Dick's entire family was dead by year's end, 1876, including Elizabeth, not pictured, and an unnamed newborn infant. Only Beaver Dick survived. By the time Jackson saw him in 1878 Beaver Dick had taken on a new wife, sixteen-year-old Susan Tadpole, a Bannack Indian. He was on the way to raising a second family (Thompson 1982, 72, 105). Jackson did photograph the second family in 1878. Courtesy National Park Service/Grand Teton National Park.

MEMORIES. n.d. Ink sketch.

William Henry Jackson's fondest memories of his many photographic accomplishments with Ferdinand Hayden's United States Geological Survey of the Territories are depicted on this postcard sketch. Included left to right are: the discovery of Two-Story House, capturing the wonders of Yellowstone with the Wind River Mountains and the Devil's Tower nearby, the mighty Grand Teton, and the Mount of the Holy Cross. William Henry Jackson looks on as his photographic outfit and an assistant approach from below. Courtesy American Heritage Center.

own lead in quest of strange and beautiful scenes in our own and other lands. None of these later experiences, however, can ever bring more delightful memories than those of earlier days, when I was doing my part to help reveal the scenic and other wonders of our Rocky Mountain region to the world. Incidentally, I was helping also, with other pioneer photographers, to blaze the trail for the great advancement that since has come in the science and art of photography.

Notes

CHAPTER ONE

1. According to the family Bible, William Henry Jackson was the first of seven children born to George Hallock Jackson and Harriet Maria Allen on April 4, 1843 (Jackson [1940] 1994, 10).

2. The photographer Frank Mowry found talented young Will Jackson through an associate photographer, Mr. C. C. Schoonmaker, who had previously hired the boy to do photographic retouching. Mowry hired Jackson to do hand tinting and other work in his photographic studio (Jackson [1940] 1994, 26, 34).

3. The Second Vermont Infantry is noted for its valor during the Battle of Gettysburg. Through a flank movement members of the brigade repelled the Confederate general, Pickett, turning the battle into a Union victory. The Vermont Twelfth Infantry Regiment guarded Washington, D.C., Alexandria, VA, Wolf Run Shoals, VA, and other nearby places. It was assigned to rear guard duties, guarding the corps train, as the Second Vermont Brigade neared Gettysburg. The regiment was mustered out of service on July 16, 1863. No casualties had been suffered, but the Twelfth lost a total of sixty-four men to disease.

4. Colonel John Singleton Mosby proved to be extremely disruptive to behind-the-lines Union activities. With twenty-nine men he rode into Fairfax Courthouse, where he reportedly arose General Edwin H. Stoughton with a slap on the rear end as he captured him. He effectively carried out a number of other guerilla raids on Union forces.

5. The Confederacy had won a decisive victory at Bull Run on July 21, 1861. For the first three months in 1863, the Twelfth Infantry did picket duty there.

6. Major General George Jerrison Stannard was the first Union soldier to volunteer from Vermont. He led the flank attack on General Pickett, helping to turn the tide of battle for the northern forces. He was severely wounded in the battle. General Robert E. Lee commanded the Army of Northern Virginia. He led the Confederate forces at the Battle of Gettysburg, where he was defeated after three days of horrific fighting. Pickett's charge was his last desperate attempt to turn the tide of battle.

7. James "Jeb" Ewell Brown Stuart was among the most famous of the Civil War cavalrymen. His death at Richmond on May 11, 1864, marked the beginning of the decline of the Confederate mounted forces.

8. Fort McHenry is the site of the Battle of Baltimore, September 3, 1814. There, Francis Scott Key wrote "The Star Spangled Banner." During the Civil War it was converted into a transfer camp for prisoners of war. In contrast to other Civil War prisons relatively few deaths occurred.

9. General George Edward Pickett had served in the United States Army, where he fought in the Mexican War. Then he joined the Confederacy, distinguishing himself in battle until the Battle of Gettysburg, in which he led an unsuccessful charge on the Union troop.

10. The Styles gallery was named the Vermont Gallery of Art. Although he worked at the gallery for over a year, Jackson never learned Mr. F. Styles's first name (Jackson [1940] 1994, 74).

11. The daguerreotype was the first commercially successful photographic process. Chemical treatment made a mirror-like silver-coated copper plate light sensitive. After exposure the plate was fixed with more chemicals to preserve the image. A tintype photographic image was made on a sheet of black-lacquered iron coated with light-sensitive chemicals. Exposed and developed simultaneously in the camera, tintypes were taken widely during the Civil War because they could be created in the field.

CHAPTER TWO

1. Jackson's companion was ". . . Rock [Rounds], so-called, perhaps, because he was by trade a marble cutter" (Jackson [1940] 1994, 85).

2. This "opportunity" came from an acquaintance of Rock's, a Harry King, who ". . . had already signed up for such a job" with the mines in Virginia City. When they ran into Mr. King, after trying for two days to land employment with the mines, he ". . . disclaimed any knowledge of the rumor which had tied him up with the silver interests. The new partnership of Rounds & Jackson was discouraged" (Jackson [1940] 1994, 85).

3. Billy's last name was Crowl (Jackson 1866–1867, April, 19, 1866). H. B. Chalfin's was the firm for which Billy worked (Jackson [1940] 1994, 86).

4. Jackson went to work with a Mr. Swift, who ". . . was not only the slowest of mortals but an old sourpuss besides. Yet I was happy to stick with him until something better should turn up. Mr. Swift had at least the virtue of paying his help punctually, and on Saturday I collected $18" (Jackson [1940] 1994, 92–93).

5. In his reconstructed diary account Jackson quotes the advertisement: "One hundred teamsters wanted for Plains. Apply at Intelligence Office on St. Francis St. between 2nd and 3rd. St. Joe Herald. June 22, 1866" (Jackson [1862–1863] 1915, June 22, 1866).

6. The boys were dreaming of gold. Virginia City was in its heyday as a wide-open mining town.

CHAPTER THREE

1. Fort Childs (later Fort Kearny) in 1847, General Stephen Kearny took command in 1848. Abandoned in 1867, it is located southwest of present-day Kearny, Nebraska.

2. Jules Reni started Julesburg as a ranch. It was burned by Indians and relocated three times.

3. Courthouse Rock, Chimney Rock, and Scotts Bluff were noted geologic landmarks on the Oregon Trail in Nebraska. Chimney Rock was considered to be one of the most spectacular landmarks on the trail. Scotts Bluff posed some serious difficulties for the wagons.

4. Fort Laramie was built in 1834 as the Fort William trading post and was the first permanent settlement in Wyoming. The U.S. military purchased it in 1849 to use as a base for protecting immigrants from hostile Sioux Indians. It was abandoned in 1890.

5. The Platte Bridge was located on the western edge of present-day Casper, Wyoming. Three weeks prior to Jackson's arrival Lt. Caspar Collins was killed by Indians at the Platte Bridge fight.

6. Commonly referred to as the Bozeman Trail, John Jacobs and John M. Bozeman created the Powder River Road as a route to connect the Montana gold-strike country with cities to the east. It crossed traditional Indian buffalo hunting territory though, and hostilities mounted. By 1868 the trail and its forts were closed because the United States did not want a protracted war with the Indians.

7. The Black Hills are known today as the Laramie Mountains.

8. The Deer Creek Station was a Pony Express stop in 1860–61 on the Oregon Trail.

9. Hams Fork (Ham's Fork) Station was a Pony Express stop on the Oregon Trail.

CHAPTER FOUR

1. When Mormon settlers established a road over Indian footpaths in 1851, Cajon Pass became a popular route to the San Bernardino Valley.

2. Father Junípero Serra (1713–1784) founded the first nine of California's twenty-one Catholic outpost missions along the Camino Real.

3. Known today as Long Beach Harbor.

4. This "comrade" was a boy named Graham. He joined Jackson and Maddern late in January and accompanied them to San Francisco (Jackson 1866–1867, January–February 1867).

5. The stage station was the Twenty Mile Ranch. Tehachapi Pass lies between Bakersfield and Mojave, California.

6. *Vaquero* is the Spanish term for cowboy.

7. The wagon road climbed from the Virgin River to the summit of Flat Top Mesa between Bunkerville and Mormon Mesa, Nevada.

8. Jackson is referencing a small community near the Beaverdam Mountains.

9. Fort Sanders was established near Laramie, Wyoming, in 1866 to guard the survey parties of the Union Pacific Railroad. It was abandoned in 1882.

10. A man named Lobeck ran two races against Sam's horse. "Sam lost the first for ten dollars and the second for twenty-five. I don't remember that any tears were shed in our party" (Jackson [1940] 1994, 168).

CHAPTER FIVE

1. President Lincoln commissioned the two companies in 1862 to construct a transcontinental railroad. The Central Pacific Railroad started from Sacramento, California, working its way east in 1863. The Union Pacific Railroad began in Omaha, Nebraska, heading west in 1865. The rails connected at Promontory Summit, Utah, a desolate stretch of desert, in 1869.

2. The Bitter Creek region is in Sweetwater County between Rock Springs and Rawlins, Wyoming.

3. The rails did not meet at Promontory Point, a peninsula in the Great Salt Lake. They met at Promontory Summit, where a temporary town mushroomed to life as the rails were being laid.

4. Ogden City (now Ogden) was chosen as the "Junction City" for the two competing railroads to meet. The Union Pacific arrived first and proceeded on to Promontory Summit where it met the advancing Central Pacific. Ogden soon became the official terminal. The town exploded into an industrial and commercial hub.

5. The Cheyenne Depot was originally called Fort Carlin. It became the second largest supply depot in the West. General Grenville Mellen Dodge (1883–1916) began surveying and building bridges, roads, and railroads in 1851. In 1866 he became chief engineer of the Union Pacific leading the construction from Omaha to Promontory Summit. Fort D. A. Russell (1867 to present), several miles north of Cheyenne, is named after the Civil War general who fell at the battle of Winchester. It was built to protect Union Pacific Railroad workers from hostile Native Americans. Today it is Warren Air Force Base. It was supplied by Fort Carlin.

6. Major General John Aaron Rawlins (1831–1869) was one of General Grant's most indispensable assistants during and after the Civil War. He died of tuberculosis only five months after becoming secretary of war. The trip with Dodge was undertaken in hopes the air of the high plains would improve his health.

7. Corrine's unique history began in 1869 as a Gentile (non-Mormon) town on the Union Pacific tracks. It was a freight transfer point for the mining towns along the Montana Trail. Established so other American business interests could compete with the Mormon Church's economic hold on Utah, the town went so far as to try to split the Utah Territory and have Corrine named as its capital. The overwhelming Mormon interests bypassed Corrine with a railroad spur, effectively ending the town's economic and political viability by the late 1870s.

8. Blue Creek was a telegraph and train station, approximately twenty miles east of Corrine. The waters of Blue Creek served several stations along the Union Pacific Railroad.

9. The formation called Devil's Slide has two vertical limestone ridges running down a steep hillside into Weber Canyon.

10. Respected Mormon pioneer Charles R. Savage (1832–1909) was a photographer known for landscapes and for portraits of members of the Mormon community. The photographer and painter George Ottinger was in partnership with Savage when Jackson visited.

11. The Thousand Mile Tree was a railroad landmark exactly one thousand miles from Omaha. The Witches Rocks, located in the Weber Valley, are a group of twisted rock columns. The well-named Pulpit Rock is near the junction of the Echo Creek and the Weber River in Echo Canyon. It projects sixty feet above the original railroad bed.

12. Although Jackson did not become part of the United States Geological Survey until 1870, he allowed his 1869 scenic photography to be added to the United States Geological Survey materials.

CHAPTER SIX

1. The American Fur Company funded Dr. Ferdinand V. Hayden to scientifically record the geology of the Upper Missouri River and its surrounding areas, beginning in 1853. In 1867 Hayden was appointed geologist-in-charge of the Geological Survey of Nebraska. His United States Geological Survey became one of the most respected and well-funded scientific endeavors of the time.

2. John Butterfield was awarded a U.S. mail contract in 1857. He founded the Butterfield Overland Stage Company, establishing a series of stations about every ten to fifteen miles. By 1866 the company had became part of Wells Fargo, which monopolized long distance coach and mail service.

3. Hyposulfate was a chemical used as a photographic fixer. The proper name for the compound is sodium thiosulfate; hence, hyposulfate is a misnomer.

4. Sanford Robinson Gifford (1823–1880) was one of the nationally known landscape artists employed by Dr. Hayden during the years of his Survey. Through his art, Gifford helped bring national attention to Hayden's work.

5. Fort Fetterman was founded in 1867 to protect workers of the Union Pacific Railroad. It became a major supply point for operations against the Indians. It was abandoned in 1882 and became an outfitting post for wagon trains and ranchers until 1886. The newly founded town of Douglass, Wyoming, had replaced it.

6. Fort Caspar, originally known as Platte Bridge Station, was built to protect the bridge and a telegraph office. The

bridge was constructed in 1859–60. The fort was abandoned in 1867. The town of Casper was later founded in 1888. "Caspar" became "Casper" when a railroad clerk misspelled the name on the town's original plat.

7. Independence Rock is considered the most famous landmark along the Oregon Trail. General Ashley's band of trappers were probably the first white men to pass the rock in 1823. Over time, thousands of travelers inscribed their names on the monolith as they traveled west. The Overland Trail lived only a short time. Supplies began traveling in wagon trains along its route in 1862. In 1869 the railroad made the trail obsolete.

8. Located to the east of the Continental Divide, St. Mary's Station was a telegraph station and a sidetrack of the railroad. In 1867, gold was discovered nearby. This led to the founding of Atlantic City in 1868. A bust hit the mines in 1872, and the population rapidly declined. Camp Stambaugh (1870–78) was constructed to protect the area's population from Indian attacks.

9. Chief Washakie (Early nineteenth century–1900) assisted the U.S. Army with operations against the Sioux and Cheyenne. He remained friendly with the Americans throughout his long career as chief, gaining land and economic aid from the American government.

10. Pacific Springs was the location of the first good water available to the pioneers as they crossed South Pass on the Pacific side of the Continental Divide. Wagon trains, Pony Express riders, and stage companies used the site.

11. The Granger Stage Station was founded in 1861–62 as a Pony Express stop. It is quite possible that this was Jackson's temporary place of employment in 1866. The Franco-German War of 1870–71 between France and Germany ended with the siege of Paris and a humiliating treaty for the French on May 10, 1871. Jackson discusses the event as though it ended in 1870 when the Hayden Survey was in Granger.

12. Church Buttes are eroded sandstone cliffs located in extreme southwestern Wyoming. They project about seventy-five feet above the surrounding hills. The Mormons named them for their steeple-like spires. Badlands, or *mauvaises terres,* are areas of eroded landscape where little vegetation grows. Early western travelers avoided them because of the rugged terrain and lack of water.

13. Jim Bridger founded Fort Bridger in 1843 as a private enterprise to serve the increasing numbers of immigrants

heading westward. The opening of overland shortcuts caused a dramatic decrease in the number of travelers using the fort. The United States government purchased it in 1857 to serve as a military outpost along the stage route. It was abandoned in 1890.

14. "Judge" W. A. Carter was the "sutler," or civilian supplier, at Fort Bridger from 1857 to 1890.

15. Other places in the Rockies were named for William Henry Jackson. Mt. Jackson, located at the southern end of Jackson Hole, Wyoming, is an example. The term Jackson Hole, however, came from an earlier fur trapper, David Jackson of the Rocky Mountain Fur Company.

16. Browns Hole, known today as Brown's Park, is a mountain-rimmed valley named by fur trappers. Because of its remote location outlaws chose it as a place in which to disappear from society.

CHAPTER SEVEN

1. Jackson tried to sell his business. Because "there was no buyer in sight, and, rather than sacrifice a growing concern, Mollie [his wife who was expecting a child] undertook to manage the studio once more" (Jackson [1940] 1994, 194), as she had the previous season.

2. The fur trappers referred to a thermal area west of Cody, Wyoming, as Colter's Hell. John Colter was probably the first white man to visit Yellowstone in 1807–08.

3. The Raynolds Survey under William F. Raynolds of the Corps of Engineers, United States Army, did some of the first organized scientific exploration and mapping of the Yellowstone region in 1859–60.

4. The Folsom-Cook-Peterson Expedition occurred in 1869. Three men (David E. Folsom, Charles W. Cook, and William Peterson) ventured into the Yellowstone wilderness for thirty-nine days. They updated older maps of the area and were the first to describe the many wonders of the region.

5. The Washburn-Langford-Doane Expedition of 1870 traced the general route of the Folsom-Cook-Peterson Expedition. The nineteen men made numerous side trips, collecting scientific data. Their lectures and articles inspired Hayden to do the in-depth follow-up survey described in this chapter in 1871.

6. The article appears as Nathaniel P. Langford. 1871. The Wonders of Yellowstone. Parts 1 and 2. *Scribner's Monthly.* May, 1–17; June, 11–29.

7. Antoine Schoenborn worked for the 1859–60 Raynolds Survey as a meteorologist and artist. Because he was an excellent cartographer and surveyor Hayden appointed him to be the Survey's topographer. Hayden as well had been in the Yellowstone basin eleven years previously with Captain William Raynolds.

8. George B. Dixon became Jackson's assistant. He was a recent University of Pennsylvania medical school graduate who had studied geology under Hayden.

9. "Last year as well as this, we have had well known artists as guests and traveling companions, S. R. Gifford first and now Thomas Moran. In each instance they took great interest in the photographic work and were my constant companions while afield" (Jackson [1871] n.d., 2, 3). Moran (1837–1926) added notoriety and credibility to the work of the Survey as Gifford had done the previous season. Moran's art was a motivating force behind the creation of the first national park, Yellowstone, in 1872.

10. Nathaniel Wyeth established Fort Hall in 1834 as a supply center for the fur-trading giant, the Hudson's Bay Company. It was located a few miles northeast of present-day Pocatello, Idaho. When beaver trapping ended it became a supply point for immigrants on the Oregon Trail. It operated until 1856.

11. Taylor's Ferry was founded in 1866 as a way across the Snake River. Taylor's Bridge, or Anderson's Bridge, was built the following year. It became the town of Eagle Rock with the arrival of the railroad, and in 1891 it became present-day Idaho Falls.

12. The Hole in the Wall area to which Jackson refers is not the famous Hole in the Wall outlaw hideout in Wyoming. See note number 10, chapter eight.

13. "Les Trois Tetons," "the three nipples," was the name given to the tallest peaks in the Teton Range by early French fur trappers.

14. Fort Ellis (1868–86), near present-day Bozeman, Montana, was established by Captain R. S. LaMotte to quell political unrest and Indian animosity. It provided escort protection for explorers, railroad personnel, and surveyors.

15. The Barlow-Heap team of eleven men joined Hayden's Survey. These topographers plus the military escort swelled the numbers of Survey personnel to a total of eighty-three men.

16. On July 11–12 Jackson and five other Survey members took a twelve-mile side trip to Mystic Lake from Fort Ellis.

17. "Botler's" is correctly spelled Bottler's. The ranch had become a staging area for expeditions and parties entering Yellowstone.

18. Jackson is mistaken. Madera and Cooper worked for Hayden during the years of the Colorado surveys between 1873 and 1875. Jackson considered them to be the two best packers of the Survey.

19. Joe Clark and "José" were the hunters. José's last name has been lost to history.

20. Earlier references to Mammoth Hot Springs exist. Captain Washington Hood's 1839 map references it. Jim Bridger's descriptions appear in the early 1850s.

21. Moran fished at Yankee Jim Canyon.

22. Thomas Hine accompanied the Barlow Expedition in 1871. This reconnaissance of the Yellowstone region took place simultaneously with Hayden's Survey. Before Hine's negatives were destroyed in the Chicago Fire some were printed, but they never gained national attention.

23. Joshua Crissman, a Bozeman, Montana, photographer, knew Jackson from Corrine, Utah, where he loaned his darkroom to Jackson and Hull. He joined the Hayden Survey for the 1871 and 1872 seasons. Some of the images catalogued by Jackson (Jackson [1875] 1978) are Crissman images.

24. Hiram Martin Chittenden wrote a guide called *The Yellowstone National Park: Historical and Descriptive* (1895).

25. Collins John "Jack" Baronett built the bridge in 1871, near present-day Tower Junction, Wyoming.

26. Lieutenant Gustavus Doane was a respected military scout whose well-done reports contributed to the creation of Yellowstone National Park. His ill-fated 1876 expedition to navigate the Snake River from Yellowstone to the Columbia River started so late in the season that his party hit an ice jam; the boat was destroyed.

CHAPTER EIGHT

1. In order to document the adventures described in chapters seven and eight, William Jackson had to rely on memory, fragmentary or indirect personal notations, and the writings of others. "I have never ceased regretting my failure to keep a diary during '71–72, the only years I did not do so while with the survey" (Jackson, January 9, 1934). In addition there are only fragmentary notes for 1878.

2. Charlie Campbell, a cousin of Jackson's late wife, became the primary photographic assistant. P. J. Beveridge, general assistant to the Survey party, also helped with photographic chores. Aleck Sibley was the packer.

3. The plateau Jackson refers to is Table Mountain. Glacier Creek is now the South Fork of Cascade Canyon.

4. "Part of the time we were camped at timber line on Table Mountain, from where the close-up views of the Grand Teton were obtained" (Jackson 1929a, 190).

5. This "plateau" on the western edge of the Tetons where the comprehensive views of the range were taken culminates to the west in a lesser summit known today as Mary's Nipple near Fred's Mountain. Jackson's famous image *Photographing in High Places* (Jackson [1875] 1978, 42: #423, 1872 series, 8″ × 10″), was taken just below this summit. It became his defining view of "the pioneer photographer."

6. The surveyor William O. Owen worked on government contracts to assess the Grand Tetons, Jackson Hole, and portions of the Snake River. He became the Wyoming State Auditor for four years, beginning in January 1895.

7. Jackson is credited for discovering Gibbon Falls. It is named after the Gibbon River, which is named for General John Gibbon. The Hayden Survey party met Gibbon briefly in 1872 while exploring near present-day Madison Junction. Gibbon had just completed a brief reconnaissance of portions of the Gibbon River.

8. Jackson busied himself for ten days photographing the Tetons, which limited his stay in the Yellowstone region. He concentrated on completing the collection of Yellowstone views he had obtained the previous season.

9. Basalt, the most common rock type on earth, is a hard, volcanic material. Breccia is a rock composed of angular stones that have been embedded in a finer material.

10. Market Lake located east of Yellowstone Park near Rexburg, Idaho was near today's Roberts, Utah. The infamous Hole in the Wall was a hideout for such notable outlaws as Jesse James, Butch Cassidy and the Sundance Kid, and others. It is not clear why Jackson refers to this place as being near Hole in the Wall, as its location is fifty miles south of Buffalo, Wyoming, near the Big Horn Mountains. Other locations are known as Hole in the Wall (see note number 12, chapter seven). The Hayden Survey was traveling through Idaho, not Wyoming, at the time of the holdup.

CHAPTER NINE

1. "Pikes Peak or Bust" was the rallying slogan painted in the covered wagons as gold seekers headed west during the Colorado Gold Rush of 1859. It was misleading as no gold had been found within a hundred miles of Pikes Peak.

2. Jackson was traveling on a route known today as the Peak-to-Peak Highway.

3. Known today as Red Rock Lake.

4. The town of Columbia was founded in 1860 as the center for the Ward Mining District. Eventually, the name Ward was applied to the town. It was one of the richest silver communities in Colorado, yet is considered a ghost town today.

5. Caribou City was organized in 1860 after the Caribou silver mine opened nearby. It was never completely rebuilt after being destroyed by fire in 1879. As the mines played out, the population dwindled until only forty-four people remained in 1900. Today it too is considered a ghost town.

6. This valley is Mammoth Gulch.

7. Jackson's diary is unclear as to what this "Deserted Village" may have been or where it was located.

8. Empire was founded as Valley City. After the gold mines played out the town became an important stage stop and supply depot for the richer mines across Union Pass.

9. The first prospectors settled in Georgetown in 1859. After the initial gold boom the town dwindled in population until silver was found nearby in 1864. The town was incorporated in 1868.

10. Jackson intends clear-cut to mean above timberline.

11. Founded in 1859 due to large gold discoveries in the area, Fairplay got its name from disgruntled miners who wanted a "fair play" in filing their claims.

12. The men were following an old Ute trail between Manitou and South Park. Ute Pass is the present-day location of Woodland Park.

13. Jackson took a side trip to an area northwest of present-day Colorado Springs. He explored the rock formations near Monument and the Garden of the Gods, and visited the waters of Manitou Springs.

CHAPTER TEN

1. The Twin Lakes Reservoir now inundates the Derry Ranch site.

2. Among the tributaries Jackson mentioned are those of the Roaring Fork River.

3. This small lake is Geneva Lake.

CHAPTER ELEVEN

1. The men were struggling to make their way up a brush-choked streambed known as Cross Creek.

2. Jackson contradicts this in his diary: "All the snow banks on the evening before were running small streams of water but now they were all hard & dry as flint. We were fortunate, however, in finding a large hollow rock that gave us a sufficiency" (Jackson 1873, August 24). Had Jackson waited for the sun to melt the snow as stated in the text it would have been too late to take the photographs.

CHAPTER TWELVE

1. Ernest Ingersoll, a well-known writer at the end of the nineteenth century, published articles in *Harper's Monthly Magazine, Scribner's Monthly, The Century,* and other periodicals. His book *Knocking around the Rockies* (Harper and Brothers, 1882) drew national attention.

2. This highway is now U.S. Route 40.

3. When Jackson refers to Mexican he is referring to Hispanic. By this time the Spanish-speaking people of the Southwest thought of themselves as United States citizens. The town of Saguache was founded in 1867. It soon became a supply depot for the booming mining communities to the west.

4. The Northern Branch of the Santa Fe Trail crossed Cochetopa Pass. Trade traffic flowed between Santa Fe and Los Angeles on the trail from 1830 to 1848.

5. The Los Pinos Indian Agency was the place Chief Ouray and his band of Ute Indians were relocated in the 1870s when their traditional tribal lands were taken by treaty.

6. The agent was a Unitarian minister named "Reverend Mr. Bond" (Jackson [1940] 1994, 224).

7. Chief Ouray of the Tabeguache Ute band led the Ute Tribe during the mid-1800s when the Utes were forced to accept resettlement as the white settlers discovered gold and other desirable natural resources.

8. Both Shavano and Guerro were sub-chiefs of the Tabeguache Ute band. Shavano was Ouray's second in command.

9. Peah, another Tabeguache Ute band sub-chief, was also known as Chief Tush-a-qui-not (Jackson [1940] 1994, 226), or Black Tail Deer (Jackson [1877] 1978, 82).

CHAPTER THIRTEEN

1. The route was through present-day Stony Pass to the south of Canby Mountain on the Continental Divide.

2. Lake Santa Maria is now Santa Maria Reservoir. It enters the Rio Grande via Clear Creek.

3. Little remains of San Juan City. It was located in Antelope Park along the Rio Grande, and was the Hindsdale County seat from its inception in 1874. It is now part of the privately owned San Juan Ranch.

4. Baker's Park is the valley to the northwest of Howardsville.

5. Howardsville, known originally as Bullion City, was in its infancy as Jackson passed through. As the mines plated out many residents moved to Silverton, a supply center for the nearby mines. Howardsville lost its post office in 1939 and today is considered a ghost town.

6. Hope Lake is just below the divide crossed by Jackson on the way to Trout Lake.

7. Del Norte was another supply center for the mines to the west.

8. Lafayette Head was Colorado's first Lieutenant Governor, from 1877 to 1879.

9. The proper spelling is Cañon City, the word "cañon" being Spanish for canyon.

CHAPTER FOURTEEN

1. Jackson crossed Ophir Pass.

2. This divide is known as Molas Pass.

CHAPTER FIFTEEN

1. Jackson never visited present-day Mesa Verde National Park in 1874. Mancos Canyon is now included in the Ute Mountain Tribal Park within the Ute Mountain Indian lands.

2. Ernest Ingersoll was given the title "naturalist" by the Survey. In reality he was a correspondent who brought timely publicity to what the Survey was doing.

3. The trail to the left of Sultan is now U.S. Route 55. The bear creek trail is now nonexistent in places.

4. Castle Springs is near present-day Durango, Colorado.

5. The Merritt Ranch was located at present-day Mancos, Colorado.

6. This area is now present-day Cortez, Colorado.

7. Today's Ute Mountain Utes are descendants of the Weminuchi Ute band.

8. Today's Aztec Divide.

9. This is not completely correct. Hovenweep is not a continuous piece of land. It is spread throughout the area where significant ruins exist. Most of Yellow Jacket Canyon is administered by the Bureau of Land Management or is privately held.

10. Lost Canyon retains the name to this day. It is the southeast branch of the Dolores River. The "back trail" to Merritt's Ranch was the Old Spanish Trail.

11. Before the photographic division departed from the La Plata region, "The Captain [Moss] insisted on entering a placer claim for Ingersoll & myself of 20 acres each. Made many plans for next year & parted with the prospect of meeting each other another season" (Jackson1874a, September 16).

CHAPTER SIXTEEN

1. Parrott City, long ago abandoned, was the relocated site of the La Plata mining operations near the confluence of the La Plata River and Parrott Creek. It became the La Plata County seat between 1876 and 1881. The Denver and Rio Grande Railroad bypassed Parrott City and chose Durango as a supply hub. By 1889, Parrott City had lost its post office.

2. Jackson traveled up the Chinle Wash. He did not see Canyon de Chelly because the expedition party cut west toward the Hopi pueblos shortly before arriving there.

3. Fort Defiance was established in 1851 to patrol the Navajo Country. It was abandoned in 1861. It was reestablished in 1863 by Kit Carson and used as a concentration camp for starving Navajos who were victims of Carson's scorched earth policy. It was abandoned again as the 8,000 prisoners were moved to Fort Sumner. After the signing of the Navajo Treaty of 1868 the old fort became the site of the Navajo agency until 1936 when Window Rock became the Navajo central agency for the entire Navajo Nation.

4. While waiting in Parrott City for supplies Jackson mentions touring the mining claim he had been gifted the previous year. "My claim on the bar that was given me by Moss last year appears to be all right—so far. One near it was sold for $800, it was said" (Jackson [1875] n.d., July 19).

5. Chief Ignacio, a Weminuchi Ute leader, remained active for some time after 1875. He is remembered for refusing an allotment of land under the 1895 Act that broke the reservation into two pieces. Instead he moved onto western Ute lands, forming what is known today as the Ute Mountain Ute Reservation.

6. Tierra Amarilla, Spanish for "yellow earth," was founded as Los Nutrinas in 1832. It was a supply center for the region as it had a railroad depot.

7. This closing in of the San Juan River is known as the Upper Narrows. Foot travel near the river becomes extremely difficult at this point due to narrow ledges and cliffs.

8. Later prints done by Jackson's Detroit Photographic Company title this ruin "Pancho House," the name by which it is known today. It is approximately ten miles up the Chinle Wash from its confluence with the San Juan River on the east bank.

9. In 1872 two men, Phillip Arnold and John Slack, conned investors into setting up a multi-million-dollar syndicate after walking into a San Francisco bank with some industrial-grade diamonds that they claimed to have found in an undisclosed location (near Black Butte, Wyoming). Part of the elaborate hoax was to spread rumors as to where the diamond fields might be. Jackson incorrectly mentions one place in the Arizona desert. It was near present-day Tez Nez Iah on the Navajo Reservation.

10. Canyon Bonito Chiquito is known today as Laguna Creek.

11. Jackson left the Chinle Wash and proceeded southwest up Laguna Creek. Comb Ridge was on the right with its large natural arch at the southern end of the formation. His photographic party proceeded south and then southeast along the western edge of Black Mesa.

12. This mesa is presently called Black Mesa because of its large coal deposits. They traveled up Polaca Wash to the Hopi villages.

13. Tewa or Hano is on First Mesa. Pueblo people who emigrated from New Mexico following the Pueblo Revolt of 1680 founded it in 1780.

14. Nampeyo lived a long and productive life. Born about 1860, she died in 1942.

15. Walpi was officially established in 1690 on First Mesa.

16. Oraybi, spelled today as Oraibi, is located on Third Mesa. It is one of the oldest continuously inhabited communities in North America.

17. Shungapavi is spelled today as Shungopavi and Shepaulavi as Sipaulovi. The villages of Shungopavi, Mishongnovi, and Sipaulovi comprise Second Mesa. Shungopavi, originally at the base of the mesa, was moved after the Pueblo Revolt of 1680 to its present location a few miles west of Second Mesa Store. It was the first of the Hopi villages to be settled.

18. William Keam and his brother Thomas were instrumental in developing the Keams Canyon Trading Post to the east of First Mesa.

CHAPTER SEVENTEEN

1. According to Gardner two mules were killed and four wounded.

2. The men headed north past present-day Monticello, Utah, and then through Dry Valley.

3. This mountainous country was west of Monticello, Utah.

4. Jackson photographed Casa Colorado Rock, the spot where Ute Indians pinned down Gardner for two and a half days. It is located in Dry Valley about four miles east of U.S. 191.

CHAPTER EIGHTEEN

1. The International Exhibition of Arts, Manufacturers, and Products of the Soil and Mines opened in the spring of 1876. Among the most visited and most controversial exhibits was that of the American Indian. Both the Powell Expedition and the Hayden Expedition added ethnographic materials and data from the Southwest to the exhibit.

2. Fort Garland, built in 1858, replaced the more vulnerable Fort Massachusetts to the north. The fort was a base of operations for keeping Ute and Jicarilla Apache Indians in check. In 1883 it was abandoned. San Luis Park is today's San Luis Valley.

3. The two Jacksons probably stayed in Taos, not the village of Ranchos de Taos, because of its proximity to the nearby Taos Pueblo.

4. Fort Defiance was an active military outpost used to keep the Navajo Indians in check between 1851 and 1868. It became the site of the Navajo Agency after being decommissioned as a fort.

5. Fort Wingate was established in 1860 as Fort Fauntleroy to control the Navajo Indians but was renamed Fort Lyon in 1861 as General Fauntleroy had defected to the Confederacy during the Civil War. Fort Wingate was in operation from 1862 to 1868 when it was abandoned. The garrison and name were transferred to Fort Wingate II. It was an active military outpost until 1921.

6. Fort Marcy, built in 1846 by General Stephen Kearny, was the first military outpost to be established in the Territory of New Mexico. It was never completed and was abandoned in 1868.

7. Jackson skirted two mountain ranges, the San Mateo Mountains and then the Zuni Mountains, on his way to Fort Wingate.

8. By "dobies" Jackson is referring to adobe or mud bricks.

9. The spelling for Canyon de Chelle varies. The most common spelling today is Canyon de Chelly.

10. The Explorer's Column is known today as Spider Rock in Canyon de Chelly National Monument.

11. White House Ruin is the most visited prehistoric site in Canyon de Chelly. Canyon del Muerto is a side branch of Canyon de Chelly located within Canyon de Chelly National Monument.

12. Sechumevay, spelled today as Sichomovi, was the last village to be established on First Mesa. It was founded in 1750. For specifics on the other pueblos see notes 13–17 in chapter fifteen.

13. The largest prehistoric site in North America, Pueblo Bonito contained over six hundred rooms and forty ceremonial kivas. It was the center of the ancestral Anasazi-Chacoan world.

14. Washington Pass is about ten miles east of present-day Sheep Springs, New Mexico, on N.M. State R. 134. It is named for Lt. Colonel John M. Washington, who organized the Simpson Expedition in 1849.

15. The Brevet Lieutenant Colonel John M. Washington led a military undertaking to force the Navajo Indians into a peace treaty. The men explored and mapped the Chaco Canyon region in 1849 as a side trip on their way to Canyon de Chelly.

16. Until 1934 the town of Cabezon existed near Cabezon Peak. It was abandoned when the United States purchased the Ojo del Espiritu Santo Land Grant.

17. Pueblo Pintado, known as Peñasco Blanco today, is the first major ruin at the upper end of Chaco Canyon. To the east of Chaco there is currently a small settlement named Pueblo Pintado.

18. Jackson means there are eleven major ruins as there are numerous lesser ruins in Chaco Canyon.

19. Josiah Gregg crossed the plains on the Santa Fe Trail in 1844. His book is considered one of the classic documents on the early American West.

20. This discovered stairway is known today as the Jackson Staircase, and Chettro Kettle is spelled Chetro Ketl.

21. "I have no idea why I made this long detour (to Laguna), for it was not as far to Santa Fe as it was to Laguna by this route. Probably something had been left there to be picked up on the return" (Jackson [1877] n.d., 22).

CHAPTER NINETEEN

1. This is not accurate. Jackson did work for the U.S. Geological Survey after the Hayden Survey was disbanded.

2. Point of Rocks is located approximately twenty-five miles east of present-day Rock Springs, Wyoming.

3. The Survey had approached the Wind River Range from the east. They were approximately fifteen miles south of Lander. The peak is on the crest of the range, bordering the Shoshone and Bridger National Forests.

4. Fremont Peak is approximately fifteen miles northeast of Pinedale, Wyoming. Because the mountains are so rugged, the men had crossed to the low lands on the west side of the range after passing Wind River Peak in order to travel to Fremont Peak.

5. John C. Fremont (1813–1890), "The Pathfinder," led his 1842 Expedition in to map the eastern portion of the Oregon Trail. He climbed Fremont Peak on August 15 and took the first barometric reading to determine the elevation of an American mountain. There is some controversy as to whether he scaled Fremont Peak or nearby Mt. Woodrow Wilson.

6. Hoback Canyon, which enters Jackson Hole from the southeast, was named for John Hoback, an early fur trapper, who guided the Astorians through the area in 1811. The Rocky Mountain Fur Company came into existence in 1826. The original partners were Jedediah Smith, David (Davie) E. Jackson, and William Sublette. Jim Bridger was leading fur-trapping expeditions for the company by 1830.

7. The Upper Gros Ventre Butte is a glacial remnant of rock that protrudes out of the middle of the Jackson Hole Valley. Jackson's best photographs of Jackson Hole were taken in 1883 when the air was clear. Some 1878 photographs exist—none are of good quality. See The Tetons from the East (page 186).

8. Mt. Sheridan was named for the Civil War hero General Phillip Sheridan, by Hayden's 1871 military escort, J. W. Barlow.

9. Mr. Jackson mentions snow, wind, and cold weather in almost every entry in his meager notes from September 22 through the Survey's arrival in the Wind River Valley on October 5: "Sep. 24. Snow—snow—snow . . . Sep. 29. Attempts at photo'g—wind and snow . . . Sept. 30. Snow" (Jackson [1878b] n.d., 2).

10. Named for General Henry D. Washburn who led the 1870 Washburn Expedition. He is given credit as making the first ascent of Mt. Washburn on August 28, 1870.

11. They crossed the Yellowstone River in the vicinity of Sulphur Mountain and the Crater Hills.

12. Camp Brown, founded as Camp Augur in 1869, had been relocated in 1871 from its original location fifteen miles southeast to a site near present-day Lander, Wyoming. It was renamed Fort Washakie in 1878 in honor of the Shoshone chief. It was closed in 1909 and became the Indian Agency in 1913.

13. Jackson is incorrect. The photograph was taken in 1872.

14. Muddy Gap is located where Wyoming Rt. 220 joins with U.S. 287. It was located near Fort Semonoe (1852–60) on the Oregon Trail.

15. Fort Steele (1868–86) was located south of present-day Ft. Fred Steele, approximately fifteen miles east of Rawlins, Wyoming. It was established to protect the railroad where the Union Pacific crossed the North Platte River. Rawlins had been founded at the site of a spring while the Union Pacific Railroad was under construction.

References

Aldrich, Lewis Cass. 2004. Vermont in the Civil War: Second Vermont Brigade, Brigade history. Available from http://www.vermontcivilwar.org/ [Accessed on February 19, 2004].

Arizona atlas and gazetteer. 1993. Freeport, ME: DeLorme mapping.

Barlow, Captain W., and Captain D. P. Heap. 1872. Reconnaissance of the Basin of the Upper Yellowstone in 1871. Washington, DC: GPO.

Bartlett, Richard A. 1962. Great Surveys of the American West. Norman and London: University of Oklahoma Press.

Bassetti, Angell E., L. Foster, and C. Foster. 1968. Developing an index for The William Henry Jackson Collection of photographs in the Colorado State Historical Society. Denver: Colorado Historical Society.

Beck, Warren A., and Ynez D. Hasse. 1969. Historical atlas of New Mexico. Norman: University of Oklahoma Press.

Blair, Bob. 1999. William Henry Jackson pioneer photographer and artist, introduced America to the Tetons with stunning images from 1872 expedition. *Jackson Hole,* Summer–Fall 1999: 46–52.

Borneman, Walter R., and Lyndon J. Lampert. 1994. A climbing guide to Colorado's fourteeners, 3rd ed. Boulder, CO: Pruett.

Bridger-Teton National Forest [map]. 1988. Ogden, UT: U.S. Department of Agriculture, Forest Service.

Canyon del Muerto quadrangle [map]. 1955. Denver and Washington, DC: U.S. Department of the Interior, Geological Survey.

Chambers, Frank, comp. 1988. Hayden and his men. Dillsburg, PA: Francis Paul Geoscience Literature.

Chittenden, Hiram M. 1895. The Yellowstone National Park: Historical and Descriptive. Cincinnati: Robert Clarke Company.

———. [1902] 1954. History of the American fur trade of the far West. Reprinted in Stanford, CA: Academic Reprints.

———. [1895] 1964. The Yellowstone National Park: Historical and descriptive. Reprinted by Richard A. Bartlett. Norman: University of Oklahoma Press.

Colorado atlas and gazetteer. 1995. Freeport, ME: DeLorme mapping.

Correlation list of new and old numbers of the descriptive catalogue of the photographs of the U.S. Geological Survey of the Territories for the years 1869 to 1875 [updated to include 1878 and 1883?]. 1951. Denver: United States Geological Survey Photo Library, United States Geological Survey, Federal Center.

Driggs, Howard R. 1942. Westward America. New York: Somerset Books.

———. 1956. The old West speaks. New York: Bonanza Books.

Elwood P. Bonney Collection of William Henry Jackson Material. 1930–1942. MS 1643. Denver: Colorado Historical Society.

Encyclopedia Britannica, 2004. Encyclopedia Britannica article. Chicago. Available from http://www.britannica.com [Accessed on February 29, 2004].

Fergusson, Erna. 1951. New Mexico: A pageant of three peoples. New York: Alfred A. Knopf.

Findley, Rowe. 1989. The life and times of William Henry Jackson; Photographing the frontier. *National Geographic.* February: 151–216.

Fritiof M. Fryxell Papers. 1853–1973. MSS 1638. Laramie: American Heritage Center, University of Wyoming.

Gardner, Jas. T. August 21, 1875. Letter to W. H. Jackson. William Henry Jackson Manuscript Collection. 1875–1942. MSS 341. Denver: Colorado Historical Society.

Godfrey, Anthony, Ph.D. August 1994. Pony Express: Historic resource study. National Park Service. Available from http://nps.gov/poex/hrs/hrst.htm [Accessed on March 14, 2004].

Grand Teton National Park Wyoming—Teton County [map]. 1968. Denver and Washington, DC: U.S. Department of the Interior, Geological Survey.

Grand Teton National Park, Wyoming. Teton County, Grand Teton Quadrangle. 1931 [map]. Denver and Washington, DC: U.S. Department of the Interior, Geological Survey. [Jackson's annotated copy of this map is found in Fryxell, F. M. 1853–1973. Papers. MSS 1638, Box 29.]

Guide to the William Henry Jackson Collection: A listing of objects from the William Henry Jackson Collection at Scotts Bluff National Monument. n.d. Scotts Bluff, NE: Print Express.

Hafen, Leroy R., and Ann W. Hafen, eds. 1959. The diaries of William Henry Jackson: Frontier photographer, to California and return 1866–1867 and with the Hayden Surveys to the central Rockies 1873, and to the Utes and cliff dwellings 1874. Glendale, CA: Arthur H. Clark.

Haines Aubrey. 1964. The Yellowstone story: A history of our first national park. 2 vols. Yellowstone National Park, WY: Yellowstone Library Museum Association.

Hales, Peter B., comp. 1988. William Henry Jackson and the Transformation of the American Landscape. Philadelphia: Temple University Press.

Harrell, Thomas H., comp. 1995. William Henry Jackson; an annotated bibliography: 1862 to 1995. Nevada City, CA: Carl Mautz.

Harrison, Tim. 2003. The American Civil War; the struggle to preserve the Union. Available from http://www.swcivilwar.com [Accessed on February 20, 2004].

Hayden, F. V., ed. 1872. Preliminary report of the United States Geological Survey of Montana and portions of adjacent Territories; being a fifth annual report of progress. Washington, DC: GPO.

———. 1873. Sixth annual report of the United States Geological Survey of the Territories, embracing portions of Montana, Idaho, Wyoming, and Utah; being a report of progress of the exploration for the year 1872. Washington, DC: GPO.

———. 1874. Seventh annual report of the United States Geological Survey of the Territories, embracing Colorado; being a report of progress of the exploration for the year 1873. Washington, DC: GPO.

———. 1876. Eighth annual report of the United States Geological and Geographical Survey of the Territories, embracing Colorado and parts of adjacent territories; being a report of progress of the exploration for the year 1874. Washington, DC: GPO.

———. 1877. Ninth annual report of the United States Geological and Geographical Survey of the Territories, embracing Colorado and parts of adjacent Territories; being a report of progress of the exploration for the year 1875. Washington, DC: GPO.

———. 1878a. Tenth annual report of the United States Geological and Geographical Survey of the Territories, embracing Colorado and parts of adjacent Territories; being a report of progress of the exploration for the year 1876. Washington, DC: GPO.

———. 1878b. Eleventh annual report of the United States Geological and Geographical Survey of the Territories, embracing Idaho and Wyoming; being a report of progress of the exploration for the year 1877. Washington, DC: GPO.

———. 1881. Geological and geographical atlas of Colorado and portions of adjacent territory. New York: J. Bien, Lith.

———. 1883. Twelfth annual report of the United States Geological and Geographical Survey of the Territories: A report of the progress of the exploration in Wyoming and Idaho for the year 1878. Washington, DC: GPO.

Historical Wyoming Tidbits. 2003. Available from http://www.wyomingbnb-ranchrec.com/History.Fort-Washakie.html [Accessed on March 11, 2004].

Holmes, William H. [1875] n.d. Hayden's Survey of the Territories (Colorado): A narrative of explorations, 1875. Fritiof M. Fryxell Papers. 1853–1973. MSS 1638. Laramie: American Heritage Center, University of Wyoming.

Hughes, Jim. 1994. The Birth of a Century. London and New York: Taurus Parke Books.

Indian Country in Arizona, New Mexico, Utah, and Colorado [map]. 1993. Los Angeles: Automobile Club of Southern California.

Jackson, Clarence S. 1957. Picture maker of the Old West. New York: Charles Scribner's Sons.

———. 1958. Pageant of the pioneers: The veritable art of William Henry Jackson, "Picture maker of the Old West." Minden, NE: Harold Warp Pioneer Village.

Jackson, William Henry. 1862–1863. "Diary." William Henry Jackson 1862–1942. Papers. New York: The New York Public Library, Manuscripts and Archives Division. Astor, Lenox and Tilden Foundations.

———. [1862–1863] 1915. "Reconstructed dairy account." William Henry Jackson 1862–1942. Papers. New York: The New York Public Library, Manuscripts and Archives Division. Astor, Lenox and Tilden Foundations.

———. 1866–1867. "Diary." The William Henry Jackson Collection. 1875–1942. Manuscript: MSS 341. Denver: The Colorado History Museum, Colorado Historical Society.

———. [1866–1867a] n.d. "Reconstructed dairy account." William Henry Jackson 1862–1942. Papers. New York: The New York Public Library, Manuscripts and Archives Division. Astor, Lenox and Tilden Foundations.

———. [1866–1867b] n.d. "Typescript." William Henry Jackson 1862–1942. Papers. New York: The New York Public Library, Manuscripts and Archives Division. Astor, Lenox and Tilden Foundations.

———. 1869. "Diary." William Henry Jackson 1862–1942. Papers. New York: The New York Public Library, Manuscripts and Archives Division. Astor, Lenox and Tilden Foundations.

———. [1867–1869] n.d. Omaha and the Union Pacific, "Typescript." William Henry Jackson 1862–1942. Papers. New York: The New York Public Library, Manuscripts and Archives Division. Astor, Lenox and Tilden Foundations.

———. 1870. "Diary." William Henry Jackson 1862–1942. Papers. New York: The New York Public Library, Manuscripts and Archives Division. Astor, Lenox and Tilden Foundations.

———. 1871. A catalogue of photographic illustrations. Washington, DC: Cunningham and McIntosh, printers.

———. [1871] n.d. The Yellowstone, "typescript." William Henry Jackson 1862–1942. Papers. New York: The New York Public Library, Manuscripts and Archives Division. Astor, Lenox and Tilden Foundations.

———. 1873. "Diary." The William Henry Jackson Collection. 1875–1942. Manuscript: MSS 341. Denver: The Colorado History Museum, Colorado Historical Society.

———. [1873] n.d. "Reconstructed dairy account." William Henry Jackson 1862–1942. Papers. New York: The New York Public Library, Manuscripts and Archives Division. Astor, Lenox and Tilden Foundations.

———. 1874a. "Diary." The William Henry Jackson Collection. 1875–1942. Manuscript: MSS 341. Denver: The Colorado History Museum, Colorado Historical Society.

———. 1874b. Miscellaneous publications—No. 5. Descriptive catalogue of photographs of the United States Geological Survey of the territories for the years 1869 to 1873 inclusive. Washington, DC: GPO.

———. [1874] n.d. "Reconstructed dairy account." William Henry Jackson 1862–1942. Papers. New York: The New York Public Library, Manuscripts and Archives Division. Astor, Lenox and Tilden Foundations.

———. 1875a. Ancient Ruins in southwestern Colorado. And: A list of photographs illustrating the ruins in southwestern Colorado and Utah. In Bulletin of the United States Geological and Geographical Survey of the territories, 1874 and 1875. F. V. Hayden, ed. vol.1, bulletin 1, second series, no. 1. Washington, DC: GPO.

———. 1875b. "Diary." The William Henry Jackson Collection. 1875–1942. Manuscript: MSS 341. Denver: The Colorado History Museum, Colorado Historical Society.

———. [1875] 1978. Miscellaneous publications—No. 5: Descriptive catalogue of the photographs of the United States Geological Survey of the Territories, for the years 1869 to 1875 inclusive, second edition. Milwaukee: reprinted by Raymond Dworczyk, The Q Press.

———. [1875] n.d. "Reconstructed dairy account." William Henry Jackson 1862–1942. Papers. New York: The New York Public Library, Manuscripts and Archives Division. Astor, Lenox and Tilden Foundations.

———. 1876. A notice of ancient ruins in Arizona and Utah lying about the Rio San Juan. In Bulletin of the United States Geological and Geographical Survey of the Territories, by F. V. Hayden. vol. 2, no. 1. Washington, DC: GPO.

———. 1877. "Fragmentary notes." William Henry Jackson 1862–1942. Papers. New York: The New York Public Library, Manuscripts and Archives Division. Astor, Lenox and Tilden Foundations.

———. April 27, 1877. Letter to William H. Holmes. Fritiof M. Fryxell Papers. 1853–1973: MSS 1638, Box 29 Correspondence file. Laramie: American Heritage Center, University of Wyoming.

———. [1877] 1978. Miscellaneous publications—No. 9: Descriptive Catalogue of photographs of North American Indians. Washington, DC: GPO, 1877. Columbus, OH: reprinted by R. M. Weatherford Books.

———. [1877] n.d. "Typescript." William Henry Jackson 1862–1942. Papers. New York: The New York Public Library, Manuscripts and Archives Division. Astor, Lenox and Tilden Foundations.

Jackson in Hayden. 1878. Report of William H. Jackson: Report on the ancient ruins examined in 1875 and 1877. In *Tenth annual report of the United States Geological and Geographical Survey of the Territories, embracing Colorado and parts of adjacent Territories; being a report of progress of the exploration for the year 1876,* by F. V. Hayden. Washington, DC: GPO.

———. [1878a] n.d. "Typescript." William Henry Jackson 1862–1942. Papers. New York: The New York Public Library, Manuscripts and Archives Division. Astor, Lenox and Tilden Foundations.

———. [1878b] n.d. Fragmentary notes of the 1878 Expedition. William Henry Jackson 1862–1942. Papers. New York: The New York Public Library, Manuscripts and Archives Division. Astor, Lenox and Tilden Foundations.

———. 1922. The Mountain of the Holy Cross. The William Henry Jackson Collection. 1875–1942. Manuscript: MSS 341. Denver: The Colorado History Museum, Colorado Historical Society.

———. 1923. Diary of a "Bullwhacker." The William Henry Jackson Collection. 1875–1942. Manuscript: MSS 341. Denver: The Colorado History Museum, Colorado Historical Society.

———. 1924. First Official Visit to the cliff dwellings. *Colorado Magazine,* vol. 1, no. 4: 151–59.

———. 1926. Photographing the Colorado Rockies fifty years ago. *Colorado Magazine,* vol. 3, no. 1: 11–22.

———. 1929a. Address regarding the first photographing of the Tetons. *Annals of Wyoming,* vol. 6, no. 1 and 2: 191–98.

———. 1929b. The pioneer photographer: Rocky Mountain adventures with a camera. Yonkers-on-the-Hudson, NY: World Book Company. [Jackson's personal annotated copy: William H. Jackson. 1866–1953. Papers: MSS 1608. Provo, UT: Harold B. Lee Library: Brigham Young University, Photographic Archives.]

———. 1931. Bullwhacking across the plains. New York: Albert and Charles Boni. Daniel W. Greenburg 1876–1940. Collection: MSS 1642. Fritiof Fryxell. M. 1853–1973. Papers: MSS 1638. Laramie: American Heritage Center, University of Wyoming.

———. 1936. With Moran in the Yellowstone: A story of exploration, photography and art. *Appalachia,* vol. 2, no. 12: 149–58.

———. 1938. A visit to the Los Pinos Indian Agency in 1874. *Colorado Magazine,* vol. 15, no. 6: 201–9.

———. [1940] 1994. Time exposure: The autobiography of William Henry Jackson. 1940. G. P. Putnam's Sons. Reprinted in Tucson: Patrice Press.

Jackson, William H., and W. H. Holmes. 1876. Ancient ruins in southwestern Colorado in *Bulletin of the United States Geological and Geographical Survey of the Territories,* vol. 2, by F. V. Hayden, U.S. geologist in charge. Washington, DC: GPO. [Jackson's personal copy, courtesy Scotts Bluff National Monument.]

Jones, William C., and Elizabeth Jones, comps. [1975] 1992. William Henry Jackson's Colorado. Golden, CO; reprinted by Colorado Railroad Museum.

Knudsen, Dean. 1998. An eye for history: The paintings of William Henry Jackson. Washington, DC: GPO.

Kuwawata. 2004. Villages, history. Available from http://hopi.nsn.us/ [Accessed on March 11, 2004].

Langford, Nathaniel P. 1871. The wonders of Yellowstone. Parts 1 and 2. *Scribner's Monthly,* May: 1–17; June: 113–29.

———. 1873. The Ascent of Mount Hayden, Grand Teton, 1872. *Scribner's Monthly.* June: 129–57.

Lapahie, Harrison, Jr. n.d. Fort Defiance, Arizona—Navajo Nation. Available from http://lapahie.com/Fort Defiance.cfm [Accessed on August 3, 2004].

La Sal Utah-Colorado [map]. 1982. Denver: United States Geological Survey.

Lawlor, Laurie. 1999. Window on the West: The frontier photography of William Henry Jackson. New York: Holiday House.

Mattes, Merrill J. 1962. Colter's Hell and Jackson's Hole. Bozeman, MT: Yellowstone Library and Museum Association, Artcraft Printers.

Merrill, Marlene Deahl. 1999. Yellowstone and the great West. Lincoln and London: University of Nebraska Press.

Miller, Helen M. 1966. Lens on the West: The story of William Henry Jackson. Garden City, NY: Doubleday.

Miller, Nina Hull. 1962. Shutters West. Denver: Sage Books.

Miller, Ted, and Carole Miller. n.d. NEGenWeb Project. From the History of the State of Nebraska: Military History, Part 8. 1882. Chicago. The Western Historical Company, A. T. Andreas, Proprietor. Available from http://www.rootsweb.com/~neresour/andreas/military/military-p8.html [Accessed on February 22, 2004].

Moran, Thomas. 1871. Diary. Available from http://www.nps.gov/yell/technical/museum/morandiary [Accessed on May 20, 2004].

Mountain Studies Institute. 2004. Silverton, CO. Available from http://www.mountainstudies.org/ [Accessed on March 2, 2004].

New Mexico atlas and gazetteer. 1998. Freeport, ME: DeLorme mapping.

Newhall, Beaumont, and Diana Edkins. 1974. William Henry Jackson. Dobbs Ferry, NY: Morgan and Morgan.

Noel, Thomas J., Paul F. Mahoney, and Richard E. Stevens. 1994. Historical Atlas of Colorado. Norman: University of Oklahoma Press.

OnlineUtah.com. n.d. History Available from http://www.onlineutah.com/ [Accessed on February 22, 2004].

Owen, W. O. Letter to W. H. Jackson. November 27, 1929. Elwood P. Bonney Collection. 1930–1942. Manuscript: MSS 1643. Denver: The Colorado History Museum, Colorado Historical Society.

Paddock, Eric. 1988. William Henry Jackson: Photographer and entrepreneur. *AB Bookman's Weekly,* vol. 82, no. 18: 1665–71.

Patterson, Michael Robert. 2004. Arlington National Cemetery website. Available from http://www.arlingtoncemetery.net [Accessed on February 20, 2004].

Pearce, T. M., Ina Sizer Cassidy, and Helen S. Pearce. 1965. New Mexico place names: A geographical dictionary. Albuquerque: University of New Mexico Press.

Pony Express Home Station. March 30, 2004. Wyoming stations; Utah stations; Colorado stations. Available from http://www.xphomestation.com/ [Accessed on March 11, 2004].

"Photography and Art Collection." n.d. [A listing of the photographs and art in storage.] Grand Teton National Park, WY.

Rathaus Reality Press. 2004. Gallery of southwestern turtle island timeless lands: Chaco Canyon, San Juan Basin, New Mexico. Available from http://www.ratical.org/southwest [Accessed on March 14, 2004].

Richardson, John. July 10, 1998. Correspondence with Bob Blair.

Robert Spurrier Ellison Papers. n.d. [In the William Henry Jackson Papers, 1843–1942.] Denver: The Denver Public Library, Western History/Genealogy Department.

RootsWeb.com. 2004. The U.S. Gen Web Project: At the big plains. Military posts in the plains states. Available from http://www.rootsweb.com/~wygenweb/index.htm [Accessed on March 3, 2004].

Rowley, Dennis, and Susan Corrigan, 1991. [Collection listings]. William Henry Jackson, 1866–1953. Provo, UT: Brigham Young University, Harold B. Lee Library, Special Collections and Manuscripts.

Rudisill, Richard. 1975. A problem in attribution: Research report no. 1. Albuquerque. [Presented at the National Convention of the American Studies Association, Fifth Biennial.]

San Luis Valley Museum Association. 2002. The Story of Fort Garland. History of the Old Spanish Trail. Available from http://www.museumtrail.org/ [Accessed on August 8, 2004].

San Luis Valley Museum Association. 2002. History of the Old Spanish Trail. Available from http://museumtrail.org/OldSpanishTrail.asp [Accessed on March 7, 2004].

SHG Resources: A guide to U.S. States. 2003. Wyoming time line of state history. Available from http://www.statehousegirls.net/wy/timeline [Accessed on March 14, 2004].

Strack, Don. 2004. Utahrails.net: Ogdenrails. Available from http://www.utahrails.net/ogden [Accessed on February 24, 2004].

Thomas, J. Noel, Paul F. Mahoney, and Richard E. Stevens. 1994. Historical atlas of Colorado. Norman and London: University of Oklahoma Press.

Thomas Moran's Diary. [1871] 1972. Typescript. Elwood P. Bonney Collection. 1930–1942. Manuscript: MSS 1643. Denver: The Colorado History Museum, Colorado Historical Society.

Thompson, Edith M. Schultz, and William Leigh. 1982. Beaver Dick: The honor and the heartbreak. Laramie, WY: Jelm Mountain Press.

Trinklein, Michael. 2003. The Oregon Trail. Available from http://www.isu.edu/%7Etrinmich/Oregontrail.html [Accessed on February 21, 2004].

United States Geological Survey. 1874. Catalogue of photographs of Indians, from the negatives in the possession of the United States Geological Survey, collected from various sources, and covering a period of twenty-five years. Washington, DC: GPO.

United States Geological Survey Photo Library, n.d. Members of Hayden Survey parties. Denver: United States Geological Survey, Federal Center.

USGS Geographic Names Information System (GNIS). 2003. U.S. Department of the Interior, U.S. Geological Survey, Reston, VA. Available from http://geonames.usgs.gov/index.html [Accessed on March 14, 2004].

W. H. Jackson Sample Album. The Denver Public Library. Western History/Genealogy Dept. W. H. Jackson Sample Album. 1881–1890.

Waitley, Douglass. 1998. William Henry Jackson: Framing the frontier. Missoula, MT: Mountain Press Publishing Company.

Weber, Wm. Hallam. 1994a. William Henry Jackson's three known negatives for his famous image "Photographing in High Places." Gaithersburg, MD: unpublished typescript.

———. 1994b. A comparative review and critique of the book "Hayden and his men." Gaithersburg, MD: unpublished typescript.

WGBH. 2004. Antiques Roadshow/Antique Speak, Available from http://www.pbs.org/wgbh/pages/roadshow/speak [Accessed on February 20, 2004].

Wheeler, Ruffner, and Simpson [map in Hayden]. 1878. Washington, DC: United States War Department.

Whittlesey, Lee H. 1988. Yellowstone place names. Helena, MT: Montana Historical Society Press.

———. January 22, 1996. Correspondence with Bob Blair.

William Henry Jackson. 1928–1947. Papers: MSS 1677. Denver: The Denver Public Library, Western History/Genealogy Department.

William Henry Jackson Papers. 1866–1966. MSS 1608. Provo, UT: Brigham Young University, Harold B. Lee Library, L. Tom Perry Special Collections.

William Henry Jackson Papers. New York: Manuscripts and Archives Division, The New York Public Library, Astor, Lenox and Tilden Foundations.

William Henry Jackson Photograph Collection. [1869–1878, and 1883] n.d. Denver: Federal Center, U.S. Geological Survey, U.S. Geological Survey Photo Library.

William Henry Jackson Collection. Gering, NE: National Park Service, Scotts Bluff National Monument.

William Henry Jackson Collection, index. 1875–1942. MSS 341. Denver: Colorado Historical Society.

William Henry Jackson Pictures. n.d. Minden, NE: Harold Warp Pioneer Village Foundation.

William Henry Jackson Photograph Collection. [1869–1878, and 1883] n.d. Photograph listings. Denver: United States Geological Survey, Federal center, U.S. Geological Survey Photo Library.

Williams, Henry T. 1877. Humanities Text Initiative. Text collections: The Pacific Tourist: Illustrated trans-continental guide of travel from the Atlantic to the Pacific Ocean. New York: Henry T. Williams, Publisher. Available from http://www.hti.umich.edu/cgi/t/text/pageviewer-idx?c=moa;cc=moa;sid=b64853cb81c0875e342025b98f7f4773;idno=afk1140.0001.001;view=image;seq=0005;size=s;page=main [Accessed on March 7, 2004].

Wright, David A. 2000. Frontier Trails adventure stories: Early Americans; Ghost towns; old West. Great Basin Research. atJeu Publishing. Available from http://www.frontiertrails.com [Accessed on March 7, 2004].

Yellowstone National Park [map]. 1993. Evergreen, CO: Trails Illustrated.

Sources of Illustrations

National Park Service, Scotts Bluff National Monument, Gering, NE.

38. *Swimming the Horses.* n.d. The William Henry Jackson Collection. SCBL #138. National Park Service, Scotts Bluff National Monument, Gering, NE. 41. *Photographing Indians of Nebraska.* 1868. The William Henry Jackson Collection. SCBL #2787. National Park Service, Scotts Bluff National Monument, Gering, NE. Photograph not catalogued by Jackson.

42. *Jackson Br's Photographers.* 1867. William Henry Jackson Papers. 1866–1966. MSS 1608, Box 3, Fd. 1, Item 2. L. Tom Perry Special Collections, Harold B. Lee Library, Brigham Young University, Provo, Utah. Photograph not catalogued by Jackson.

43. *La-Roo-Chuck-A-La-Shar* (Sun Chief). 1868. National Anthropological Archives. BAE GN 01285 06250400. National Museum of Natural History, Smithsonian Institution, Washington, DC. Originally catalogued by Jackson ([1877] 1978, 76) as #534.

44. *Pawnee, Jackson Bros.* 1868. The William Henry Jackson Collection. SCBL #2762. National Park Service, Scotts Bluff National Monument, Gering, NE. Photograph not catalogued by Jackson.

47. *Corinne, Utah.* July 1–8, 1869 (Jackson 1866–1867). William Henry Jackson Photograph Collection. [1869–1878, and 1883] n.d. WHJ #45. U.S. Geological Survey Photo Library, U.S. Geological Survey, Federal Center, Denver. Originally catalogued by Jackson ([1875] 1978, 8) as #45, 1869 series, 8″× 10″.

48. *Promontory Point, Utah.* June 31–July 1, 1869. William Henry Jackson Photograph Collection. [1869–1878, and 1883] n.d. WHJ #712. U.S. Geological Survey Photo Library, U.S. Geological Survey, Federal Center, Denver. Originally catalogued by Jackson ([1875] 1978, 9) as #65, 1869 series, stereoscopic view.

49. *Main Street, Salt Lake City.* September 10, 1868. William Henry Jackson Photograph Collection. [1869–1878, and 1883]. WHJ #811. U.S. Geological Survey Photo Library, U.S.

Geological Survey, Federal Center, Denver. Originally catalogued by Jackson ([1875] 1978, 10) as #156, 1869 series, stereoscopic view. The original negative is listed in Jackson's photographic catalogue (1978b) as #156. The United States Geological Survey lists it as #160 (United States Geological Survey Photo Library [1869–1878, and 1883] n.d.). Number 160 is missing in Jackson's catalogue. This may be simply a transcription error. However, the lack of catalogue information casts some doubt as to who took the photograph. It may have been Jackson's assistant, Arundel Hull. He took other photographs in the summer of 1868 that have been attributed to Jackson.

50. *The 1,000-Mile Tree.* August 3, 1869 (Jackson 1869). The William Henry Jackson Collection. SCBL #2769. National Park Service, Scotts Bluff National Monument, Gering, NE. Originally catalogued as (Jackson [1875] 1978, 9) as #98, 1869 series, stereoscopic view.

51. *Green River Butte.* 1869. William Henry Jackson Photograph Collection. [1869–1878, and 1883] n.d. WHJ #11. U.S. Geological Survey Photo Library, U.S. Geological Survey, Federal Center, Denver. Originally catalogued by Jackson ([1875] 1978, 6) as #11, 1869 series, 8″× 10″.

53. *The Camp of the United States Geological Survey.* August 11–12, 1870 (Jackson 1870, 8). William Henry Jackson Photograph Collection. [1869–1878, and 1883] n.d. WHJ #247. U.S. Geological Survey Photo Library, U.S. Geological Survey, Federal Center, Denver. Originally catalogued by Jackson ([1875] 1978, 11) as #47, 1870 series, 6 1/2″× 8 1/2″.

54. *Dr. Hayden and his favorite horse Patsy.* Circa 1872. Yellowstone National Park Archives. YELL #24165. National Park Service, Yellowstone National Park, WY. Originally catalogued by Jackson ([1875] 1978, 46) as #513–525, 1872 series, 8″× 10″.

55. *My first packing outfit with the Geological Survey.* 1870. The William Henry Jackson Collection. SCBL #2781. National Park Service, Scotts Bluff National Monument, Gering, NE. Photograph not catalogued by Jackson.

56. *W. H. Jackson on Independence Rock.* Circa 1950. (Original art work done by Jackson in 1932). William Henry Jack-

son Pictures. WARP #52. Harold Warp Pioneer Village Foundation, Minden, NE. Litographic print by Clarence Jackson. Original photograph from which the painting was created was catalogued by Jackson ([1875] 1978, 11) as #81, 1870 series, 6 1/2″× 8 1/2″.

58. *The emigrant's grave.* August 29, 1870 (Jackson 1870, 28). William Henry Jackson Photograph Collection. [1869–1878, and 1883] n.d. WHJ #300. U.S. Geological Survey Photo Library, U.S. Geological Survey, Federal Center, Denver. Originally catalogued by Jackson ([1875] 1978, 15) as #98, 1870 series, 6 1/2″× 8 1/2″.

60. *Washakie, Chief of the Shoshones.* September 3, 1870 (Jackson 1870). Yellowstone National Park Archives. YELL #8164. National Park Service, Yellowstone National Park, WY. Originally catalogued by Jackson ([1877] 1978, 76) as #661–2.

61. *Badlands—Blacks Fork.* September 9–11, 1870 (Jackson 1870, 39–41). Andrew Smith Gallery, n.d. Commercial collection of W. H. Jackson photographs. Santa Fe, New Mexico. Originally catalogued by Jackson ([1875] 1978, 16) as #109–110, 1870 series, 6 1/2″× 8 1/2″.

62. *Jackson Cañon.* September 1870. William Henry Jackson Photograph Collection. [1869–1878, and 1883]. WHJ #279. U.S. Geological Survey Photo Library, U.S. Geological Survey, Federal Center, Denver. Originally catalogued by Jackson ([1875] 1978, 14) as #78, 1870 series, 6 1/2″× 8 1/2″.

63. *From Photograph Ridge.* September 18, 1870 (Jackson 1870). William Henry Jackson Photograph Collection. [1869–1878, and 1883]. WHJ #319. U.S. Geological Survey Photo Library, U.S. Geological Survey, Federal Center, Denver. Originally catalogued by Jackson ([1875] 1978, 17) as #123, 1870 series, 6 1/2″× 8 1/2″.

64. *The Flaming Gorge, Green River.* September 9, 1870 (Jackson 1870). William Henry Jackson Photograph Collection. [1869–1878, and 1883] n.d. WHJ #332. U.S. Geological Survey Photo Library, U.S. Geological Survey, Federal Center, Denver. Originally catalogued by Jackson ([1875] 1978, 18) as #139, 1870 series, 6 1/2″× 8 1/2″.

66. *Naturalists at work.* 1870 or 1871. Courtesy U.S. Geological Survey. William Henry Jackson Photograph Collection. [1869–1878, and 1883] n.d. WHJ #896. U.S. Geological Survey Photo Library, U.S. Geological Survey, Federal Center, Denver. This photograph may have been taken during the 1870 Survey expedition. It was included with the 1871 images in the first edition of *The Pioneer Photographer.* Number 378 is written on the stereograph negative. The numbers in Jackson's catalogues of photographs (Jackson 1871 and Jackson [1875] 1978) end with #377 in 1870 and begin with #380 in 1871. All of the men pictured were with the survey during both seasons.

69. *Franklin Butte and the north end of Cache Valley.* 1878. The lithograph is found in the Eleventh Annual Report of the Survey (Hayden 1878b, plate 75a). The photograph from which the lithograph was created was catalogued by Jackson ([1875] 1978, 22) as #169, 1871 series, 8″× 10″. The original listing was "Camp on Warm Creek …" #169 (Jackson 1871). The photograph was taken on June 13–14, 1871 (Merrill 1999, 75).

70. *A successful fisherman.* July 20, 1871 (Merrill 1999, 125). NPS Museum Handbook Part III. GRTE #332. National Park Service, Grand Teton National Park, Moose, WY. Originally catalogued as (Jackson [1875] 1978, 33) as #423, 1871 series, stereoscopic view.

71. *Boteler's* [Bottler's] *Ranch.* July 17, 1871 (Merrill 1999, 125). Yellowstone National Park Archives. YELL #50330. National Park Service, Yellowstone National Park, WY. Originally catalogued by Jackson ([1875] 1978, 24) as #203, 1871 series, 8″× 10″.

72. *Family Group.* September 13, 1871 (Merrill 1999, 188). Yellowstone National Park Archives. YELL #37775. National Park Service, Yellowstone National Park, WY. Originally catalogued by Jackson ([1877] 1978, 70) as #48, Shoshones.

74. *Mammoth Hot Springs.* July 21, 1871 (Jackson [1940] 1994, 201). Yellowstone National Park Archives. YELL #50468. National Park Service, Yellowstone National Park, WY. Originally catalogued by Jackson ([1875] 1978, 25) as #217, 1871 series, 8″× 10″.

75. *Tower Falls.* July 26, 1871 (Moran 1871). Yellowstone National Park Archives. YELL #50342. National Park Service, Yellowstone National Park, WY. Originally catalogued by Jackson ([1875] 1978, 26) as #233, 1871 series, 8″× 10″.

76. *The Lower Falls of the Yellowstone.* July 28–30, 1871 (Moran 1871). The William Henry Jackson Collection. SCBL #675. National Park Service, Scotts Bluff National Monument, Gering, NE. Originally catalogued by Jackson ([1875] 1978, 27) as #239, 1871 series, 8″× 10″.

77. *Crater of Castle Geyser.* August 8, 1871 (Merrill 1999, 149). Yellowstone National Park Archives. YELL #50438. National Park Service, Yellowstone National Park, WY. Originally catalogued by Jackson ([1875] 1978, 31) as #295, 1871 series, 8″× 10″. The original negative, residing with the U.S. Geological Survey, is incorrectly numbered as #294 (William Henry Jackson Photograph Collection [1869–1878, and 1883] n.d.).

81. *A precarious passage.* Circa 1929. William Henry Jackson Papers. 1866–1966. MSS 1608, Item #832. L. Tom Perry Special Collections, Harold B. Lee Library, Brigham Young University, Provo, UT.

82. *Hayden's Peak or the Great Teton.* Circa July 20, 1872. NPS Museum Handbook Part III. GRTE #788. National Park Service, Grand Teton National Park, Moose, WY. Originally catalogued by Jackson ([1875] 1978, 46) as #503, 1872 series, stereoscopic view.

82 (left). *One of the bighorns of the Teton Mountains.* Circa 1929. William Henry Jackson Papers. 1866–1966. MSS 1608, Item #831. L. Tom Perry Special Collections, Harold B. Lee Library, Brigham Young University, Provo, UT.

83. *Photographing in high places.* Circa July 10, 1872. The William Henry Jackson Collection. SCBL #841. National Park Service, Scotts Bluff National Monument, Gering, NE. Originally catalogued by Jackson ([1875] 1978, 42) as #423, 1872 series, 8″× 10″.

84. *The bivouac above camp.* Circa 1929. NPS Museum Handbook Part III. GRTE #114. National Park Service, Grand Teton National Park, Moose, WY.

86. *Interior of Sawtell's ranch at Henrys Lake, Idaho.* August 1872. William Henry Jackson Photograph Collection. [1869–1878, and 1883] n.d. WHJ #950. U.S. Geological Survey Photo Library, U.S. Geological Survey, Federal Center, Denver. Originally catalogued as (Jackson [1875] 1978, 47) as #533, 1872 series, stereoscopic view.

87. *Group of all the members of the Survey.* August 15, 1872. The William Henry Jackson Collection. n.d. SCBL #671. Scotts Bluff National Monument. Originally catalogued by Jackson (1978b, 46) as #510, 1872 series, 8″× 10″.

88. *Old Faithful in eruption.* August 1872. William Henry Jackson Photograph Collection. [1869–1878, and 1883] n.d. WHJ #1572. U.S. Geological Survey Photo Library, U.S. Geological Survey, Federal Center, Denver. Originally catalogued as (Jackson [1875] 1978, 47) as #546, 1872 series, stereoscopic view. Courtesy U.S. Geological Survey.

89. *Gibbon Falls.* Circa 1872–73. Yellowstone National Park Archives. YELL #751. National Park Service, Yellowstone National Park, WY.

90. *Bannack Indians.* August–September 1872. W. H. Jackson. 1868–1883. MS 914: WHJ 996. Federal Center, U.S. Geological Survey Library. Originally catalogued as (Jackson [1875] 1978, 48) as #626–636, 1872 series, stereoscopic view.

93. *Longs Peak from Estes Park.* May 28, 1873 (Jackson 1873, 6). J. V. Howell Collection 1853–1968. MSS 1684, #B-J 139-wh-ph. American Heritage Center, University of Wyoming, Laramie. Originally catalogued as (Jackson [1875] 1978, 62) as #6, 1873 series, 5″× 8″.

94. *In the snow.* June 15, 1873 (Jackson [1875] 1978, 65). The William Henry Jackson Collection. SCBL #3075. National Park Service, Scotts Bluff National Monument, Gering, NE. Originally catalogued as (Jackson [1875] 1978, 65) as #656, 1873 series, stereoscopic view.

95. *The Snowy Range of Colorado.* Circa 1920–1930. Rocky Mountain National Park Museum Collection, ROMO #10195. National Park Service, Rocky Mountain National Park, Estes Park, CO. Originally catalogued by Jackson

([1875] 1978, 52) as #51, 1873 series, 11˝× 14˝. The photograph was taken on June 5, 1873 (Jackson 1873, 9).

96. *The twin peaks.* June 18, 1873 (Jackson 1873, 14). William Henry Jackson Photograph Collection. [1869–1878, and 1883] n.d. WHJ #1310. U.S. Geological Survey Photo Library, U.S. Geological Survey, Federal Center, Denver. Originally catalogued by Jackson ([1875] 1978, 54) as #65, 1873 series, 11˝× 14˝.

99. *Chicago Lake.* June 23, 1873 (Jackson 1873, 15). The William Henry Jackson Collection. SCBL #794. National Park Service, Scotts Bluff National Monument, Gering, NE. Originally catalogued as (Jackson [1875] 1978, 65) as #673, 1873 series, stereoscopic view.

101. *Columns in Monument Park.* 1874. The lithograph is found in Hayden's Seventh Annual Report (1874b, fig. 5. U.S. Geological Survey, Field Records Library). It was created from the photograph *Eroded Sandstones in Monument Park* (Jackson [1875] 1978: #72, 1873 series, 11˝× 14˝) on July 1, 1873 (Jackson 1873, 17).

102. *Pikes Peak.* July 4, 1873 (Jackson 1873, 17). William Henry Jackson Photograph Collection. [1869–1878, and 1883]. WHJ #1223. U.S. Geological Survey Photo Library, U.S. Geological Survey, Federal Center, Denver. Originally catalogued by Jackson ([1875] 1978, 56) as #78, 1873 series, 11˝ × 14˝.

103. *The Upper Twin Lake, Colorado.* 1874. The lithograph is found in Hayden's Sixth Annual Report (Hayden, 1873, fig. 17, U. S. Geological Survey, Fields Record Library). It was created from the photograph "Upper Twin Lake, Near View" (Jackson [1875] 1978: #699, 1873 series, stereoscopic view).

107. *Hayden Survey party at Rock Creek.* August 8, 1873 (Jackson 1873, 30). Museum of New Mexico Photo Archives. Neg. #22911. Museum of New Mexico, Santa Fe. The photograph is not catalogued by Jackson.

108. *Snow Mass Mountain and Elk Lake* [Snowmass Lake]. August 13, 1873 (Jackson 1873, 30). William Henry Jackson Photograph Collection. [1869–1878, and 1883] n.d. WHJ

#1335. U.S. Geological Survey Photo Library, U.S. Geological Survey, Federal Center, Denver. Originally catalogued by Jackson ([1875] 1978, 53) as #98, 1873 series, 11˝× 14˝.

109. *Looking north over the Sawatch Range.* August 17, 1873 (Jackson 1873, 35–36). William Henry Jackson Photograph Collection. [1869–1878, and 1883]. WHJ #393. U.S. Geological Survey Photo Library, U.S. Geological Survey, Federal Center, Denver. Originally catalogued as (Jackson [1875] 1978, 63) as #31, 1873 series, 5˝× 8˝.

110. *Red Rock Falls, Elk Mts.* August 14, 1873 (Jackson 1873, 34). William Henry Jackson Photograph Collection. [1869–1878, and 1883] n.d. WHJ #1465. U.S. Geological Survey Photo Library, U.S. Geological Survey, Federal Center, Denver. Originally catalogued as (Jackson [1875] 1978, 63) as #698, 1873 series, stereoscopic view.

112. *Valley of the Sheep Back Rocks* [Roches Moutonées] *and the Mountain of the Holy Cross.* August 25, 1873 (Jackson 1873, 41). William Henry Jackson Photograph Collection. [1869–1878, and 1883] n.d. WHJ #1340. U.S. Geological Survey Photo Library, U.S. Geological Survey, Federal Center, Denver. Originally catalogued by Jackson ([1875] 1978, 60) as #105, 1873 series, 11˝× 14˝.

114. *The Mount of the Holy Cross.* August 24, 1873 (Jackson. 1873, 40). William Henry Jackson Photograph Collection. [1869–1878, and 1883] n.d. WHJ #1485. U.S. Geological Survey Photo Library, U.S. Geological Survey, Federal Center, Denver. Originally catalogued as (Jackson [1875] 1978, 65) as #718, 1873 series, stereoscopic view.

115. *Some of the group that made the trip to the Mountain of the Holy Cross.* August 25, 1873. (Jackson 1873, 41). Rocky Mountain National Park, Museum Collection. Photograph Album, ROMO #4050 p. 14.

117. *A line-up of the photographic division of the Survey.* 1874. William Henry Jackson Photograph Collection. [1869–1878, and 1883] n.d. WHJ #359. U.S. Geological Survey Photo Library, U.S. Geological Survey, Federal Center, Denver. Originally catalogued as (Jackson [1875] 1978, 72) as #177, 1874 series, 5˝× 8˝.

119. *Falls at the foot of Round Mountain.* August 1, 1874 (Jackson 1874a). Rocky Mountain National Park Museum Collection, ROMO #4017, p. 9. National Park Service, Rocky Mountain National Park, Estes Park, CO. Originally catalogued as (Jackson [1875] 1978, 66) as #73, 1874 series, 5˝× 8˝.

120. *View in the Middle Park.* August 6, 1874 (Jackson 1874a). William Henry Jackson Photograph Collection. [1869–1878, and 1883] n.d. WHJ #443. U.S. Geological Survey Photo Library, U.S. Geological Survey, Federal Center, Denver. Originally catalogued as (Jackson [1875] 1978, 67) as #82, 1874 series, 5˝× 8˝.

121. *Piah* [Peah] *and other Ute Chiefs.* August 20, 1874 (Jackson 1874a). Smithsonian Institution. National Anthropological Archives. #SPC BAE 4605 01603609. Originally catalogued as Utes, Utah and Colorado, #801, Various Groups (United States Geological Survey 1874). Also catalogued by Jackson as Utahs, #960–63 ([1877] 1978, 76).

122. *Chief Peah's papoose.* Disputed date. William Henry Jackson Manuscript Collection. 1862–1942. MSS 341, Indians Notebook, CHL 8764. Colorado Historical Society, Denver. The Colorado Historical Society lists it as "Indian Papoose" with other dry plate views taken in the 1880s. There is no apparent reference to it in Jackson's North American Indian catalogue, *Miscellaneous Publications, No. 9* (Jackson [1877] 1978).

124. *The Rio Grande.* September 27, 1874 (Jackson 1874a). William Henry Jackson Photograph Collection. [1869–1878, and 1883] n.d. WHJ #516. U.S. Geological Survey Photo Library, U.S. Geological Survey, Federal Center, Denver. Originally catalogued as (Jackson [1875] 1978, 68) as #122, 1874 series, 5˝× 8˝.

126. *Baker's Park and Sultan Mtn.* August 29, 1874 (Jackson 1874a). William Henry Jackson Manuscript Collection. 1862–1942. MSS 341, 83.400.3029-3026. Colorado Historical Society, Denver. Originally catalogued as (Jackson [1875] 1978, 69) as #137, 1874 series, 5˝× 8˝.

127. *The photographic dark tent on the summit of Sultan Mountain.* August 31, 1874 (Jackson 1874a). William Henry Jackson Photograph Collection. [1869–1878, and 1883] n.d.

WHJ #1103. U.S. Geological Survey Photo Library, U.S. Geological Survey, Federal Center, Denver. Originally catalogued as (Jackson [1875] 1978, 73) as #827, 1874 series, stereoscopic view.

128. *Sierra San Miguel* n.d. Western History Genealogy Department, The Denver public Library. WHJ 213. Jackson's later Detroit Publishing Company lists this photograph as No. 2833.

130. *The Survey entertains a guest at dinner.* 1874. The William Henry Jackson Collection. SCBL #2774. National Park Service, Scotts Bluff National Monument, Gering, NE. Originally catalogued as (Jackson [1875] 1978, 73) as #828, 1874 series, stereoscopic view.

131. *John, the cook baking slapjacks.* October 6, 1874 (Jackson 1874a). William Henry Jackson Photograph Collection. [1869–1878, and 1883] n.d. WHJ #1644. U.S. Geological Survey Photo Library, U.S. Geological Survey, Federal Center, Denver. Originally catalogued as (Jackson [1875] 1978, 74) as #842, 1874 series, stereoscopic view.

131 (left). *Study of picturesque pine and castellated rocks.* October 6–8, 1874 (Jackson 1874a). Fritiof M. Fryxell Papers 1853–1973. MSS 1638, Oversize F-20 Shares Box. American Heritage Center, University of Wyoming, Laramie. Originally catalogued as (Jackson [1875] 1978, 68) as #120, 1874 series, 5″× 8″.

132. *The travois at Fisher's Ranch.* October 12, 1874 (Jackson 1874a). Museum of New Mexico, Photo Archives. Neg. #22914. Museum of New Mexico, Santa Fe. If Jackson catalogued this image the number is unknown. It is a 5″× 8″image as that was the only size image made in 1874. The 5″× 8″ "Camp-studies" were listed simply as "Nos. 173 to 239" with no further descriptions (Jackson [1875] 1978, 72). There is no identifying information on the print.

134. *The big camera in peril.* 1929. This image was reproduced from the first edition of *The Pioneer Photographer.*

135 (right). *Interior of the dark tent.* Circa 1929. William Henry Jackson Papers. 1866–1966. MSS 1608, Item #834. L. Tom Perry Special Collections, Harold B. Lee Library, Brigham Young University, Provo, UT.

135. *Head of Astra* [Arrastra] *Gulch.* July 11, 1875 (Jackson 1875b). William Henry Jackson Photograph Collection. [1869–1878, and 1883] n.d. WHJ #551. U.S. Geological Survey Photo Library, U.S. Geological Survey, Federal Center, Denver. Originally catalogued as (Jackson [1875] 1978, 78) as #267, 1874 series, 5″× 8″.

136. *Camp of the Miners.* July 12, 1875 (Jackson 1875b). William Henry Jackson Photograph Collection. [1869–1878, and 1883] n.d. WHJ #566. U.S. Geological Survey Photo Library, U.S. Geological Survey, Federal Center, Denver. Originally catalogued as (Jackson [1875] 1978, 77) as #252, 1874 series, 5″× 8″.

136 (right). *Trail in the San Juan Mts.* July 13, 1875 (Jackson 1875b). Fritiof M. Fryxell Papers 1853–1973. MSS 1638, Oversize F-20 Shares Box. American Heritage Center, University of Wyoming, Laramie. Originally catalogued as (Jackson [1875] 1978, 78) as #255, 1875 series, 5″× 8″.

137. *Falls at Rio San Miguel.* n.d. The William Henry Jackson Collection. SCBL #188. National Park Service, Scotts Bluff National Monument, Gering, NE.

139. *Aerial Habitation.* 1876. The lithograph was reproduced from William Jackson's personal copy of the *Report on the Ruins of Colorado, Arizona, Utah Examined in 1874-'75 and '77, Eighth Annual Report,* "Ancient Ruins in Southwestern Colorado." (Hayden 1876, Plate II, Fig. 7).

141. *John Moss—our guide to the cliff ruins.* September 6, 1874 (Jackson 1874a). William Henry Jackson Photograph Collection. [1869–1878, and 1883] n.d. WHJ #1114. U.S. Geological Survey Photo Library, U.S. Geological Survey, Federal Center, Denver. Originally catalogued as (Jackson [1875] 1978, 74) as #850-897, 1874 series, stereoscopic view.

142. *Merritt's Ranch.* September 15, 1874 (Jackson 1874a). William Henry Jackson Photograph Collection. [1869–1878, and 1883] n.d. WHJ #1628. U.S. Geological Survey Photo Library, U.S. Geological Survey, Federal Center, Denver. Originally catalogued as (Jackson [1875] 1978, 73) as #793, 1874 series, stereoscopic view.

144. *Cliff ruin, Mancos Cañon, Colorado.* September 10, 1874 (Jackson 1874a). Museum of New Mexico, Photo Archives.

Neg. #49787. Museum of New Mexico, Santa Fe. Originally catalogued as (Jackson [1875] 1978, 71) as #156, 1874 series, 5″× 8″.

145. *Mancos Canyon near its outlet to the San Juan Valley.* September 11, 1874 (Jackson 1874a). Museum of New Mexico, Photo Archives. Neg. #29973. Museum of New Mexico, Santa Fe. Originally catalogued as (Jackson [1875] 1978, 71) as #160, 1874 series, 5″× 8″.

146. *Cave dwellings near the Fortified Rock on the McElmo.* September 13, 1874 (Jackson 1874a). William Henry Jackson Manuscript Collection. 1862–1942. MSS 341, Albumin Prints on USGS Mounts. Colorado Historical Society, Denver. Originally catalogued as (Jackson [1875] 1978, 72) as #167, 1874 series, 5″× 8″.

147. *Old tower near the McElmo.* September 11–13, 1874 (Jackson 1874a). Andrew Smith Gallery, Santa Fe. Originally catalogued as (Jackson [1875] 1978, 72) as #168, 1874 series, 5″× 8″.

148. *The Photographic Division of the Geological Survey.* 1875. NPS Museum Handbook Part III. GRTE #141. National Park Service, Grand Teton National Park, Moose, WY. Originally catalogued as (Jackson [1875] 1978, 80) as #303-308, 1875 series, 5″× 8″.

149. *Gold-mining in Boren's Gulch.* July 23, 1875 (Jackson 1875b). William Henry Jackson Photograph Collection. [1869–1878, and 1883] n.d. WHJ #544. U.S. Geological Survey Photo Library, U.S. Geological Survey, Federal Center, Denver. Originally catalogued as (Jackson [1875] 1978, 78) as #372 [catalogue error: it should read #272], 1875 series, 5″× 8″.

151. *Cliff dwellings.* August 2, 1875 (Jackson 1875b). The William Henry Jackson Collection. SCBL #108. National Park Service, Scotts Bluff National Monument, Gering, NE.

152. *Casa del Echo.* August 4, 1875 (Jackson 1875b). William Henry Jackson Manuscript Collection. 1862–1942. MSS 341, W. H. Jackson Stereographs 84-192.863. Colorado Historical Society, Denver. Originally catalogued as (Jackson [1875] 1978, 81) as #957, 1875 series, stereoscopic view.

153. *Cave town of the Rio De Chelly, Arizona.* August 7, 1875 (Jackson 1875b). George Eastman House, #74:041:442.

Rochester, NY. Originally catalogued as (Jackson [1875] 1978, 78) as #958–962, 1875 series, stereoscopic view.

156. Pueblo maiden. Circa 1875. The William Henry Jackson Collection. SCBL #95. National Park Service, Scotts Bluff National Monument, Gering, NE. The original photograph used to create the sketch is catalogued as (Jackson [1875] 1978, 81) as #970, 1875 series, stereoscopic view.

157. She-Paul-A-Wee [Sipaulovi]. August 14, 1875 (Jackson 1875b). Long Island Historical Society Collection. #3086. Box 1, BJ-139-whph. American Heritage Center, University of Wyoming, Laramie. Originally catalogued as (Jackson [1875] 1978, 80) as #299, 1875 series, 5″× 8″.

158. Patio of a pueblo. 1875. The William Henry Jackson Collection. SCBL #102. National Park Service, Scotts Bluff National Monument, Gering, NE.

159. Plate XLVII. 1878. Museum of New Mexico History Library. In Hayden 1878. Museum of New Mexico, Santa Fe.

161. Cave rocks. August 27, 1875 (Jackson 1875b). William Henry Jackson Photograph Collection. [1869–1878, and 1883] n.d. WHJ #1159. U.S. Geological Survey Photo Library, U.S. Geological Survey, Federal Center, Denver. Originally catalogued as (Jackson [1875] 1978, 81) as #948, 1875 series, stereoscopic view.

163. Perfectly inaccessible. 1878. Museum of New Mexico, History Library. In Hayden 1878. Museum of New Mexico, Santa Fe.

164. Ruins in Montezuma Cañon. August 30, 1875 (Jackson 1875b). William Henry Jackson Manuscript Collection. 1862–1942. MSS 341, Albumin prints on USGS Mounts, 83-400.3029-3026. Colorado Historical Society, Denver, CO. Originally catalogued as (Jackson [1875] 1978, 79) as #288, 1875 series, 5″× 8″.

167. A lucky fall. n.d. William Henry Jackson Papers. 1866–1966. MSS 1608, Item #838. L. Tom Perry Special Collections, Harold B. Lee Library, Brigham Young University, Provo, UT. The incident occurred on September 2 (Jackson 1875b).

169. A Restoration of a portion of an ancient cave town on the Rio De Chelly, Arizona. n.d. Harold Warp Pioneer Village. In Jackson, C. 1958, 84.

172. Adobe Dwellings. March 26, 1877 (Jackson to Holmes, April 27, 1877. Fritiof M. Fryxell Papers. 1853–1973. MSS 1638, Box 29, correspondence file). The William Henry Jackson Collection. SCBL #98. National Park Service, Scotts Bluff National Monument, Gering, NE.

174. Pueblo Woman. Circa 1875-1877. The William Henry Jackson Collection. SCBL #93. National Park Service, Scotts Bluff National Monument, Gering, NE.

176. Fort Defiance, Arizona. Circa 1929. William Henry Jackson Papers 1866-1966. MSS 1608, Item #982. L. Tom Perry Special Collections, Harold B. Lee Library, Brigham Young University, Provo, UT.

178. Pueblo Bonito. 1878. The William Henry Jackson Collection. Jackson in Hayden 1878a, vol. 2, plate LXXII. National Park Service, Scotts Bluff National Monument, Gering, NE.

179. Ancient stairway. 1878. Museum of New Mexico, History Library. Jackson in Hayden 1878a, plate LXII.

181. Pueblo Alto, Chaco Cañon, NM. 1878. Museum of New Mexico, History Library. Jackson in Hayden 1878a, plate LX.

182. Laguna. May 1877. The William Henry Jackson Collection. SCBL #105. National Park Service, Scotts Bluff National Monument, Gering, NE.

184. Wind River Peak. August 2, 1878 (Jackson [1878b] n.d., 1). William Henry Jackson Photograph Collection. [1869–1878, and 1883] n.d. WHJ #1251. U.S. Geological Survey Photo Library, U.S. Geological Survey, Federal Center, Denver.

186. The Tetons from the east. August 1878. NPS Museum Handbook Part III. GRTE #110. National Park Service, Grand Teton National Park, Moose, WY. Jackson's incomplete notes for 1878 do not specify the date for the creation of this photograph.

186 (right). Columbia Spg., Red Mtn. Basin. August–September 1878. William Henry Jackson Photograph Collection. [1869–1878, and 1883] n.d. WHJ #622. U.S. Geological Survey Photo Library, U.S. Geological Survey, Federal Center, Denver. Jackson's incomplete notes for 1878 do not specify the date for the creation of this photograph.

187. Lower Basins, Mammoth Hot Springs. 1883 (Hayden 1883. Vol. 2, Plate IV). The lithograph duplicates an 1878 photograph entitled *Mammoth Hot Springs, Lower Basins, looking up* (William Henry Jackson Photograph Collection. [1869–1878, and 1883] n.d. WHJ #518. U.S. Geological Survey Photo Library, U.S. Geological Survey, Federal Center, Denver, CO).

188. Upper Fire Hole From Old Faithful. 1878 or 1883. The William Henry Jackson Collection. SCBL #677. National Park Service, Scotts Bluff National Monument, Gering, NE.

189. We meet bruin "silver tip." n.d. The William Henry Jackson Collection. SCBL #120. National Park Service, Scotts Bluff National Monument, Gering, NE.

190. View from Togwotee Pass. October 4–5, 1878 (Jackson [1878b] n.d., 3). William Henry Jackson Photograph Collection. [1869–1878, and 1883] n.d. WHJ #607. U.S. Geological Survey Photo Library, U.S. Geological Survey, Federal Center, Denver.

191. Beaver Dick and his family. 1872. NPS Museum Handbook Part III. GRTE #582. National Park Service, Grand Teton National Park, Moose, WY. Originally catalogued by Jackson ([1875] 1978, 46) as #513-525, 1872 series, 8″× 10″.

193. Memories. n.d. Fritiof M. Fryxell Papers 1853–1973. MSS 1638, Box 29, Correspondence File. American Heritage Center, University of Wyoming, Laramie.

COLOR PLATES

COLOR 1 *Winter quarters.* February 22, 1863 (Jackson 1862–1863). The William Henry Jackson Collection. SCBL #233. National Park Service, Scotts Bluff National Monument, Gering, NE.

COLOR 2. *Yoking up.* Circa 1920–1930. The William Henry Jackson Collection. SCBL #748. National Park Service, Scotts Bluff National Monument, Gering, NE.

COLOR 3. *California Crossing.* Circa 1950 (Original artwork done by Jackson in 1936). William Henry Jackson Pictures. WARP #44. Harold Warp Pioneer Village Foundation, Minden, NE. Lithographic print by Clarence Jackson.

COLOR 4. *Mitchell Pass, Nebraska.* Circa 1950. William Henry Jackson Pictures. n.d. WARP #46. Minden, NE: Harold Warp Pioneer Village Foundation. Lithographic print by Clarence Jackson. Original artwork done by Jackson in 1936.

COLOR 5. *Our wagon train passing Chimney Rock.* December 2, 1866 (Jackson 1866–1867). The William Henry Jackson Collection. SCBL #53. National Park Service, Scotts Bluff National Monument, Gering, NE.

COLOR 5 (bottom). *Intersection of Echo and Weber Canyons.* December 30, 1866 (Jackson 1866–1867). The William Henry Jackson Collection. SCBL #125. National Park Service, Scotts Bluff National Monument, Gering, NE.

COLOR 6. *Our last attempt.* Circa 1930–1940. Fritiof M. Fryxell Papers 1853–1973. MSS 1638, #15-788-WHJ. American Heritage Center, University of Wyoming, Laramie.

COLOR 7. *Views of Omaha.* 1869. Albumin stereoview. Union Pacific Historical Collection. WHJ-A. Union Pacific Railroad Museum, Council Bluffs, IA. Jackson photograph catalogue number unknown.

COLOR 8. *Expedition of 1870.* Circa 1920–1930. The William Henry Jackson Collection. SCBL #703. National Park Service, Scotts Bluff National Monument, Gering, NE. Originally catalogued by Jackson ([1875] 1978, 14) as #80, 1870 series, 6 1/2″ × 8 1/2″.

COLOR 9. *Virginia Dale Station.* October 1870. William Henry Jackson Pictures. WARP #32. Harold Warp Pioneer Village Foundation, Minden, NE. The photograph from which the painting was created was entitled *The Robbers' Roost,* catalogued by Jackson ([1875] 1978, 19) as #150, 1870 series, 6 1/2″ × 8 1/2″.

COLOR 10. *The 1871 expedition en route in Yellowstone Park.* Circa 1920–1930. The William Henry Jackson Collection. SCBL #705. National Park Service, Scotts Bluff National Monument, Gering, NE. Originally catalogued by Jackson ([1875] 1978, 31) as #303, 1871 series, 8″ × 10″. The photograph was taken on August 24, 1871 (Merrill 1999, 171).

COLOR 11. *The Anna.* Circa 1920–1930. The William Henry Jackson Collection. SCBL #728. National Park Service, Scotts Bluff National Monument, Gering, NE. Originally catalogued by Jackson ([1875] 1978, 29) as #273, 1871 series, 8″ × 10″. The photograph was taken on July 28, 1871 (Merrill 1999, 142).

COLOR 12. *Hayden Survey* (1871) 1935. U.S. Department of Interior Museum Collection. INTR #46. U.S. Department of Interior, Washington, DC.

COLOR 13. *Pawnee Indian Naming Ceremony.* Circa 1950. William Henry Jackson Pictures. WARP #35. Harold Warp Pioneer Village Foundation, Minden, NE. The photograph (Jackson [1877] 1978, 68 catalogued as #523) was later hand tinted and duplicated by Jackson's son, Clarence. The flag seen in the left center portion of the lithograph does not exist in the original photograph.

COLOR 14. *Photographing in high places.* 1936. NPS Museum Handbook Part III. GRTE Acc #06. National Park Service, Grand Teton National Park, Moose, WY.

COLOR 15. *Adventure of Mr. Stevenson.* Circa 1872–73. Yellowstone National Park Archives. YELL #752. National Park Service, Yellowstone National Park, WY.

COLOR 15 (bottom). *Self-portrait.* 1873. William Henry Jackson Papers. 1866–1966. MSS 1608, Item P66, series 2, box 4. L. Tom Perry Special Collections, Harold B. Lee Library, Brigham Young University, Provo, UT.

COLOR 16. *Holy Cross.* 1936. Courtesy National Park Service/Scotts Bluff National Monument. Scotts Bluff National Monument Museum. The William Henry Jackson Collection: SCBL #2130. This and the painting *Photographing the Mount of the Holy Cross* (114) were done as a pair. Jackson donated them to Rocky Mountain National Park. In 1971 the paintings were moved to Scotts Bluff National Monument.

COLOR 17. *Photographing the Mount of the Holy Cross.* 1936. The William Henry Jackson Collection. SCBL #2129. National Park Service, Scotts Bluff National Monument, Gering, NE.

COLOR 18. *The Summit of Berthoud Pass, Colorado.* Circa 1920–1930. Rocky Mountain National Park Museum Collection, ROMO #10188. National Park Service, Rocky Mountain National Park, Estes Park, CO. Originally catalogued as (Jackson [1875] 1978, 66) as #65, 1874 series, 5″ × 8″. The photograph was taken on July 27 (Jackson 1874a).

COLOR 19. *Fisherman's cabin, on Grand Lake.* Circa 1920–1930. Rocky Mountain National Park Museum Collection, ROMO #10196. National Park Service, Rocky Mountain National Park, Estes Park, CO. Originally catalogued as (Jackson [1875] 1978, 66) as #68, 1874 series, 5″ × 8″. The photograph was taken on August 2 (Jackson 1874a).

COLOR 20. *Discovery of Two Story Cliff House, Mancos Canyon.* 1936. Mesa Verde National Park Museum Collection. #5599. Mesa Verde National Park, CO.

COLOR 21. *Racing.* Circa 1920–1930. The William Henry Jackson Collection. SCBL #737. National Park Service, Scotts Bluff National Monument, Gering, NE. The incident occurred on August 31 (Jackson 1875b).

COLOR 22. *5 Porches, 1 Door.* March or May 1877. The William Henry Jackson Collection. SCBL #106. National Park Service, Scotts Bluff National Monument, Gering, NE.

COLOR 23. *Indian woman.* Circa 1877. The William Henry Jackson Collection. SCBL #97. National Park Service, Scotts Bluff National Monument, Gering, NE.

COLOR 24. *The Rock Citadel at the summit of Fremont Peak, Wyoming.* Circa 1920–1930. The William Henry Jackson Collection. SCBL #722. National Park Service, Scotts Bluff National Monument, Gering, NE. The photograph was taken on August 9, 1878 (Jackson [1878b] n.d., 1).